THE PRACTICAL AND THE PIOUS

THE
PRACTICAL
AND THE PIOUS

Essays on Thomas Chalmers (1780-1847)

Edited by
A C CHEYNE

THE SAINT ANDREW PRESS: EDINBURGH

First published in 1985 by
THE SAINT ANDREW PRESS
121 George Street, Edinburgh EH2 4YN

Copyright © A C Cheyne 1985

ISBN 0 7152 0582 X

The Practical and the Pious: Essays on Thomas Chalmers (1780-1847)
  1. Chalmers, Thomas   2. Free Church of Scotland—Clergy—Biography
  I. Cheyne, A. C.
  285'.2'0924   BX9225.C4

Printed in Great Britain by Macdonald Printers (Edinburgh) Limited

Contents

Preface

The essays which follow took their origin in the Chalmers Bicentenary
Conference which was held in the University of Edinburgh in March,
1980. While thanks are due to all the contributors, not least for their
patience in the face of an ever-receding publication date, special
mention should be made of Margot Butt, who (over and above her
other services) gave us our title, and of Olive Checkland and John
McCaffrey, whose enthusiasm helped to launch the project and whose
encouragement has upheld the editor in carrying it to completion
despite many unforeseen difficulties.

I am also deeply indebted to the Senate of New College and the
trustees of the Hope Trust for valuable financial help, to the staff of
New College Library, John Howard, Joyce Barrie and Iain Hope, for
their prompt and cheerful assistance at every stage of the venture, to
Mary Kerr of The Saint Andrew Press for her scrupulously careful
editing of the typescript, to May Hocking, whose secretarial expertise is
almost but never quite taken for granted, and to my brother George,
who compiled the index.

A C Cheyne,
New College, Edinburgh
October 1984

Introduction
Thomas Chalmers: Then and Now
A C Cheyne

In his own day, and for some decades thereafter, the greatness of Thomas Chalmers seems to have been well-nigh universally acknowledged. Karl Marx, it is true, referred to him, in a phrase which was presumably meant to be uncomplimentary, as 'the arch-parson' [1]; and Thomas Carlyle, at his sourest, could avow that 'Such an intellect, professing to be educated, and yet so ill-*read*, so ignorant, in all that lay beyond the horizon in place or time, I have almost nowhere met with.' [2] They may be seen as anticipating the less adulatory verdict of a subsequent age. At the other end of the scale, many contemporary estimates strike us today as excessive or even ludicrous. 'Bury me beside Chalmers' was the death-bed plea of that 'earnest student', the hero-worshipping John Mackintosh [3]; while John Cairns of Berwick (the only 19th-century representative of the Seceding tradition who came anywhere near Chalmers in stature and influence) dared to compare him with Plato, Descartes, Pascal, Leibnitz and Kant as combining 'an intellect essentially and characteristically scientific' with 'that intuition of moral genius which sounds the depth of human nature and the destinies of human society.' [4]

Most assessments, though more moderate that those just quoted, were considerably nearer panegyric than denunciation. Even Carlyle remarked that 'It is not often that the world has seen men like Thomas Chalmers, nor can the world afford to forget them', and supposed that 'there will never again be such a preacher in any Christian Church'. [5] If Melbourne, Peel, Sir James Graham and (latterly, at least) Lord Aberdeen were not among his admirers, some eminent statesmen certainly were. According to the eighth Duke of Argyll, he was one of the best and greatest men he had ever known [6]; according to Mr Gladstone, 'an admirable man . . . one of nature's nobles' [7]; according to Lord Rosebery, 'the most illustrious Scottish churchman since John Knox.' [8] The acidulous John Morley referred to 'mighty Chalmers'. [9] Lord Cockburn spoke of 'four men who in my time have made Scotland illustrious—Dugald Stewart, Walter Scott, Thomas Chalmers, and Francis Jeffrey'. [10] Sydney Smith exclaimed, 'He was not one man; Dr Chalmers was a thousand men.' [11]

Perhaps less remarkably, churchmen over several generations united to honour him. That patron saint of modern Evangelicalism, Charles Simeon, observed of Chalmers with characteristic portentousness, 'Truly I regard him as raised up by God for a great and peculiar work'[12]; while the Scottish Episcopalian Dean Ramsay remarked that 'His highest praise, but, at the same time, his *just* eulogium is, that his fervency of spirit, his sensibility, and his energy, were all exercised and called forth in the one great and magnificent cause—promoting the glory of God and the welfare of Mankind.'[13] Again, whatever post-Disruption Auld Kirkers might think of other dignitaries of the Free Church, they united to honour the man whom Norman Macleod referred to as 'dear old Chalmers'[14]; while from the rival denomination Robert Rainy, Chalmers' late Victorian successor in the leadership of both Church and Assembly, spoke for nearly all when he described him quite simply as the greatest man he had ever met.[15] And the note of admiration continued to echo—in Scotland, at any rate—far into our own iconoclastic century. 'He had,' wrote James Denney, 'the greatness of the nation in him as well as that of the Church, and it is an immense gain to a churchman when he has such an interest in the State as keeps his ethics from becoming ecclesiastically narrow in range'[16]; and this view was apparently shared by the author of a delightful little essay which appeared as recently as 1960. 'It is easy to criticise,' wrote Professor Ian Henderson in Dr Selby Wright's compilation, *Fathers of the Kirk*, 'not so easy to think of many since his day who have conceived for our country a pattern of life at once so Scottish and so permeated by spiritual values.'[17]

How do we account for the unique place which Chalmers won for himself among his contemporaries and his immediate successors? The basis of his reputation, in an age whose appetite for the spoken word seems almost incredible today, was an oratorical power that verged on wizardry. John Brown the essayist (who left a memorable account of one of Chalmers' sermons and the impression it made on its hearers) reported that 'His eloquence rose like a tide, a sea, setting in, bearing down upon you, lifting up all its waves—"deep calling unto deep"; there was no doing anything but giving yourself up for the time to its will.'[18] After hearing him in the Assembly, Francis Jeffrey of the *Edinburgh Review* exclaimed that there was 'something altogether remarkable about that man'.[19] Hazlitt, testifying to Chalmers' 'prophetic fury' in the pulpit, told how he 'never saw fuller attendances or more profound attention' than at St John's, Glasgow, in 1822: 'It was like a sea of eyes, a swarm of heads, gaping for mysteries and staring for elucidations.'[20] What happened during one of the early visits to London, in 1817, was only a slightly exaggerated version of the normal course of events wherever he went to preach or to lecture. 'All the world wild about Dr Chalmers,' noted Wilberforce in his diary, and went on: 'Sunday, 25th [May]. Off early with Canning, Huskisson, and Lord Binning to the Scotch Church, London Wall, to hear Dr Chalmers. Vast crowds . . . Lords Elgin, Harrowby, etc. . . . I was surprised to see how greatly Canning was affected; at times he was quite melted into tears.'[21] That was in the morning. Of the afternoon service in the Scots Church, Swallow Street, another enthusiast reported: 'I never witnessed the place so full in my life, pews, passages, pulpit stairs, windows, etc., etc., all crowded to excess; and some noblemen, members of Parliament, and even some most beautiful young ladies of distinction hauled through the vestry window. . . . The carriages stood from the head of Vigo Lane to near Sackville Street in Piccadilly.'[22]

Such an extraordinary impact is hard to explain. Neither originality of thought nor grace of style could be claimed for the speaker: the content of his preaching differed not a whit from that of much less gifted colleagues (though he was perhaps more indifferent than they to the subtler nuances of Calvinist orthodoxy), and of its form it has been said that 'he trampled underfoot every accepted canon of pulpit success.'[23] Hazlitt took refuge in a quotation, 'There's magic in the web'[24]; and maybe we should leave it at that. But presumably the secret lay in the cumulative effect of a great variety of things. We think of his fertile imagination and his skill at creating atmosphere. We note his fondness for vivid and arresting phrases: 'moonlight preaching ripens no harvest', 'the expulsive power of a new affection', 'rather save a single soul than deliver an empire from pauperism', 'a house-going minister, a church-going people', 'who cares for any Church, but as an instrument of Christian good?', and so on. We recall his ability to surpass all his contemporaries at dressing up a single idea in a dozen different guises without ever wearying his audiences, as well as his occasional willingness to challenge accepted notions. We do not forget his unequalled force of conviction and (as important as anything) the indefinable charisma of a personality which, though genial and benign, was at the same time strangely elusive and inaccessible. Or are we perhaps to ground Chalmers' appeal not so much in his own outstanding gifts as in the psychology of his hearers: their need to find some stable foothold amid the torrent of revolutionary change, their hopes of escape, in spirit if not in flesh, from the crowding horrors of social convulsion, their tendency to transpose the economic struggle into a religious key, their search for entertainment, and the divine, in a dreary world? There is still room here for worthwhile debate, and the outcome still remains doubtful.

Whatever our verdict upon it, Chalmers' preaching never constituted his sole title to fame. As an administrator he had something which came little short of genius, combining (in John Cairns' phrase) 'absorption in great principles' with 'interest in the minutest details'.[25] Examine the record of his dealings with the Town Council of Glasgow before and during the so-called 'St John's experiment', as well as the multitudinous injunctions and memoranda which he drew up for the guidance of his beloved 'agency'; consider the depth and the range of his investigations into poor law administration, not only in Scotland but throughout Great Britain; study his reports to the General Assembly as convener (from 1834 to 1840) of its Church Extension Committee, discerning behind the statistical tables in the appendices the driving force of a superb organiser—the father, surely, of the modern committee system in the Kirk. Remember, finally, how even in his last years, when sick and old and sometimes dispirited by the collapse of so many cherished enterprises, he was capable of conceiving and bringing to maturity the Sustentation Fund which made possible the continued existence of the Free Church and entitles him to be called Scotland's first and greatest teacher of Christian stewardship. If you do these things, you will have gone a long way towards uncovering the secret of the spell he cast on both his own and subsequent generations.

There is yet more to be said, however. To his outstanding gifts as orator and administrator he added a quite exceptional breadth of interests. He began his academic career by holding an assistantship in mathematics; the greatest sensation of his Glasgow ministry was caused not by ordinary sermons but by the *Astronomical Discourses* and the *Commercial Discourses*, which sought to relate the Faith to contemporary intellectual concerns; he was competent in chemistry, physics and botany, and keenly interested in geology; he held a chair in Moral Philosophy; and although his hopes of achieving recognition as an economist were never realised, John Stuart Mill remarked of his *Political Economy* that at least he always had the merit of studying phenomena at first hand. [26] And as an attractive little story from his old age would seem to suggest, he never lost a certain openness and generosity of mind. Dean Stanley, meeting him just 11 days before his death, discovered that Chalmers had recently finished reading Gibbon's *Decline and Fall*, and later told how 'the old man's face, Evangelical devout Scotsman as he was, kindled as he spoke of the majesty, the labour, the giant grasp displayed by that greatest and most sceptical of English historians.' [27]

Over and above all these things, we must reckon with a character—sometimes domineering, often unpredictable, nearly always compellingly intense and vital—which impresses by its unusual combination of dynamism and charm. The dynamism comes home to us when we examine Professor Hugh Watt's descriptive list of *The Published Writings of Dr Thomas Chalmers*, a whole volume devoted to recording the titles of some 200 separate publications, sermons, tracts, lectures, reports and many 100-page treatises, which poured from his

pen between 1805 and 1847[28]; when we realise that beyond this
printed material there lies the vast repertory of manuscript letters in
New College Library, Edinburgh, whose cataloguing has already
occupied several years; and when (to select only one example from
many such relationships) we read David Keir's history of *The House of
Collins*, and observe how even a man of William Collins' superb
business gifts could find himself driven almost to the limits of
endurance by his greatest author's never-ending flow of new projects,
his vigilant attention to detail (not least where profits were concerned),
and his invariable assumption that what seemed central to him must
seem central to everybody. [29]

The magnetic charm is equally undeniable, as Collins' long-suffering
fidelity bears witness. He was only one of many, famous and not so
famous, who felt its influence. John Anderson heard Chalmers preach
in Edinburgh during the early summer of 1815, and, like Boswell with
Johnson, was enslaved for ever. His *Reminiscences of Dr Chalmers* are
the fruit of a sedulous, life-long garnering of the great man's utterances,
public and private, important and less important. [30] Contemporaries of
stature such as David Stow the educational pioneer and Robert Story
the minister of Rosneath (friend of Edward Irving, Thomas Erskine of
Linlathen and John Macleod Campbell) clung to his friendship
through many vicissitudes. Generations of students, including
Alexander Duff the missionary pioneer and Robert Murray McCheyne
the influential Evangelical preacher, acknowledged him to be one of the
shaping influences (in quite a few cases, *the* shaping influence) in their
lives. Professor David Masson, whose *Memories of Two Cities,
Edinburgh and Aberdeen* contains a lively introduction to Chalmers, was
not unrepresentative of all these when, telling of the unforgettable
impression made by the famous preacher on a raw lad from
Aberdeenshire, he wrote: 'Till he flashed casually before me in that
perambulation of benevolence which led him into our bleakish parts,
never had I felt such power, never had I conceived the possibility of
such prodigiousness of energy in human form. He answered all one's
young notions, and more, of what "greatness" might be; and from that
day the whole of that part of our island to which my vision was as yet
pretty much bounded, seemed to me full of him, and almost of him
only. Scotland was but a platform to and fro on which there walked a
Chalmers.' [31]

Perhaps Dr John Brown the essayist got even nearer than that to
Chalmers the man. 'There was,' he tells us:

> no separating his thoughts and expressions from his person, and
> looks, and voice. How perfectly we can at this moment recall him!
> Thundering, flaming, lightening, in the pulpit; teaching,
> indoctrinating, drawing after him his students in the lecture room;
> sitting among other public men, the most unconscious, the most

king-like of them all, with that broad leonine countenance, that beaming, liberal smile; or on the way out to his home, in his old-fashioned great-coat, with his throat muffled up, his big walking-stick moved outwards in an arc, its point fixed, its head circumferential, a sort of companion and playmate, with which doubtless he demolished legions of imaginary foes, errors and stupidities in men and things, in Church and State. His great look, large chest, large head, his amplitude every way; his broad, simple, childlike, in-turned feet; his short, hurried, impatient step; his erect royal air; his look of general good-will; his kindling up into a warm but vague benignity when one he did not recognise spoke to him; the addition, for it was not a change, of keen speciality to his hearty recognition; the twinkle of his eyes; the immediate saying something very personal to set all to rights, and then sending you off with some thought, some feeling, some remembrance, making your heart burn within you; his voice indescribable; his eye—that most peculiar feature—not vacant, but asleep—innocent, mild, and large; and his soul, its great inhabitant, not always at his window; but then, when he did awake, how close to you was that vehement, burning soul! how it penetrated and overcame you![32]

So Brown's appreciation (written, be it remembered, only a few years after Carlyle had published his *Heroes and Hero-worship*) reaches its memorable climax: 'Dr Chalmers was a ruler among men: this we know historically; this every man who came within his range felt at once. He was, like Agamemnon, a native ἄναξ ἀνδρῶν, and with all his homeliness of feature and deportment, and his perfect simplicity of expression, there was about him "that divinity that doth hedge a king." You felt a power in him, and going from him, drawing you to him in spite of yourself. He was in this respect a *solar man*, he drew after him his own firmament of planets. They, like all free agents, had their centrifugal forces acting ever towards an independent, solitary course, but the centripetal also was there, and they moved with and around their imperial sun— gracefully or not, willingly or not, as the case might be, but there was no breaking loose: they again, in their own spheres of power, might have their attendant moons, but all were bound to the great massive luminary in their midst.'[33]

Such, then, was the man who stood so near the centre of our country's secular and religious life during the first half of last century. His prominence cannot be questioned. But what of his effectiveness? There would seem to be good grounds for arguing that, despite the talents he possessed, the influence he wielded, the respect bordering on veneration generally accorded him, the story of Chalmers' life is in the last analysis a story of failure: failure in the matters which concerned him most, failure of a kind that may well cast doubt upon the soundness of the principles which shaped his ministry and perhaps still shape the ministry of the Kirk in the 1980s. Let me explain. When the word 'failure' is used in connection with Chalmers, one's immediate reaction is probably to think of the Disruption and of what it implied for his vision of a popularised Church of Scotland, allied with the State but independent of it, evangelical, national and free. The events of 1843 were indeed a tragedy, for Chalmers as well as for Scotland; but they are not what I have chiefly in mind. I am thinking rather of what happened, even before the Disruption, to the ideals which had more to do with shaping his churchmanship than Non-Intrusion, and as much even as Spiritual Independence: I mean, of course, his devotion to the parochial system and to the principle of Establishment, the great hinges on which all his thinking and acting turned.

First, Chalmers and the parochial system. Chalmers believed that the two great evils of his day were irreligion and poverty. He also believed that the two were intimately connected, the former being the root cause of the latter. And he contended that the only way of eliminating either was to revive, within the context of modern industrial society, the ancient virtues of rural and small-town life in Scotland: awareness that we are all 'members one of another'; recognition of a providential ordering, perhaps we should say stratification, of society; unselfconscious philanthropy on the part of the rich, and grateful but never subservient acceptance of it by the deserving poor; family loyalty; sturdy independence; hard work; thrift; temperance; and of course piety—all of them, it may be, somewhat idealised in retrospect.

But how was the much-needed recovery of these desirable characteristics to be achieved? For his answer, Chalmers turned to the territorial parish as he had known it in the Anstruther of his boyhood and the Kilmany of his first ministry. A manageably small area housing a community of some two thousand souls who lived, worked and worshipped together, with a church and a school at its centre and a minister and a kirk session to attend to both its spiritual and its temporal necessities: here, he argued, was the basic—he would even have said redemptive—unit of Scottish society. Here was the means of national regeneration. Admirably suited to coping with the traditional problems of country life, it also (in his opinion) constituted the only remedy for the horrifying conditions created during his lifetime by industrialisation, the population explosion, and the rise of large towns: the destitution, crime, squalor and disease, all on a massive scale, which not only defied sanitary and moral control but even seemed to be undermining the very foundations of civilised life and Christian faith in Glasgow, Edinburgh, and the Central Lowlands of Scotland generally.

Broadly understood, Chalmers' profound regard for the parochial system may be said to underlie all the major interests and activities of his long ministry. It was a close ally of his devotion to 'the Establishment principle'. It strengthened his enthusiasm for Church Extension, his antipathy to pluralities, his emphasis upon the need for improvement in the training of ministers. It was not unconnected with his adherence to the Non-Intrusion movement and his belated support for the abolition of patronage. But if Chalmers' advocacy of the parochial ideal extended over almost his entire adult life, his practical demonstration of its effectiveness was confined to two relatively brief periods: one near the beginning of his career as a national figure, the other at its close. I refer, of course, to the 'St John's experiment' from 1819 to 1823 and the 'West Port operation' from 1844 until his death in 1847. Whether or not he made his case will depend largely upon the success or otherwise of those two great-hearted but very diversely-regarded enterprises. The earlier was much the more important of them, and attention may be confined to it, leaving those who are interested to consider the later by means of S J Brown's excellent article in a recent number of the *Scottish Church History Society Records*.[34]

The news of Waterloo was only a few weeks old when Chalmers was inducted to the charge of Glasgow Tron. Four years later, having attained a fame which, at least in some quarters, almost rivalled that of the great Duke himself, Scotland's most celebrated preacher was ready to provide a dramatic and (as he believed) utterly cogent demonstration of the adequacy of the parish system to meet even the fiercest challenges that urban life could offer to the Christian Faith and the Christian Church. All that he demanded for the achievement of his purpose was an area of operations as representative as possible of the worst that 'slumdom' could do, together with freedom to tackle things in his own way, untrammelled by any interference from the civic and ecclesiastical authorities. Both were granted him, and in the late summer of 1819 he entered upon his labours as minister of the newly-created parish of St John's. Carved out for him by the Council from three overgrown East End parishes, and crowded with some 10 000 exceptionally poor people, it presented all the difficulties—and all the opportunities—which even he might have desired. The great experiment could begin.

The distinctive thing about Chalmers' ministry at St John's was that it took the traditional features of parochial administration—spiritual oversight, education, and poor relief—more seriously, and dealt with them more efficiently, than had perhaps ever been done before.

The task of spiritual supervision, which was quite beyond the minister's own unaided powers, was tackled by adopting the simple expedients of sub-division and devolution. Chalmers parcelled out the area in 25 districts or 'proportions', containing from 60 to 100 families apiece; and to each he assigned an elder, charged with the oversight not only of St John's members but of every household not effectively connected with some other congregation, Seceding or Roman Catholic, within the city. These men went where he could not find time to go, 'ministering,' as he put it, 'from house to house in prayer and in exhortation and in the dispensation of spiritual comfort'[35]: helping to keep alive the people's contact with their local church and its activities, informing the minister of problems as they arose, and binding the whole parish together by innumerable filaments of spiritual and social intercourse. Through their labours, it was hoped, some sense of individual worth and significance might be restored to the bewildered and degraded inhabitants of an overgrown city; and certainly there is nothing far-fetched in seeing the 'proportion' as a kind of successor to the intimate parish community of earlier days. (The scheme, incidentally, was more than just a successful exercise in the delegation of duties and the deepening of Christian fellowship. It also pioneered what would now be called the training of the laity; for the congregation of St John's learned to regard itself as being less an assemblage of hearers than a body of workers, its mission to the parish planned and directed by the clergy but managed and carried through by a subordinate band of elders, deacons, Sunday and day school teachers, and others—the NCOs, as it were, of a Christian army.) All in all, no part of Chalmers' work in Glasgow was more impressive than what he did in this matter of spiritual supervision.

High priority was also given to the task of education. At St John's, as at the Tron, the religious instruction of every child in the parish was enthusiastically promoted: each 'proportion' had at least one Sunday school, and some had two or even three. But this did not satisfy Chalmers. He often pointed out how great an obstacle illiteracy or semi-literacy could be to a true understanding of the Bible, and in any case he firmly believed that a measure of elementary education was the best possible defence against the wiles of political agitators. As early as September 1819, therefore, he set about providing his new parish with modestly-endowed day schools after the pattern which he most admired: the parochial schools of the Scottish countryside, where, to quote his own words, 'the education is so cheap as that the poor may pay, but at the same time . . . so good as that the rich may receive.'[36] The effects were soon evident. An education committee was formed in the congregation; the immediate construction of two schools and two masters' houses was agreed upon; and within about two years four salaried teachers were in charge of over 400 scholars. By the time of his departure from Glasgow the number of pupils had risen to nearly 800.

Most difficult and controversial of all Chalmers' activities at St John's was his handling of the immense, mind-boggling, problem of poverty. Conditions in early 19th-century Glasgow were more like those now obtaining in Calcutta or Hong Kong than anything we know in the West; and most onlookers were baffled or terrified or driven to despair by the abject misery and degradation of the new urban proletariat. An increasingly popular response (imported, it seems, from the South) was to levy a poor-rate on the city's property owners and

B

distribute the proceeds as 'indoor' (poorhouse) or 'outdoor' relief to the needy. In Chalmers' eyes, however, this was an altogether deplorable expedient—a palliative, not a cure, undermining the traditional self-respect and self-sufficiency of the Scottish people, and leading in the long run to an increase rather than a diminution of the distress. In opposition to it, he advocated a return to what we might call 'the Anstruther solution', and what he himself described as 'the principle of locality'. This involved reliance, within the parish, and under the supervision of the minister and kirk session, upon the self-help of the poor, the assistance of relatives, the kindness of neighbours, and the discriminating charity of the rich to achieve what could never be looked for from a compulsory national scheme with its multiplicity of officials, its impersonality, and its tendency to demoralise the beneficiaries.

Central to Chalmers' scheme was the revival of the ancient office of the diaconate; and the instructions which he issued for the guidance of the new deacons clearly indicate how he hoped to reduce a vast problem to manageable proportions. 'When one applies for admittance through his deacon upon our funds,' ran the memorandum:

> the first thing to be inquired into is, if there be any kind of work that he can yet do so as to keep him altogether off [the poor roll] or as to make a partial allowance serve for his necessities; the second, what his relatives and friends are willing to do for him; the third, whether he is a hearer in any dissenting place of worship, and whether its session will contribute to his relief. And if after these previous inquiries it be found that further relief is necessary, then there must be a strict ascertainment of his term of residence in Glasgow, and whether he be yet on the funds of the Town Hospital, or is obtaining relief from any other parish. If upon all these points being ascertained the deacon of the proportion where he resides still conceives him an object for our assistance, he will inquire whether a small temporary aid will meet the occasion, and state this to the first ordinary meeting. But if instead of this he conceives him a fit subject for a regular allowance, he will receive the assistance of another deacon to confirm and complete his inquiries by the next ordinary meeting thereafter, at which time the applicant, if they still think him a fit object, is brought before us, and received upon the fund at such a rate of allowance as upon all the circumstances of the case the meeting of deacons shall judge proper. [37]

Impostors had little chance of obtaining relief under such conditions, while the genuinely distressed were unlikely to become destitute.

For a time at least the scheme seemed to be highly successful. The burden of assistance borne by the parish was reduced from £1400 to £280 per annum; after only two years it became possible to relieve the Town Hospital (or poorhouse) of responsibility for any St John's parishioners who were still on its books; and such confidence had been generated that a supplementary place of worship, paid for by loans raised on the security of its seat-rents, was built to carry still further the 'principle of locality' and the practice of self-help. As Professor L J Saunders has commented, 'even if the secular rulers of Glasgow refused to spend money on churches and schools, a way seemed open for a self-supporting and limitless church extension; if the state continued indifferent or became hostile, the Church would attempt to fulfil its national mission by its own enthusiastic effort.'[38] In 1823, however, Chalmers was appointed to the Chair of Moral Philosophy at St Andrews, and thence, five years later, he migrated to the Chair of Divinity in Edinburgh. The great St John's experiment—or at least his intimate association with it—was over.

What verdict are we to pass upon it? His own and subsequent generations seem pretty well convinced that Chalmers' attempt to revitalise the parochial system produced commendable results in the areas of pastoral oversight and the instruction of the young; though it is a serious criticism that the fees charged in the schools excluded the poorest children, and that the integrity of the parish (on which he always laid great stress) was constantly threatened by an influx of pupils from outside. But in the crucially important matter of poor relief, the number one issue of the day, judgments have on the whole been unfavourable, and that despite Chalmers' obvious conviction that failure there meant failure all along the line.

Even in the early years, with their undoubted triumphs, the current of opinion tended to go against him. On a fairly superficial level, it was argued (by Carlyle, for example) that such success as his methods did enjoy was due not to their intrinsic excellence but to their author's quite exceptional gifts: the oratory which attracted huge crowds and so ensured substantial offerings for the poor fund; the charm and dynamism which recruited and organised a host of able and wealthy office-bearers to administer the St John's experiment; the masterfulness which overbore all resistance; and the optimism which made light of tremendous difficulties. More searchingly, men like Professor W P Alison of Edinburgh University suggested that Chalmers did not understand, or take sufficient account of, the environmental factors in early 19th-century poverty, factors which called for Christian compassion rather than the somewhat censorious moralism which he sometimes displayed. [39] And of course the verdict of events (doubtless not unaffected by such strictures) was equally unfavourable. In 1837, St John's ceased to be an enclave within the poor law administration of Glasgow. In 1843, the Disruption—in which, ironically, Chalmers played a central part—extinguished all hope that official support would ever be given to an implementation of his ideas throughout the country. (In S J Brown's words, 'By assuming a leading role in the Disruption of the Church of Scotland, he had helped deprive the nation of perhaps the only institution capable of mobilising sufficient resources for

organising an effective national, social and ecclesiastical structure based
upon his parochial ideal.'[40]) In 1845, the Poor Law Amendment Act
finally took responsibility for the care of the poor out of the Church's
hands. Britain had begun its journey away from 'the ideal of parish
communities and church-directed social services'[41] toward the social
welfare state, and the great experiment had failed.

Today, over 150 years later, the criticisms directed against the St
John's project and Chalmers as a social reformer are many and various.
His plans have been called 'speculative and over-confident'.[42] His
concentration on the individual and the family, though praised as
foreshadowing the 'family casework' approach of our own time, is seen
as blinding him to the wide interdependence—impersonal but
nonetheless real—of all citizens in a great commercial and industrial
centre like Glasgow. He is accused (Dr Lee of Edinburgh's Old Kirk
began it in the 1830s)[43] of failing to reckon with the new facts of social
and geographical mobility; of encouraging, through the inquisitorial
methods which he recommended to his deacons, the concealment
rather than the relief of poverty; of discriminating with undue rigour
between the deserving and the undeserving poor. He is dismissed
because of his attachment to a view of economic relations which did not
reckon with the emergent world of strikes, lock-outs, booms and
slumps; he is denounced for his coolness towards Trade Unions, his
paternalism, his amateurism, his petit-bourgeois sentiments and
sympathies. His dependence on *laissez-faire* theorists and the gloomy
harshness of Malthusianism is noted and deplored: 'It may be
surmised,' writes Dr Mechie, 'that others, neglecting his example and
concentrating on his economic teachings, derived from them a positive
discouragement to active effort for social betterment.'[44]

Perhaps most serious of all, a strange heartlessness underlay the
treatment of poverty worked out by Chalmers and his supporters. That
in itself may sufficiently explain the lack of enthusiasm which is now
felt for his social teaching (though its profoundly clerical flavour may
also have something to do with it). And if Professor Saunders is right it
probably also accounts for the massive reaction against all that he stood
for which set in long before his death in 1847. At the close of an
invaluable discussion of 'The Christian and Civic Economy', Saunders
remarks: 'In his understanding of industrial conflict and industrial
failure alike Chalmers seemed to exhibit such a contrast between
principle and application that many turned away from what seemed to
them too much a "business Christianity". . . . Some sought out more
satisfying forms of social faith or were caught up by utopian
enthusiasms. Others, in hope or in bitterness, adopted a secularism that
seemed a blasphemy to the orthodox. . . . It was only as a workingman
achieved success and emerged from his class that Chalmers' rhetoric
began to carry with it something of the conviction of experience.'[45]

Alongside Chalmers' enthusiasm for the parish must be set his equally great devotion to the Establishment principle and the ideal of a National Church. But just as the parish was being subjected to unprecedented pressures and strains during his lifetime, so the age-old notion of an Established Church was also coming under increasing criticism.

That there should be one Scottish Church just as there was one Scottish State, and that the former had a right to all the economic and political assistance it might require from the latter, seems to have been something like an axiom for Knox and his reforming associates. Inherited from medieval times, it was acted upon in the 1560s, survived all the vicissitudes of Stuart rule, and commanded general support in the country down to the Revolution Settlement. From then on, however, it underwent a process of slow but almost unceasing erosion. The continued survival of the Roman alternative had always been an embarrassment to those who held that there should be only 'one face of the Kirk' in Scotland; but it was even more disturbing when all Protestants could not be gathered within the fold of the Established Church. In 1690, the Cameronians held themselves aloof from an uncovenanted Kirk. In 1712, Parliament's grant of toleration to the Episcopalians meant the official acceptance of religious dissent. Thereafter, the decline of the old 'one State—one Church' ideal was accelerated by the Presbyterian secessions of the mid-18th century and the rise (during the Moderate hegemony) of what we might call a 'live and let live' attitude within the Establishment itself. Even more important, towards the close of the century the Seceding heirs of Ebenezer Erskine gradually abandoned their original respect for the idea, if not the actuality, of Establishment. Joining hands with the descendants of Thomas Gillespie, the founder of the voluntarist Relief Church, they manifested increasing hostility to the very idea of a National Church and, in particular, to the special pretensions and privileges of the Church of Scotland. (Chief among the influences which brought about their change of heart were the continuing difficulties created by patronage, the American example of ecclesiastical freedom from state control, the liberating effects of the French Revolution, and the intellectual ferment which eventually led to social and political reform in the 1830s.) This new attitude came violently to the surface in the so-called Voluntary Conflict, touched off in 1829 by Andrew Marshall's famous sermon, 'Ecclesiastical Establishments Considered'.

Marshall, who was a United Secession minister in Kirkintilloch, called for the abolition of every form of religious Establishment throughout Great Britain, employing arguments which were to be repeated again and again during Chalmers' lifetime. The starting-point of his case was the situation then confronting the Churches: a situation where the authorities were generally favourable to the Christian mission but where most of the common people remained unaffected and unresponsive. What was to be done? 'Shall we,' he asked, 'have recourse to the secular arm? Shall we solicit the aid of the law—not only placing ourselves under its protection but arming ourselves with its force? Shall we repair to our unenlightened brethren with the imposing apparatus of a religious Establishment—showing them our Confession of Faith which they are henceforth to adopt—showing them the act of the legislature sanctioning that Confession—telling them that, by the orders of a paternal government which cares for their best interests, they are distributed into parishes—that by the order of government provision is made for erecting churches among them, and endowing clergymen—and that by the same order each particular division of them is to receive a minister, whom someone will send them and whose business will be to teach them the way of salvation?'[46] To all these questions Marshall's answer was a resounding negative, which he supported with a perfect battery of arguments.

The Lord of the Church, he reasoned, had not set up a religious Establishment, nor did the early Christians know anything resembling one. The institution fosters religious exclusiveness, leads almost inevitably to persecution, nourishes dissatisfaction among those excluded from its benefits, secularises the Church and discourages Christian liberality. It is almost inevitably inefficient, and has been shown to be so by the superior vigour of American voluntaryism. As for a line of reasoning much used in defence of establishments by Chalmers and others, Marshall had this comment to make:

> It is said that unless we send the Gospel to men they will never seek it; it is none of the things they naturally desire, none of the things they are apt to deem essential to their comfort, or which, of their own accord, they will endeavour to provide. Means must therefore be employed to continue it among them; and what means are so suitable or promise to be so efficient as a national establishment? To this argument we reply by admitting the premise but denying the conclusion. We admit that the expense of sending it, and in all probability of preserving it among them for a time, must be defrayed; but we deny that the interposition of the civil power is either necessary for the purpose or to be desired. Let the gospel emanate from those who have been put in trust with the gospel; let it emanate from the church to which the Lord Jesus has given the commission; and if the ministers of the church require assistance in the work, pecuniary assistance or assistance of any other kind, let them look for that assistance, let them confidently expect it, from their Christian brethren.[47]

Needless to say, there was no dearth of apologists for the Church of Scotland and the Establishment principle on which it was founded.

Among them Chalmers figured prominently. Of his many writings on the subject three are particularly relevant: his treatise, *On the Use and Abuse of Literary and Ecclesiastical Endowments,* first printed as early as 1827; his sermon, *On Ecclesiastical Endowments,* preached just after Marshall's in 1829; and his *Lectures on the Establishment and Extension of National Churches,* delivered in London, at the height of the controversy, in 1838. The treatise, which was written in defence of university endowments (then under attack), argued against those who would leave the provision of schools and colleges—and churches—to the operation of the laws of supply and demand, and contended that the remedy for both ignorance and impiety was a national Establishment, with a schoolmaster and a minister in every parish: only thus would men become conscious of their needs, and find close at hand the means for satisfying them. The sermon concerned itself with two of Marshall's chief allegations against Establishment: that it was a corruption of the Church, unknown before Constantine, and that it involved state control and the secularisation of religion. In reply, Chalmers argued that, just as the supporters of a missionary society may give it their financial assistance without exercising any control over its message or its ministers, so with the State's relation to the Church. 'For the sake of an abundant gospel dispensation we are upheld in things temporal by the State. For the sake of a pure gospel dispensation we are left in things spiritual to ourselves.'[48] The famous London lectures have a special, almost melancholy, interest for the historian in view of the comment which events were soon to pass on optimistic phrases like the following: 'It should never be forgotten that, in things ecclesiastical, the highest power of our Church is amenable to no higher power on earth for its decisions. It can exclude, it can deprive, it can depose at pleasure. . . . There is not one thing which the State can do to our independent and indestructible Church but strip her of her temporalities. *Nec tamen consumebatur,* she would remain a Church notwithstanding.'[49] At the time, however, the most impressive aspect of the Lectures was their central contention that pure Voluntaryism (Voluntaryism *ab intra,* as Chalmers liked to call it) was incapable of reclaiming the heathenised masses for Christianity, and that only an adequately-endowed state Church could do so.

In drawing attention to this point we really move from the Voluntary Controversy, properly so-called, to the great debate about Church Extension which grew out of it. From the Middle Ages almost until Chalmers' lifetime the ecclesiastical map of Scotland had changed very little, at least so far as the number of parishes, their boundaries, and the size and location of the parish churches were concerned. But now it was being transformed by the population explosion and the growth of large towns which accompanied the Industrial Revolution. How were the Churches to react? The Dissenting bodies were happily free to respond to demand—if not to need—whenever it arose: they grasped the opportunity with both hands and called many new congregations into being. But their flexibility was not possible for the Establishment, which had to tackle its problems without contravening the numerous regulations imposed by the State in order to safeguard the interests of existing parishes and the rights of heritors. One device which enjoyed official approval was to increase the number not of parishes but of ministers in a hard-pressed area: St Andrew's in Edinburgh, for example, became a collegiate charge in 1800 and so provided two pastors instead of one for the rapidly developing New Town. Another was to find stipends for new charges by uncollegiating old ones in less populous districts: an idea which encouraged the city fathers to erect some of the capital's handsomest churches in the decades immediately after 1815.

Despite their attractions, however, collegiating and uncollegiating proved to be mere palliatives of the situation. Especially favoured by those who wished to extend the Church's influence was the provision of 'chapels of ease': sanctuaries erected and supported by the people in the hope of their complete incorporation, sooner rather than later, into the official system. Unfortunately, the suspicious attitude of Moderate Assemblies baulked this hope for many years. Only a few dozen chapels were admitted between 1707 and 1833, whereas Presbyterian Dissent erected 500 places of worship in the same period; and even when a chapel was accorded recognition, the status of its minister remained markedly lower than that of his colleagues. In Hugh Watt's words, 'Though trained in the same University Faculty as the average parish minister, licensed by the same presbytery, called by a congregation of considerable numbers, and regularly ordained to the ministry, he had not only no defined field of labour, and no seat in any Church court, he had not even a kirk session of his own.'[50] To Evangelicals like Chalmers this was an intolerable situation; and one of the earliest consequences of their at last attaining an Assembly majority (in 1834) was the passage of the Chapels Act, which sought to remove all the disabilities just referred to. Church Extension on a large scale was now a real possibility, and it became a certainty with Chalmers' appointment that same year as convener of the Church Accommodation Committee.

In his first address to its members the new convener expressed his enthusiasm for the assignment. 'I can truly affirm,' he declared, 'that had I been left to make a choice among the countless diversities of welldoing, this is the one office that I should have selected as the most congenial to my taste.' He then went on to describe the aims of Church Extension as he conceived them:

I trust the Committee will not relax its exertions, and not relinquish them, even though it should require the perseverance of a whole generation, till we have made it a sufficiently thick-set Establishment, and brought it into a state of full equipment—till churches have been so multiplied, and parochial charges so sub-divided, that there will not one poor family be found in our land who might not, if they will, have entry and accommodation in a place of worship and religious instruction, with such a share in the personal attentions of the clergyman as to claim him for an acquaintance and a friend. [51]

'A sufficiently thick-set Establishment': that (in Chalmers' quaint phraseology) was the target which he set himself and his committee, and only the even more remarkable record of Church Extension in the period after 1843 has dimmed the lustre of the great campaign which followed. Appeals of a kind previously unknown in the Kirk were directed to both individuals and congregations; collections were made, and congregational associations of penny-a-week contributors formed; a programme of special meetings was organised; and in his report to the Assembly of 1838 the convener was able to intimate that in four years over £205 000 had been raised and 187 churches added to the strength of the Church of Scotland. [52]

It was an astonishing achievement, and most men would have been inclined to rest on their laurels at that point. Not so Chalmers. To have built the churches was, in his estimation, only a beginning. Ministers must now be provided for them, and although recruitment would present no problems (there was a glut of candidates at the time) payment was a different matter. The clergy already at work in Scottish parishes were mainly provided for either out of the ancient teinds or, in larger towns, out of seat rents; but there was little likelihood of the old endowments being stretched to cover the new livings, and it ran counter to Chalmers' deepest convictions to charge for accommodation in such a way as to exclude poor parishioners from worship. The only way forward was to take the fact of Establishment seriously and turn to the State for assistance. Nor was there an absence of precedents for so doing. As recently as 1818 the sister Establishment south of the Border had benefited to the extent of £1 million from a government grant for church-building; and another £500 000 had been made available six years later. At that time, the Kirk itself received £100 000 towards the erection and endowment of 40 or so 'Parliamentary Churches' (as they came to be called) in the remote Highlands. It was therefore decided to make application to the Whig ministry of Lord Melbourne for another such grant, and in July 1834 the first of several Scottish deputations visited London. The friendly reception accorded them made hopes run high; but the parliamentary session was too far advanced for anything to be done immediately, and the Kirk's envoys returned home with nothing to show save 'good words and comfortable promises'. [53] Before the opening of the next session the Whigs had fallen from power and been succeeded by Sir Robert Peel and the Tories; yet even that turn of events was not really discouraging. The Tories were more of a Church party, and more friendly to Church Extension, than their opponents; and Chalmers received positive encouragement to renew the application for aid. In February 1835 the King's Speech, which was, of course, a statement of government policy, foreshadowed imminent legislation in the Church's favour. Success seemed to be within its grasp.

And then the blow fell. The announcement of the Government's intentions had been greeted with 'a veritable tornado of protest',[54] in which the Voluntaries of both England and Scotland took the lead. They accused the General Assembly, and Chalmers in particular, of blatant deception. Their real aim, obviously, was not the evangelisation of the poor and the unchurched but the annihilation of every religious body in Scotland except the Kirk. If their schemes were fully realised, Dissent could not possibly survive; and in any case, was the Church of Scotland even making adequate use of its existing endowments? Such statistics as were available suggested that it was not! Bombarded by allegations of this kind, the Government (friendly though it was) hesitated; and while it hesitated another turn of fortune brought Melbourne, the very antithesis of Chalmers in politics and religion alike, back to office. By this time, some measure of a temporising kind was almost inevitable; and despite the pleas of another Scottish deputation at Westminster the appointment of a Royal Commission to investigate the whole situation was announced soon afterwards.

The disappointment and alarm of the Kirk were only increased when the names of those who would serve on the Commission became known. They included several outspoken and aggressive Voluntaries. 'A restless, locomotive, clamorous minority,' commented Chalmers, 'by the noise they have raised, and by the help of men irreligious themselves, and therefore taking no interest, but the contrary, in the religious education of the people, have attained in the eyes of our rulers a magnitude and an importance which do not belong to them—while the great bulk of the population, quiet because satisfied, are by an overwhelming preponderance on the side of the Establishment.'[55] (An early reference, this, to the 'silent majority' so familiar to us in the present century!) He did not refuse, however, to collaborate in the inquiry, for it was his belief that a sufficiently rigorous investigation would reveal the Church's aims to be exactly as he had always described them: not clerical enrichment and enhancement of status, and certainly not the diminution or elimination of Dissent, but simply the uplift of the neglected poor and the betterment of the nation's life as a whole.

The Commission, which had also been asked to report on religious facilities within the Dissenting Churches, made its various reports in due course. From the Establishment's point of view they proved to be somewhat more favourable than might have been expected. Despite all that the Secession and the Relief had done, church accommodation in the great cities was revealed as having fallen far behind the increase in population: in Edinburgh, for example, there was room for only 48 per cent of the people. On the other hand, this was not to say that all the available sittings were let: far from it. In Edinburgh alone, 11 000— mostly the cheapest—had not been taken up at all. Over one-third of the inhabitants of the capital, and an even higher proportion in Glasgow, were living in entire neglect of religious ordinances. The opponents of Establishment drew their own conclusions from such evidence; but in Chalmers' eyes it served only to underline the clamant need for government help so that the Church, properly endowed at last, might be empowered to enter upon 'aggressive' evangelism which only an Established Church could perform.

Unfortunately for the Kirk and its spokesmen, the ambiguous findings of the Commission—inadequate accommodation insufficiently utilised—failed to move Lord Melbourne's Government in the desired direction. Whatever else the agitation of the last few years had done, it had certainly convinced the Prime Minister and his colleagues that this was not the time to alienate their valuable supporters, the Dissenters of England and Scotland. The most they would do, therefore, was to bring in a Bill which was quite unsatisfying so far as the Church Extension Committee were concerned; and yet another official deputation from the Kirk failed to alter things. To the complaint that the proposed legislation would inflict a grievous wound upon the Church of Scotland, Melbourne replied: 'That, gentlemen, is your inference. You may not be the better for our plan, but—hang it—you cannot surely be worse.' [56] There was no guarantee that the Tories, though full of promises while out of office, would be any more generous; and in any case, by the time they had a chance to do something the Ten Years' Conflict (by 1841 in its last stages) had irretrievably blurred the issues. The chances that the Church would obtain what it considered an adequate addition to its endowments had become slight indeed. During the next few years, Church Extension enthusiasts were obliged to rely, like their Dissenting antagonists, on the freewill offerings of the faithful; in the early spring of 1843 the law-courts' belated condemnation of the Chapels Act deprived many of the new Church Extension charges of their hard-won status; and a month or two later the Disruption finally put an end to Chalmers' surviving hopes.

Just as Chalmers' faith in the parochial system had scarcely been upheld by the crucial experiments at St John's and the West Port, so now his advocacy of the Establishment principle was rebuffed, and his reliance on a Christian government to support the missionary outreach of the Church disappointed, by the fate of the great endowment appeal. At both the local and the national level it is difficult not to see him—despite all the many successes which attended his exertions—as being, in the last analysis, a failure: a magnificent failure, admittedly, but a failure nevertheless. That this was so may be explained partly by the character and convictions of the man himself, partly by the circumstances of the time. With all his endearing qualities, he alienated not a few by his overbearing manner and his almost monomaniacal obsession with whatever happened to be the scheme of the moment. His personal relationships could be presented as a sad succession of conflicts and misunderstandings: from the early confrontations with local landowners in the East Neuk of Fife, the gentleman to whose children he was briefly a tutor, the professor of mathematics and the University Senate at St Andrews, and the presbytery of Cupar, [57] to the appallingly bitter controversy with Dr Lee over the moderatorship in the 1830s, the breach with Lord Aberdeen at the height of the Ten Years' Conflict, and the animosities which he aroused in many of the politicians with whom he had to negotiate over endowment. [58] He could be disturbingly illogical: failing, for example, to see the possible incompatibility of Non-Intrusion and 'the Establishment principle'. In his social philosophy, as a man like Patrick Brewster of Paisley realised, he was frequently more bourgeois than Christian, more indebted to Adam Smith and Malthus than to the humanitarian insights of the Gospels and the Epistles. At two crucial moments in his career he was revealed, once by Professor Alison and once by Dr Lee, to be doctrinaire, and lacking in both realism and compassion. He was by no means untouched by the fanaticism which is so disturbing a characteristic of some embattled Evangelicals. Above all, perhaps, he failed his country and his Church by presenting them both with an anachronistic ideal—of Scotland as an aggregation of Anstruthers, meeting the problems of the 19th century with the solutions of the 16th.

At the same time, however, we should remind ourselves of the well-nigh overwhelming problems which confronted him and his beloved Scotland in that tragic generation. Changes greater than any known to Western man since the fall of Rome—changes for which we today have still no satisfactory answer—were putting an almost intolerable strain on Church and society alike; and if Chalmers failed to retrieve the situation, at least he helped to minimise some of the difficulties as well as putting heart into many thousands of those who had to contend with them. As we leave behind the bicentenary of his birth we salute him as a true genius, if a flawed one. And we recall (we who are small failures only because we have never attempted anything very big) Carlyle's wise words at the close of his essay on Burns: 'Granted, the ship comes into harbour with shrouds and tackle damaged; the pilot is blameworthy; he has not been all-wise and all-powerful; but to know *how* blameworthy, tell us first whether his voyage has been round the Globe, or only to Ramsgate and the Isle of Dogs.'[59]

Notes to Introduction

1 K Marx, *Capital* (trans. Moore and Eveling, ed. F Engels, 3rd edn., 1896), p.630 note.

2 T Carlyle, *Reminiscences* (ed C E Norton, intro. I Campbell, 1972), p.216.

3 N Macleod, *The Earnest Student, being Memorials of John Mackintosh* (pop. edn., 1863), p.476.

4 J Cairns, *Thomas Chalmers* (n.d.), p.5.

5 G D Henderson, *Heritage* (1943), p.113; D A Wilson, *Carlyle Till Marriage (1795-1826)* (1923), p.134.

6 A T Innes, *Studies in Scottish Church History, Chiefly Ecclesiastical* (1902), p.184.

7 J Morley, *The Life of William Ewart Gladstone* (1905 edn.), vol. I, p.110.

8 Lord Rosebery, *Miscellanies, Literary and Historical* (1921), vol. I, p.238.

9 Morley, *Gladstone*, vol. I, p.169.

10 Henderson, *Heritage*, p.109.

11 I Henderson, 'Thomas Chalmers, 1780-1847', p.130, in R S Wright, *Fathers of the Kirk* (1960).

12 A Philip, *Thomas Chalmers, Apostle of Union* (1929), p.21.

13 E B Ramsay, *A Biographical Notice of the late Thomas Chalmers, DD, LLD* (1850), p.46.

14 D Macleod, *Life of Norman Macleod*, vol. I (1876), p.263.

15 P C Simpson, *The Life of Principal Rainy* (1-vol. edn., 1909), p.92.

16 Philip, *Chalmers*, p.16.

17 Henderson, 'Thomas Chalmers', p.140.

18 J Brown, *Horae Subsecivae* (3-vol. edn., 1908), 2nd series, p.133.

19 D Masson, *Memories of Two Cities: Edinburgh and Aberdeen* (1911), p.57.

20 W Hazlitt, *The Spirit of the Age, or Contemporary Portraits* (4th edn., 1894), p.63 note.

21 W Hanna, *Memoirs of the Life and Writings of Thomas Chalmers* (1849-1852), vol. II, p.102.

22 H Watt, *Thomas Chalmers and the Disruption* (1943), p.48.

23 ibid., p.49.

24 Hazlitt, *Spirit of the Age*, p.75.

25 Cairns, *Chalmers*, p.6.

26 J Shield Nicholson, Preface (p.5) to G C Wood, *The Opinions of Dr Chalmers Concerning Political Economy and Social Reform* (1912).

27 Philip, *Chalmers*, p.73.

28 H Watt, *The published writings of Dr Thomas Chalmers (1780-1847): a descriptive list* (1943).

29 D E Keir, *The House of Collins: the story of a Scottish family of publishers from 1789 to the present day* (1952).

30 J Anderson, *Reminiscences of Thomas Chalmers* (1851).

31 Philip, *Chalmers*, pp.19-20.

32 Brown, *Horae Subsecivae*, 2nd series, pp.122-3.

33 ibid., pp.117-8.

34 S J Brown, 'The Disruption and Urban Poverty: Thomas Chalmers and the West Port Operation in Edinburgh, 1844-47', *Records of the Scottish Church History Society*, vol. XX, pt I (1978), pp.65-89.

35 Hanna, *Memoirs*, vol. II (Appendix), p.508.

36 ibid., pp.239-40.

37 ibid., p.299.

38 L J Saunders, *Scottish Democracy, 1815-1840. The Social and Intellectual Background* (1950), p.216.

39 cf. Olive Checkland's study, infra; also S J Brown, *Thomas Chalmers and the Godly Commonwealth in Scotland* (1982), pp.289-96, and R A Cage, *The Scottish Poor Law, 1745-1845* (1981), pp.126-30.

40 Brown, 'The Disruption and Urban Poverty', p.66.

41 ibid., p.88.

42 Saunders, *Scottish Democracy*, p.217.

43 *Dr Lee's Refutation of the Charges brought against him by the Rev Dr Chalmers and Others in reference to the Questions on Church Extension and University Education* (1837).

44 S Mechie, *The Church and Scottish Social Development, 1780-1847* (1960), p.57.

45 Saunders, *Scottish Democracy*, p.221.

46 A Marshall, *Ecclesiastical Establishments Considered. A Sermon* (1829), pp.15-16.

47 ibid., pp.41-42.

48 *The Works of Thomas Chalmers* (1835-1842), vol. XI, p.450.

49 Hanna, *Memoirs*, vol. IV, pp.45-46.

50 Watt, *Chalmers*, p.137.

51 Hanna, *Memoirs*, vol. III, pp.451-52.

52 *Fourth Report of the Committee of the General Assembly of the Church of Scotland on Church Extension, Given in and read on the 22nd of May 1838 by Thomas Chalmers, DD, Convener* (1838), p.12.

53 N L Walker, *Robert Buchanan, DD. An Ecclesiastical Biography* (1877), p.47.

54 Watt, *Chalmers*, p.146.

55 Hanna, *Memoirs*, vol. III, p.483.

56 ibid., vol. IV, p.23 note.

57 cf John McCaffrey's study, infra; also Brown, *Chalmers and the Godly Commonwealth*, ch1.

58 cf. the studies by Iain Maciver and Ian Muirhead, infra; also Brown, *Chalmers and the Godly Commonwealth*, esp. chs. 5 and 6.

59 T Carlyle, *Critical and Miscellaneous Essays*, vol. I (Centenary edn, 1899), p.318.

I

The Life of Thomas Chalmers

John McCaffrey

Thomas Chalmers was born in Anstruther in Fife in March 1780 and died in Edinburgh in May 1847. Between these two dates and places he lived a varied life, crammed with incident and, for much of it, in the public eye. [1] He was a student at St Andrews from 1791 to 1799. He attended classes in Edinburgh from 1799 to 1801. From 1801 to 1823 he was a parish minister, first as an assistant in Roxburghshire, then at Kilmany in Fife from 1803 to 1815 and in Glasgow from 1815 to 1823. He next became a university professor, first in Moral Philosophy at St Andrews from 1823 to 1828, then in Divinity at Edinburgh from 1828 to 1843, and finally in Divinity for the Free Church at New College, Edinburgh, and as its first Principal, from 1843 to 1847. His personal and intellectual influence was extensive both at home and abroad. If a man's life is measured by the range of his acquaintances and friends and by the impression he made on them then Chalmers' was a rich one. For instance, Andrew Fuller, the secretary of the Baptist Missionary Society, once remarked that could Chalmers only speak without notes 'he might be king of Scotland'. [2]

From about 1810 he began to make a considerable and increasing impact on the public mind through his preaching and writings on the social and ecclesiastical issues of his time. In his 30s and 40s he won increasing renown for his parochial experiments in social reform and was fêted as a thinker who could popularise scientific discovery and harmonise it with the religious outlook of the age. He gained national fame through the vehemence with which he urged his vision of re-invigorated ecclesiastical Establishments altered to meet the changing state of 19th-century society. He was honoured by centres of learning. Glasgow University made him a Doctor of Divinity in 1816. In 1834 he was elected a corresponding member of the Royal Institute of France. Oxford University awarded him the honorary degree of Doctor of Civil Law in 1835. His views on ecclesiastical and social issues were solicited and listened to by the leading members of society. He published extensively, his collected works, when produced in a uniform edition between 1836 and 1843, running to 25 volumes.

31

From 1816 he assumed an increasingly prominent role in ecclesiastical courts. His advocacy in this sphere led to a stricter view of parochial responsibility being adopted. He masterminded a great surge of church extension in the 1830s. He was embroiled in the controversies which led to the Disruption, and played a part in creating the elements which formed the Free Church of Scotland as a standing challenge to the dominant political outlook of the time. In addition to his public work as a professor, to his work in Church courts, to his writing and preaching as a minister, and to his private responsibilities as a family man, he travelled quite extensively. He made 15 journeys through England, he toured Scotland on several occasions, he visited Ireland twice and France once. The overall outline of his career is therefore clear enough. From a provincial background in the later 18th century he became a prominent figure by the second decade of the 19th century. The 1820s, 30s and 40s saw him emerge as a man of national stature and when he died his passing received the attention which is generally given only to great figures of state. Hugh Miller summed up the public mood at his demise when he expressed the view that: 'Chalmers, like all the truly great, may be said rather to have created than to have belonged to an era.'[3] For Henry Cockburn, too, that other acute observer of the contemporary scene, Chalmers was one of the four men (the others being Dugald Stewart, Walter Scott and Francis Jeffrey) 'who in my time have made Scotland illustrious'.[4]

Yet for all the public fame and action over a long life-span there is a sense in which he never left the geographical and intellectual orbit of that Forth region in which he began and ended his days. Amid the impressive titles under which he was listed in the commemorative conference held at Edinburgh on the bicentenary of his birth, namely Evangelical preacher, social reformer, Disruption leader, Professor of Divinity and first Principal of New College, there is one missing, perhaps because it is so obvious: Thomas Chalmers, human being. The definitive biography by his son-in-law, William Hanna, was the first to set the tone in the 1850s: 'the more minute, exact and faithful in all respects the narrative of his life can be rendered, it will only excite the more affectionate admiration, while more fully accomplishing the still higher object of making his life subservient in representation to the high Christian ends to which it was consecrated in act.'[5] Where Hanna led, other 19th-century biographers in general followed, interpreting Chalmers in terms of the hero figure struggling against odds. Much of this is understandable in the aftermath of the Disruption, but it can lead to distortion, a figure without blemishes or blot, impelled to a consistent course of action as if following out an almost preordained plan.

Chalmers, however, was a man of strong personality, of strong feelings which if bottled up or thwarted could explode in bursts of indignation: he was deeply impressionable and warmed to affection and companionship, but he was conscious of a need to stand on his own feet, aware of his own powers and abilities but driven too, as his diaries reveal, by feelings of insecurity and provincial inadequacy. Because of his abilities he became increasingly involved in public affairs, and public events often seem to give the shape and direction to his life. But concentration on these aspects hides the man behind the public mask. Only by taking into account his own sense of identity, how he saw events and issues and made decisions on them from his own limited viewpoint, can we get an insight into the totality of his outlook as a human being. His early environment was an important formative influence shaping his personality. So, too, were the efforts to school his will as his intellectual perceptions deepened. Throughout his life he had a constant sense of responsibility, of acting with a conscious end in view. He had a deep urge to play an active role, not to be moulded by events but to try to meet them at least half-way in a conscious effort to improve himself.[6] There was something in him, too, of the public performer compelled not by a desire for applause but by an inner need to dramatise his emotions. Associated with this there was his feeling that he stood at the crossing of two worlds, that it was his duty to make his contemporaries aware of the changing nature of their society and readier to accept change in such a way that the human values he himself prized so highly would be preserved intact in an increasingly uncertain world. He saw himself as a bridge-builder. He sensed from a quite early date that his life and actions had to be validated by a wider set of values than the merely contemporary. He took initiatives in public life not from a sense of his own importance (indeed, in his private journal he often deprecated the fame which contemporaries ascribed to him[7]), but because he consistently struggled with all his failings to be true to himself. His analysis of a contemporary issue could, thus, often fail to be sufficiently flexible but this inflexibility came precisely because he approached each different issue, amidst the cares of a busy life, honestly with the weapons he had to hand in his own intellectual powers and his own reading. In a changing world he had only his own judgment and faith to steer by.

Hence the apparent contrast between the sure dogmatic utterances in public and the exasperating tendency to switch front and deal with the matter in a different light. For instance, he could be seen as the advocate of the most grudging treatment of the poor; but at the same time he was the man opposed to T F Kennedy's Bill in 1824 to abolish the poor rates.[8] Or again, he was the consistent public proponent of toleration for Roman Catholics but at the same time the implacable theological opponent of that religion.[9] Yet again, he was the paternalist mistrustful of giving initiative to the ideas of labouring men but at the same time convinced he was the best friend and advocate of their

C

claims. He was the man who thought politics less important than religion but who imagined he could deal with politicians as if they too shared the same convictions as he did with no regard for party considerations or the compromises necessary in public life. His was the mind essentially of the 18th-century man to whom all knowledge was a unity seeking stability in general systems and theories. But in his most public phase in the early 19th century he had to face the challenge of a more individualistic age when the old unities in society and thought were breaking up and the various elements were being forced into a new balance.

He seems a man of contradictions, therefore, but the contradictions were present in his earliest environment which shaped him and in his strong character which sought always to break out of any constraints in which he felt himself placed. Of him it could indeed be said 'the childhood shows the man'. The family he was born into had a strongly-developed sense of locality and status and an equally firmly-held conviction that it was each member's duty to strive with the gifts he had been given to make a place for himself in the world. His family displayed the virtues most warmly appreciated in that environment: adherence to principle based on independent judgment, religious sincerity, sociability, use of talent, communal responsibility. He was the sixth of 14 children born to John and Elizabeth Chalmers. The father was a small-town merchant and shopkeeper. The mother was the daughter of wine merchants in Crail and had been educated in Edinburgh under the superintendence of the famous Miss Nicky Murray. Both were strict in religious outlook, with an emphasis in the mother's case on the need to marry works with grace in practical concern for her less fortunate neighbours, and a predilection for the views of the New Testament rather than the Old. With eight other babies to care for in quick succession to Thomas there could have been little time for undivided attention to him alone in his early years. He recalled her as a hard-working, dutiful mother, though he had to learn to fend for himself in a large family with its fair share of strong personalities. Her letters show her as shrewd, observant and humorous, deeply interested in the welfare of her children and, like her husband, anxious that they become industrious, pious citizens through the cultivation of regular habits and moderate tastes. [10]

Although his father was relatively well-to-do and inherited a position of some financial soundness (and became a respected magistrate and Lord Provost of Anstruther), he never seemed to attain any great prosperity. [11] Through the period 1780-1810 there was little left over from the business to relieve any of the children of the need to make their own way. Thomas' elder brothers left home early to make careers for themselves in business or at sea. When he went with William, who was one year older, to St Andrews, it was Thomas who undertook the role of adviser. There was always something of the elder son's mantle about him. When he became a parish minister after 1802 he was the one to whom the family turned. He cared for his unmarried sisters who kept the manse for him. He superintended the education and prospects of the youngest brothers, Patrick, Charles and Sandy in turn. He acquired that rather anxious air of paternalism which he would never quite shed. He had had to make his own way amid the competing claims of a large family, and much of its 'no nonsense' practicality seems to have rubbed off on him. He was obviously affectionate by nature and could be hurt by criticism and insecurity. His constant search for approval, and that prickly sense of his own importance which later led to many tempestuous encounters, probably stemmed from the way he had to fit into the family pecking order. An instance in 1804 when he was 24 years old shows how something of this still remained. He was returning Patrick, who had been studying under him, back to Anstruther, having concluded he lacked ability in book learning. However, in a revealing passage to his father he sought to shield Patrick from the disappointed expectations of his family. 'I would by all means check the irritating reflections in which the rest of the family and particularly sisters are apt to indulge,' he wrote. 'I have myself a most distinct recollection of the pernicious effect that the impertinence of my sisters had upon my own feelings when of his age [about 14 years, when his own lack of progress at St Andrews was giving cause for concern]. It . . . is apt to give a disgust at home and at relations which even absence and a length of years may not be able to efface.'[12] Perhaps this explains that restless propensity shown in the readily undertaken visits to his brother James in England in 1796, 1799 and 1801, and in his refusal to settle down quickly in Fife after he was licensed to preach in 1799 when he spent much of his time in Edinburgh. He wanted to break free of the smothering influences of Fife.

He became self-reliant. In later life he often showed he could act without too much regard for the consequences of his actions on others, resolving difficulties by deeds dutifully performed. He could exaggerate opposition and anticipate offence. His strong sense of family combined with an equally strong streak of individualism. This may explain the curious circumstance that, when he attained the notoriety of running alternative mathematics classes in 1803 in St Andrews in rivalry with the university, his own sisters, who were keeping house for him at this time, only heard of Thomas' venture accidentally by seeing a report of the furore in a local newspaper.[13] At the same time he was anxious to give precedence to his father by informing him beforehand of his intentions in an effort to reconcile him with the stance he was taking.

Much of his confidence in making decisions like this came from a self-reliance in intellectual matters which he had hewed out for himself in the experiences of his youth. It was never enough for Chalmers to rely on opinions delivered by others. He had to be convinced in his intellectual pilgrimage by his own reading and reflections as to conclusions which were only painfully arrived at. His schooldays seem to have been happy and marked by companionship and a love of games. Probably the lessons were not too demanding, for both he and his brother James thought the Anstruther school had not prepared him well for university. [14] However, he must have shown some promise for he matriculated at St Andrews when he was only 11 years old. He was remembered there at first as keener on games than books (hardly surprising at that age) and 'for entertaining with excellent teas at which there was an abundance of shortbread'. [15] (Evidence here of a life-long attraction to the pleasures of the table.) However, when about 14 years of age he gained three things. One was a resolve to work hard to attain intellectual distinction: evidence of a growing realisation of his mental powers. The second was a glimpse into the wider world beyond Fife through teachers like Dr James Brown in mathematics and Brown's friends, [16] in whose company the events in revolutionary France in the 1790s and the great questions of national policy were discussed. The third thing sprang from this. Admiration for these men and their subjects led to a desire to excel in mathematics and science. His reading, at this time, of a contemporary philosopher like Godwin on *Political Justice* (1793) opened up the interesting speculation that man's nature is determined by environment rather than Providence. It must have been attractive to read in Godwin that 'he who regards all things . . . as links of an indissoluble chain will find himself assisted to reflect upon the moral concerns of mankind with the same firmness of judgment . . . as we are accustomed to do upon the truths of geometry', [17] and comforting to be assured that the movements of men's hearts could be explained by reference to Euclid and Pythagoras. There is still greater significance in the fact that writers like Godwin who saw society in static terms should have been attractive to Chalmers, even when the particular message they preached was ultimately rejected by him. They induced him to view human beings in all their complexity as being capable of reduction to self-regulating units in an axiomatic social context. When the message and the view were both congenial—as in Malthus—his intellectual adherence was unwavering.

In St Andrews, therefore, he learned to go back to sources and large original ideas to work things out for himself. (It says something for the supposed backwardness of St Andrews at this period that a boy of 14 or 15 years should have been able to study such texts.) He became aware that the virtues enshrined in the family setting of Anstruther were already becoming too restrictive for his developing outlook. This readiness to work things out on his own occurs in two other instances. When he drifted (as Professor Watt points out [18]) into study for the ministry, ideas derived from Godwin came up against Professor Hill's rational, orthodox presentation of Calvinist theology. How was Chalmers to reconcile benevolence and free will with grace? Typically he again refused to rely simply on his lecture notes and turned instead to an intensive study of Jonathan Edwards' difficult treatise on *Freedom of the Will* (1754). The intellectual struggle this involved burned into his mind a view which was both comprehensive and static. His reading of Edwards presented him with a view in which the Lockean world of the senses and the Newtonian order of material elements could be understood as part of God's providential plan, and so allowed him to reconcile science and religion in terms of a beneficent God.

The second example of this approach came in the interval between the end of his divinity course and his presentation to Kilmany in 1802. Scientific advance had been so extensive in the 18th century as to lead some minds to deny the need for a beneficent creator. The answer for Chalmers came during his attendance at Professor Robison's Natural Philosophy lectures in Edinburgh in 1800-1801. Robison transformed Chalmers into a Baconian by showing that scientific facts could be fitted into a metaphysical scheme by working from the known to the unknown. Spirit and matter could thus be reconciled and so Chalmers was able to defend Christianity in terms of 18th-century natural religion: proving it from the universal adaptation in nature of means to ends, and the moral adaptation of men's minds to the expectation of constancy in nature. [19]

As David Masson pointed out, it was this width derived from scientific reading which enabled Chalmers to temper the theology of the 19th-century Scottish Church and point it forward imperceptibly in a more liberal direction. [20] His penchant for natural religion and scientific discovery and his struggle to reconcile faith and reason equipped him particularly well to bridge the gap between the rationalistic world of the 18th century and the individualism and uncertainty of the 19th century. [21] That man could reduce the magnitudes of time and space to ordered sequences and abstract mathematical formulae in his own small mind was evidence itself to Chalmers of the divine origins of mind, spirit and nature. His ability to translate the ordered phraseology of 18th-century thought into the language of commercial and scientific society in the early 19th century enabled him to address it in terms, it seemed, of almost prophetic insight. Hence the popular success of his *Astronomical Discourses* delivered and published in Glasgow in 1816 and 1817.

His strength did not lie so much in discovering new insights as in a willingness to link metaphysics and science in ways which could be popularly understood. This was precisely because he himself had had to arrive at a personal conviction of their validity by going back to first principles. The struggle to work out ideas for himself had an effect on a man with a warm and generous temperament. The experience compelled him to communicate the lessons he had learned to others with increased vehemence.

There was a merging of the old and the new in Chalmers' early development here which he never quite lost and equally never fully elaborated. Conviction came to him not only through reason. It involved in his case something approaching a 19th-century struggle in the recesses of the soul. We know from his friends' recollections that this period saw him rely more and more on his inner life and its growth through prayer. Faith had its place as well as reason. 'Under all the difficulties and despondencies of such a state,' he wrote to a friend, 'I would still encourage you to prayer. Cry as you can. With real moral earnestness and a perseverance in this habit light will at length arise out of darkness.'[22] Other elements in the conflict between old and new, which appear later in his social thinking, are also to be discerned emerging at this time. There is the awareness of communal responsibility for godliness, discharged by means of the links between Church and society. At the same time there emerges an emphasis on the individual struggle where godly status can be all too easily equated with observable success and where those still struggling to make the transition can be dismissed as feckless.

By the 1800s, then, he appeared a bundle of contradictions to his contemporaries. He was absorbed in strange reading and given to bouts of deep introspection, but he delighted, too, in companionship and sought approval. He mixed easily with his fellow students and ministers, but he was conscious of an awkwardness in more extended company. He did not fit easily into groups or parties. He was aware of his intellectual powers and determined to play the part of an enlightened minister, but equally determined to be responsible for his actions and valued for himself rather than for his office.[23] A sense of prickly self-importance and a willingness to act regardless of the consequences for others became a fixed trait in his twenties and thirties.

This showed itself early in his first public venture as a tutor in Arbroath in 1798. His father had secured the post partly to offset his son's bookishness and to develop his social graces. Thomas felt, however, that the family under whose roof he found himself undervalued him. Rather than dissimulate because of his lowly position, however, he felt compelled by honesty to speak his mind. Taxed by his new master for having too much pride, he retorted: 'There are two kinds of pride . . . that which lords it over inferiors and . . . that which rejoices in repressing the insolence of superiors. The first I have none of—the second I glory in.'[24] Inevitably the contract was terminated. The well-known episode in 1803-4 when he ran rival mathematics classes alongside those of the university shows the same insistence on proving himself right. When presented to Kilmany in

1802 the antipluralist of later years also secured appointment as assistant to the Mathematics professor in St Andrews. His hopes of using this as a means to attain his dearest wish, a university chair, were dashed when the engagement was not renewed. Rather than brood, however, he set out to prove his point by running his own classes. The challenge to the Establishment set the town by the ears. It hurt his family. More important for Chalmers was the need to vindicate his reputation. The diary he kept of this episode is very revealing, showing the extent of his emotional involvement. Each victory on his side was noted meticulously, just as was every scrap which suggested the lack of teaching ability in the official university classes.[25] The storm thus raised left him unperturbed, however, and, typically, once he had made his point by 1804, he dropped the project. It was as if a tremendous force built up which had to be released: but once the storm was over it subsided as quickly, waiting only for the next episode to reawaken it.

Intellectual ambition continued to embroil others. When he published his first book on economics on the *Extent and Stability of National Resources* in 1808, letters showered on the publishers and on his brother James in London, stressing the need to publicise it and the vital truths of the arguments it contained. 'I find that booksellers require to be urged to anything like exertion,' wrote the exasperated Thomas, and to supplement their efforts his brother James, amid the cares of his own business, was directed to distribute copies to influential public figures and place advertisements in the London newspapers. Thomas even proposed that James might pilot a second London edition through the press, placidly reassuring him that all he would have to spare was an hour each day correcting the proofs.[26] The storm then subsided as quickly as it arose leaving James and the bookseller to pick up the threads of their interrupted lives as best they could.

The same driving energy in pursuit of a single aim reappeared in his dealings with his congregation and the public authorities when he moved to Glasgow in 1815. In the earlier episodes he had been impelled by a secular desire for fame as a mathematician or an author. By 1815 and the Glasgow phase he had subordinated these ambitions to a religious end. By then he had developed a strategy which combined economics, religion and Malthusian theory in a unique answer (as he believed) to the social and political challenges of the 19th century. But the same need to justify his views runs through both the earlier Moderate and later Evangelical behaviour, and in the later as in the earlier it involved not merely himself but others in a series of abrasive encounters and left them in a radically different position to that obtaining before he came on the scene. Finally, having raised the storm, he then withdrew to propagate his views by different means.

In Glasgow he let it be known at the outset that as far as possible he would confine himself to strictly parochial endeavours and eschew secular cares such as attending the committee meetings of public bodies and benevolent institutions on which the city ministers customarily sat. Thwarted in this purpose of giving his sole attention to parish duties, he next organised a band of helpers to share the load of visitation and began to affect their lives by welding them into a cohesive group under his leadership. He then persuaded the Town Council to appoint him to a new parish which they had just created, St John's, and to make separate arrangements for education and poor relief therein.

The echoes from these actions resounded both during and after his period in Glasgow. The General Session of all the Glasgow parishes protested at his proposals for separate management in 1819, argued among themselves and finally ceased to co-operate with the city magistrates in the administration of poor relief. Then in 1822 Chalmers started another project by trying to persuade the Town Council to provide a chapel of ease in St John's. (This was urged on the grounds that very few of his parishioners had seats in St John's. Yet one of the grounds on which he had urged the Council to make the new parochial arrangements for him in 1818 had been that his parishioners would have priority there. The magistrates must have wondered what they had let themselves in for in 1815 when they appointed a man who said he wanted to restrict himself as much as possible to purely spiritual matters!) The Town Council were next advised by their poor relief managers that new arrangements would have to be made. The latter's report of December 1823 in fact implicitly upheld Chalmers' critics' arguments and recommended the reinstitution of the system which had been abandoned at his insistence in 1819. Finally, when matters seemed to be reaching an impasse, Chalmers accepted an appointment as Professor of Moral Philosophy in St Andrews in 1823 and left others to carry on the day-to-day work in the St John's experiment. This prompted the rather barbed comment by one of his fellow ministers that he could see little benefit to the Church in a man of Chalmers' talents taking himself off to a situation where he would be idle for at least half the year. [27]

There is a revealing entry in his diary for 15 May 1810. It concerns a minor matter but it suggests where this consistent attitude in both his earlier and later life came from. He had been anxious about the settlement of an estate of which he was an executor. He had expected opposition, but things went smoothly and he wrote: 'Settled matters with Mr Ballardie's legatees and *have to record for my own encouragement and direction in all future causes* that a *steady, unyielding determination* to carry through what is *your right* and *your justice* is far less formidable in the act than in the anticipation' (italics mine). [28] Clearly, to steel himself against feelings of his own inadequacy, he had to become more determined in sticking to what he thought was right.

This suggests that such normal episodes were seen by him as performances before which he suffered in anticipation, like an actor, from a fit of nerves. Did he, thus, harden himself to overcome imagined opposition because he felt his provincial background, or feared that his appearance and manner might not be sufficiently imposing to convince people as to his worth, status, and capacity? Notes which he made at this period and the recollections of his friends suggest that he was conscious of defects in his appearance and manner.[29] His emotional extremes betray a sense of insecurity. He was ready to imagine himself slighted by social superiors. At the first sign of acceptance, however, his warm retraction of earlier suspicions of others could lead to equally extreme social conformity. He resented the indifference of social superiors but on one occasion when he was invited to dine with rather well-off relatives he recorded: 'my unpleasant impressions . . . softened for this day by the style of their reception and this bye the bye is an argument against evil-speaking. There is a fascination in the attention of superiors and I feel a conscious weakness upon contrasting the bitterness of my former invective with the elevation inspired by their civil and respectful manners this day.'[30] This shows how he wanted to be accepted for himself and how ready he was to suppress past resentments for the sake of present approbation. But he did not immediately impress others. Hearers at his sermons confessed themselves disappointed at first with his accent, appearance, manner and delivery. Only once he had launched himself in his subject were they caught up in the fire of his oratory. His feelings of social awkwardness induced him therefore to summon up all his energies in an ever more determined fashion to impose his will.

By the time he was 30 years old this pertinacity had become a fixed, conscious habit. It was reinforced in turn by a deepening religious conviction. This phase developed from about 1806 and by 1811 had stripped him of his earlier tolerant outlook and left him a convinced Evangelical. By 1811 and 1812 he had experienced a change from a state in which he relied on his own efforts to improve himself to one where he now placed all his trust in God's providence. The change occurred for various reasons. Partly it came because he was at that age in which every individual faces a reassessment as the seemingly endless years of youth recede before the warning approach of middle age. Partly it was due to the sobering effect of a series of closely-linked family bereavements. The darkening tone in his correspondence at this time shows this.[31] And the glimpse of death he himself had caught during his own long, serious illness of 1809-1810 hastened the process.[32] In addition there was the gathering effect of his involvement in a study of Christian authors for the article on Christianity which his growing fame had led David Brewster to request for the *Edinburgh Encyclopaedia*. His reading of William Wilberforce's *Practical*

Christianity (1797) at this time made a powerful impression, chiming as it did with his own growing conviction and his penchant for practical application of the ideas and emotions influencing him. In 1810, too, his journal shows he was contemplating the security which marriage would afford. A broken love affair distressed him and there is a more mature self-knowledge shown when he records that the lady was likely to make another match. 'This certainty has gone far to disburden my mind,' he wrote, 'of the anxieties which have so often oppressed it. Such is the mysteriousness of love. It is hope and fear and ignorance and uncertainty which feed and influence it. Let me cherish this certainty and it will not only tranquillise me. It will induce a more Christian frame of mind upon this subject for it was the keen interest which anxious and aspiring love communicated to my feelings that lay at the bottom of all the heat and acrimony which have so often transported me.' [33] Here is the human side of Chalmers, uncertain, capable of sorrow, but struggling too to rise above adversity. Domestic tranquillity eventually came in 1812 with marriage to Grace Pratt and in the affectionate relationship he developed with his six daughters. His letters to his family, the accounts by his friends of his playful habits in his children's company, the interest and concern he showed for each of his family in turn, all testify to this.

After 1811 his new determination to act whatever the consequences was sustained by his reading. The lives of 17th-century divines amidst trials and tribulation, he confessed, 'put the present [age] to shame.' [34] He became increasingly reluctant to suffer any distraction or interruption from his religious duties: a trait which surfaced clearly in the Glasgow ministry. He became concerned, too, about maintaining his health and as he grew older complained of the pressures to which he felt himself subjected. [35] Fear of unpopularity only made him more determined. In 1812 he wrote to a friend (John Honey) about the problems facing those who, like himself, had resolved to follow a strict regimen in public and private life. 'You offer to keep me in countenance. It is the dread of being laughed at which keeps men from announcing themselves.' Nevertheless, he continued, 'embark with energy in this new career and you will find it the most splendid and animating you have ever tried. . . . Nor can I see . . . how we can stop 'till we have found our conclusion and our repose in the peculiar doctrines of the Gospel.' [36]

The last phrase is important for it expresses total commitment without heed as to consequences. These could now be left to the workings of Providence. This aspect of Chalmers' life, his new religious state, is important in explaining his motivation. It was so personal and so continuously monitored by him that he often seemed to take decisions on grounds different from those apparent to others. It could lead him into courses which sometimes seemed to contemporaries at best contradictory, and at worst devious. The issues to be faced up to were so momentous that no time could be found for a long period of reflection, nor for the spirit of compromise needed in dealing with major issues in which the actions of self-interested men were involved. Religious conviction swamped pragmatism. In the church conflicts he was anxious to find common ground in private conversation, but when principle had to be demonstrated in public this personal compromise gave way to public obstinacy. The reason was that personal religious responsibility demanded in the last analysis total commitment. Thus, along with greater certainty came a certain recklessness as to temporal consequences, a trait he had already shown in his early days. At the end of 1811 he wrote: 'Let the impression grow on me as the years roll by that I am here on a journey; and let me carry about with me the same faith . . . the same nearness of perception as to the things of eternity as if I knew that in half an hour I were to be summoned by the last messenger.'[37]

The strategy he adopted from 1814 onwards to change the policy of the Church of Scotland derived its consistency from this religious motivation. It is exemplified in his opposition to pluralities in 1814 and 1816. It determined the outstanding features of his Glasgow ministry of 1815-23. It lay behind the more sustained attack he made on pluralities in the Assembly in the 1820s, his proposals for the modification of patronage in 1833, his work on Church Extension during the years 1834-41, and above all his role in the events leading to the Disruption. Whether the question concerned pluralities, veto, or church extension, one idea was common to all and in publicising it he made his reputation. Two things were essential to it: character and locality. The quality of the population would be assured by an effective teaching Church. The appointment of ministers to parishes and popular assent to these appointments had to be reconciled to ensure orderly progress. The common man and his attitudes were the key. The 18th-century 'enlightenment' tradition inclined Chalmers to envisage this in somewhat static terms as part of a natural law rather than as a developing situation in which flexibility was required. But it did encourage him to try to marry economics and morality. If the quality of people depended on their resourcefulness then this led him to a more obdurate defence of the means whereby he thought this resourcefulness could be guaranteed, viz. an effective territorial Establishment; a close alliance between Church and society. Unfortunately, society was beginning to be dominated by an individualistic ethic where respectability depended on the free-for-all of achievement. In trying to bridge the gap between community and individual values Chalmers' background inclined him to lay more emphasis on the latter.[38]

This social and religious outlook led him directly into a consideration of the condition of the labouring population and the issues affecting it in a period of transition. However, his very real concern for labouring men was not widely enough based to give him any real insights into their popular political aspirations. Thus, Chalmers' attitude to working-class radicalism and to the major movements in British politics from the 1800s to the end of his life was at best cautious, ambivalent, at worst suspicious and downright reactionary. Some of his companions in his youth had thought he was attracted to radical political notions in the 1790s, but his life-long friend and correspondent, Thomas Duncan, more shrewdly and drily recalled that whatever early leanings towards Whiggism he had had were soon replaced by 'an admiration for that state of society in which a generous aristocracy shower blessings on the poor and the poor look up with gratitude to the aristocracy'. [39]

Chalmers' political views were a mixture of solicitous care for the struggling poor and a concern that any amelioration of their lot should not threaten the existing social structure. These sentiments had already matured in Fife before 1815. His attitudes to economic, social and political issues were based on the belief that human progress could only come through an inner reformation in the population, not through an outer change in the political structure. The former gave reality to the hope of progress, the latter the shadow without the substance. The lower orders would be the agents of change only when guided by a paternal instruction in religion and economics to a right view of their condition and potential. Political agitation was a delusion and, worse, it would almost always lead, in his opinion, to the overweening influence of a demagogue.

He believed that the vitality of the modern state depended on the freedom of each individual. That true freedom, however, would only come from the power of religion informing each individual's conscience. Persuasion and education were, therefore, essential. So, too, was the concern of each class or group for the other, and especially the responsibility of the higher for the lower. 'We feel quite assured,' he wrote in 1832, 'of every land of law and liberty that with an order of men possessing large and independent affluence, there is a better security for the general comfort and virtue of the whole, than when society presents an aspect of almost unalleviated plebeianism.' [40] Initiatives from working men were only acceptable when they came as a result of paternalistic guidance.

His first reaction to the growing economic instability and social unrest after 1815 was to underplay its significance. On holiday in Anstruther in 1815 he wrote: 'in towns all is clamour and noise and broad manifestation . . . my impression is that it is more bawled and belaboured about, both in print and conversation, than it ought to be.'

After some residence in Glasgow, however, his response by 1819 had become more positive. While he regarded the radical outbreaks of 1819 and especially of 1820 as 'an aspect of infidelity and irreligion', he was more inclined to emphasise the need to find lasting solutions. Military force was not the best means of ensuring peace, he observed in 1819, and a better method of conciliating the lower classes would be to repeal the Corn Laws. He also seems to have envisaged government grants to relieve distress being used for some form of industrial retraining, 'a sum to draw away labourers from the loom to other employments'. [41] Above all, he recognised the *anomie* emerging in manufacturing centres. In this period he wrote, 'there is a mighty unfilled space interposed between the high and the low of every large manufacturing city . . . and a resentful feeling is apt to be fostered of disdain and defiance which it will require all the expedients of an enlightened charity effectually to do away.' [42]

This enlightened charity would be accomplished, he thought, through responsible effort in the locality, through district visiting and daily concern undertaken by the better off, above all through a reinvigorated national Church. Hence the intensity with which he carried out his social experiments in Glasgow. By them, social and political strains would be lessened and the true path to progress signposted. 'If power and popularity shall ever stand in hostile array against each other, we are not to wonder though the result should be, a church on the one hand, frowning aloof in all the pride and distance of hierarchy upon our population, and a people on the other, revolted into utter distaste for establishments and mingling with this a very general alienation of heart from all that carries the stamp of authority in the land.' [43] Thus some compromise arrangement over patronage and Church Extension would be needed in the immediate future. Here in all these responses of Chalmers to political discontent published in 1821 lay the seeds of the later Ten Years' Conflict.

He was a Liberal Tory with all the blend of basic inflexibility and cautious pragmatism typical of that creed. He had long advocated the abolition of the Corn Laws and the imposition of a progressive income tax. His attitude to the great question of Reform between 1830 and 1832 was, however, sceptical and grudging. When the 1830 revolution in France was 'the subject of daily thought, meditation and converse', Chalmers observed to his Quaker friend J J Gurney: 'I am not one of those who underrate the value of civil and political liberty, but I am well assured that it is only the principles of Christianity which can impart true security, prosperity and happiness, either to individuals or to nations.' [44]

He was even less in favour of the 1832 Reform Act. While welcoming some electoral modification he deplored the prevailing tendency to see in it the ultimate solution to all contemporary problems. Material improvements would not be achieved 'amid the uproar of a furious and discordant politics', but by 'the fruit of a moral warfare whose weapons are not carnal but spiritual. . . . We should rejoice in . . . higher wages for the labourer . . . but this cannot be effected . . . by any assertion, however successful, of a political equality with the other orders of the state. . . . It will be the aggregate effect of a higher taste, a higher intelligence, and above all a widespread Christianity throughout the mass of the population.' [45]

Self-help efforts undertaken by working men in this period, like the development of Trade Unions, the Ten Hours movement and Chartism, were viewed with the same mixture of Liberal Toryism. He had welcomed the repeal of the Combination Laws in 1824 but more as a sign of lessening governmental intervention in economic affairs than as a gateway to the freedom of organised labour. He was even more insistent on curbing any undue assumption of power on the part of the now legalised unions. [46] He was scathing, however, in his indictment of child labour: 'the enormity unheard of till these modern times, of children from nine years old and upwards doomed to fourteen hours of every day of confinement and hard labour amid the dust, and the steam and the dizzying sounds of a crowded manufactory.' [47]

With such an outlook his view of Chartism was inevitably unsympathetic. Finding himself engaged to lecture in 1840 to a mechanics' institute where George Combe and Patrick Brewster had recently spoken, he publicly dissociated himself from the secularism of the former and the Chartism of the latter.[48]And in 1846, when laying the foundation stone for New College, he addressed these coldly reproving remarks to the workmen present:

> It delights me to observe that so many of the working class in our city now stand within reach of my voice. Within the walls now to be raised by their hands there may or there may not in time be delivered the lessons of general science. But from the very outset, we hope, there will be the lessons of the higher wisdom which is often hid from the wise and prudent and revealed to babes. We leave to others the passions and politics of this world; and nothing will ever be taught, I trust, in any of our halls, which shall have the remotest tendency to disturb the existing order of things, or to confound the ranks and distinctions which at present obtain in society. [49]

Yet he consistently expressed his sympathies for the labouring population. In 1840 he blamed Chartism directly on the defects of the governors: 'Should the fearful crisis of a sweeping and destructive anarchy be now awaiting us, it will lie as much, we think culpably and inexcusably more so, at the door of the highest as of the lower orders in the commonwealth.' [50] But his sympathies were starved of life by the mistrust with which he viewed the political initiatives of the working classes. [51]

His outlook was not entirely negative. One area in which he did favour government intervention was that of providing a national system of education. [52] And again, just before his death he took up his pen once more to call for a national effort to solve the problems of the 1845 famine in Ireland by direct government legislation and intervention. [53]

He increasingly declared a wish, in the 1830s, to be less involved in public questions and play a more private role, especially after he had suffered what seems to have been a form of stroke or seizure in 1834. His insistence on his views of Church and society, however, drew him increasingly yet unwillingly into the Ten Years' Conflict. The success of his London lectures on the necessity of National Establishments in 1838 was such as to make this almost inevitable. His argument for a strong Establishment was not based on a precise sense of history or patristic learning, nor was it formulated to convince scholars. It was a call to action and vigilance, and as such succeeded in generating triumphal enthusiasm. [54] But it also tended to brush aside difficulties. Its vision of a national recognition of religion which would include Dissenters and Voluntaries in a united crusade placed Chalmers somewhat outside of a narrow denominational spectrum. He declared to his friend J J Gurney, 'I do not plead very earnestly for any particular church; but I would have a well-formed machinery fixed in every country.' [55] This breadth and lack of definition could lead him still to claim in 1838, when events were proving otherwise, that 'external force might make an obnoxious individual the holder of a benefice, but there is no external force in these realms that could make him a minister of the Church of Scotland.' [56]

Despite the apparent intransigence in such statements he had always been in favour of compromise. His views had never really altered from 1814 when he declared that it was up to the church courts to exercise responsibility in judging the fitness of a candidate. But by 1840 issues like the weight to be given to the views of parishioners, which had seemed so clear cut in 1814, were now capable of a variety of interpretations, of differing emphases: tailor-made, in fact, to create misinterpretation and suspicion. Because of this politicians like Lord Aberdeen and Sir James Graham felt he had tricked them by seeming to say one thing to them in private and then denouncing their proposals when they became public. [57] Aberdeen wrote to him in May 1840 before he presented his compromise bill in Parliament, saying, 'I believe the peace of the church is in your hands'. [58] But was Aberdeen just deceiving himself and hoping to flatter Chalmers into a more neutral position? James Robertson of Ellon sensed something of the conflicting pressures when he recorded in February 1840: 'I had several long conversations [with Dr Chalmers] upon the subject; and though he said nothing which could commit him to the view which I have all along entertained he did not seem very adverse to the plan which I submitted in the October Synod . . . I thought he might have done much to bring his own party to terms of reason. . . . He is, I do believe, a good man; but I think it must be admitted by his best friends that he is extravagantly rash.'[59] Alexander Campbell of Monzie, MP for Argyll, also wrote in May 1840, obviously in some haste, in much the same terms as Aberdeen in an effort to secure Chalmers' support for Aberdeen's proposals. In Campbell's letter, however, there is a more open recognition of the inadequacies in Aberdeen's measure and of the influence of political calculation on negotiations at this stage:

> I therefore eminently hope that you will give this measure your powerful support. I feel assured that you in common with many of the Church's best friends will be disappointed with it but yet I fondly hope that the awful position we shall be placed in, if the Conservative party failing in obtaining the co-operation of the church in this measure are, as well as the Whigs, obliged to give up attempting to legislate in the matter, will weigh with you. Let me assure you the object and intention of the Whigs (now that they have seen Lord Aberdeen's motion) aim again to profess affectionate regard for the Church of Scotland, again to tempt her sons to believe them sincere in their professions and as certainly to desert them the instant they effect a split between them and the Conservatives. In plain words then . . . I call upon you to stand forth in that prominent and commanding position in which Providence has placed you, to rally round you all who really love their church and disregarding alike the backwardness of the timid and the imprudence and rash zeal of some of the 'modern martyrs' take and keep the lead in this struggle.[60]

Was Chalmers a leader then, but vacillating? After receiving letters such as this it must have been difficult for him to pick his way between the conflicting claims of friendship, natural inclination, party advantage and principle. In any case contemporaries were probably wrong to regard him by that stage (the later 1830s and early 1840s) as a leading figure capable of determining events. His diary shows he was reluctant to become involved in the specific points raised by the veto in the courts. On 1 April 1840 he wrote, 'I long for my own deliverance from the turmoils of public life'; and again on 13 April, 'To Edinburgh against my will on Non-Intrusion.' By 31 January 1841, after a call from Sir George Sinclair, he was deploring the 'strong probability that I may be implicated more than I like with the church question', and on 14 March in that year he was 'sadly exercised . . . by the urgencies that I should again mingle in the fray to the hazard of my health and serious injury of my literary undertakings'.[61] He was becoming an old man less and less inclined to take up new causes and increasingly conscious of the passage of time. In addition younger and wilder spirits were taking over in the Non-Intrusion struggle who wanted cut and dried solutions.

Chalmers must have sensed that his larger view, with its tendency to look for compromise, would fail if persisted in and would make him lose with both sides. There is a lack of sympathy in his diary at this period for the more bustling attitudes of his younger colleagues. Thus on 11 April 1840 he comments on 'the impracticableness of my committee on Lord Aberdeen's proposition'. [62] In 1840, too, as well as influences from the politicians on the one side, from the other churchmen like Robert Buchanan were writing to press on him the necessity for all Non-Intrusionists to unite to show the government they could not be trifled with. [63] Chalmers, too, recorded a feeling at times of being bypassed. On 4 March 1841 he wrote: 'Surprised at want of communication . . . on the affairs of the church. Mr Cunningham's non-appearance particularly striking after introduction I gave him to the Bishop of London.' And on 6 October 1841 he wrote: 'Every feeling of offence [must be struggled against] at the silence of the ecclesiastics towards me respecting the affairs of our church.' [64] Perhaps, to use Disraeli's phrase, he was becoming one of those 'men who lead rather than guide'.

In such a situation it was not surprising that pressure should be brought to bear on him, nor that he should come to identify himself publicly with the side he was in closest daily contact with—the Non-Intrusionist. A H Gordon in his biography of Lord Aberdeen goes so far as to suggest that Chalmers' adoption of a firmer stance and his rejection of Aberdeen's proposals in 1840 was forced on him by untoward pressure, even blackmail: 'Violent discussions, it is said—in which complaints of Chalmers' so-styled secret communications with Lord Aberdeen and even threats founded on some equivocal propositions in his lectures are stated to have been freely uttered—took place in his presence.' [65] Chalmers' journal entries for this period fail to throw more than a tantalisingly vague glimmer on this charge. But an examination of the issue shows that Chalmers' stand on the church question evolved in a more human and painful way than has been indicated in standard accounts of the Disruption where events seem to take place in a series of inevitable steps.

He increasingly sought refuge in Burntisland from the pressures present in Edinburgh. There is a peremptory tone (surprising in addressing a figure of his stature) in a letter he received in April 1840 from Non-Intrusionists who, finding he had gone over to Burntisland, requested 'in a particular manner that, if possible, you will make it convenient to be in Edinburgh tomorrow for the meeting'. [66] But the only entries in his journal (not cited by Hanna) which might suggest conflict on his theological teaching do not occur until 1841. On 24 January 1841 he was 'Brooding I fear especially on the injustice done me by certain members of Presbytery in regard to my Theological teaching. Exploded in on my family in the evening.' On 1 February

1841 he 'called on Mr Buchanan, Messrs Candlish and Cunningham there. Made an appointment with the latter; and pray that God may enable me to acquit of my intended explanation in a way that may resound to His Glory and the good of His Church.' And on the next day, 2 February 1841, 'Two days lost to study by my anxieties about a public meeting and my brooding anent an injustice which has so far been softened by the explanation of Mr Cunningham with whom this morning I had a long conversation that I desire to be quit of it for ever.'[67] Were the explanations exchanged on 1 and 2 February connected with the injustices done him with regard to his theological teaching a week earlier? The entries occur too long after the Aberdeen negotiations of 1840 to substantiate Gordon's charge. However, there is an admission here which shows he had been touched to the quick by some imputations about his teaching. There is not enough in the Journal to prove Gordon's point one way or the other. However, given the single-mindedness and intransigence of men like Candlish and Cunningham it would not be surprising if strong efforts had been made, even without any hint of untoward pressure, to ensure that Chalmers' weight was thrown into the Non-Intrusionists' side in the faction fray which was now increasingly splitting the Establishment.

Whatever the reason, he was unhappily launched on a course from 1840 which broke up the Church he had spent a lifetime serving. He could comfort himself with the hope that it might lead eventually somehow to a better Establishment. It meant, however, that despite the fame which he enjoyed in the Free Church he ended his days as something of an exile, as the figurehead of movements in reality led by younger and different men, in a situation in which his broad appeal (his main strength) was necessarily circumscribed. In his last days he retained his appetite for action. As late as 1841 he could still reproach himself in his Journal for becoming too involved in a public question like the Corn Laws. His activities in fund-raising for the Free Church involved him in fresh public controversy with the Anti-Slavery movement over the question of maintaining links with slave-holding Churches. As has been mentioned, he was active too, at this time, in calling for a national effort for famine relief in Ireland. At the same time, however, he was concentrating increasingly on spiritual essentials, jettisoning the accumulated lumber of a lifetime's worldly business and retaining only the essential faith by which he had tried to live since the awakening of 1811.[68] His death went unrecorded by the General Assembly of the Church of Scotland in May 1847. Nevertheless, it made a deep impression among the members of all Churches. His funeral was something of a state occasion. 'No private death could produce a deeper or more general feeling of public sorrow,' wrote Cockburn. His fame, the latter remarked, depended not on his reputation as a party leader but rather on the fact that he was superior to parties and derived 'his authority by the way he addressed himself to the whole Scotch mind'. [69] In a narrowing situation it was his width and weight (what he himself would have called 'wecht') which was remembered.

In order to assess the importance of his life we have to measure in some way his influence on others. His advocacy of the social gospel is well known. At the same time his insistence on personal commitment could easily encourage the narrower 19th-century individualistic outlook with its emphasis on personal worth in terms of 'respectability', and thus give men a selfish excuse for avoiding an analysis of the root causes of recalcitrant social problems. However, what were the alternatives open to him as early as 1815? To condemn him for callousness is to condemn the age. Even W P Alison at this period was 'mournfully inclined to Mr Malthus' doctrine'. [70]

It is impossible to ignore the fact that Chalmers did have an immediate effect on the society around him. Looking at the long rows of his publications today we may wonder at this. Who can have read these volumes with their over-ornate prose? The answer must be many because they had an enormous vogue at the time, enjoying tremendous sales and giving Chalmers a substantial income. [71] More directly and personally his preaching and encouragement stimulated contemporary activists and their later imitators like William Collins and David Stow, William Logan, James Begg, Thomas Guthrie and Sir Michael Connal.[72] His influence in England through visits, correspondence, lectures and sermons must also have been immense. There were few who directly imitated the exact details of his St John's experiment except in small ways like the Revd J M Cunningham [73] of Harrow, but he helped add to that general reappraisal of society and the individual's responsibility in it which was influencing men like S R Bosanquet and Bishop Blomfield. Bosanquet derived encouragement from the *Christian and Civic Economy*, [74] while Blomfield incorporated some of Chalmers' ideas into his diocesan charge to his clergy in 1830 when undertaking his big drive to make the parochial system in the metropolis more effective. [75] Henry Bathurst, Bishop of Norwich, was an admirer of Chalmers. [76] The Rector of Sunderland was anxious to introduce Chalmers' plan of local schools in his area and, according to the Scottish clergyman there, Chalmers was the inspiration of the Evangelical clergy of the Church of England. [77] He had particularly good relationships with English Dissenters like the Quaker J J Gurney, and the Baptists Andrew Fuller, John Foster and Robert Hall. From the Continent figures like Merle d'Aubigné hailed Chalmers as the Scottish representative of the Reformed tradition in Europe, and his influence was also felt in Germany. [78]

His ideas were not original in the sense of striking contemporaries with their novelty. And it is impossible to isolate them as a distinct force among the influences which, from Hannah More to William Wilberforce, were turning men's minds to the serious nature of the challenges facing them. However, it might be claimed, as the success of his sermons on public occasions demonstrated, that he was able to pull ideas together and give them sharper focus and authority through the originality and force of his oratory, his vehement conviction and practical action. [79] In J J Gurney's view he occupied the same position in Scotland as Simeon had done in England. [80]

His oratory convinced contemporaries of his sincerity and depth. Cockburn made a shrewd comment on his veto speech in 1833. By it Chalmers 'raised himself above most modern orators . . . [it] blazed with the fire of his volcanic imagination. Yet his, after all, is chiefly the triumph of intensity of manner . . . it is only when his feelings are brought out in his emphasis . . . in the general look and air of the speaking man that his oratory can be understood. How he burns! I shed more tears of genuine imagination than I have done since they were forced from me by the magnificence of Mrs Siddons.' [81] It was this ability as a performer that raised him above contemporaries. Those who came to hear him speak confessed to a feeling of disappointment at first at the Fife accent and low key of the speaker at the outset. And then as if by some inner histrionic transformation they all became transfixed as his vehemence and intensity rose and he began to glow. [82] The heat of that impression burned contemporaries. To Cockburn his glowing vehemence 'carried people's minds off their legs . . . even Robertson [the great 18th-century Moderate leader] would have withered in his furnace.' [83] An American visitor, Nathaniel H Carter, caught the same mood. When he went to hear Chalmers speak to raise funds for a school for the poor Roman Catholics in Glasgow he was repelled at first by the short, thickset clumsy form, with heavily pock-marked face, by the broad Scots accent, the whole 'exhibiting few external indications of talent.' His gestures and elocution were:

> positively bad . . . [but] the effect of his preaching arises from vigour of thought, boldness of conception and earnestness of manner. He throws himself forward as if he would pitch headlong out of the pulpit; he clenches his white pocket handkerchief firmly in his fist, and brings down his hand as if smiting something at his feet: this gesture is uniform answering fully to what Hamlet calls 'sawing the air' and nothing but the conviction that it is wholly involuntary can reconcile it to the hearer: the orator seems convulsed with the throes of thought, and the grandeur of his periods, rolling out one after another in rapid succession, leaves the mind little time for dwelling on minor considerations. . . . I cannot illustrate his manner better, than by comparing him to a torrent of his native hills, which at one time rushes impetuously down its rugged bed and then glides away in a deep and silent current. [84]

That unconscious ability to act (and his ability to smile at himself too) was glimpsed by the artist John Kelso Hunter in the more informal artistic setting of the Royal Scottish Academy exhibition in Edinburgh, in April 1844. 'On that day,' he recalled:

> I had the pleasure for the first and last time of seeing in the flesh and spirit the celebrated Dr Chalmers. His portrait by Thomas Duncan was in the exhibition and the doctor came in with five young ladies [his daughters?]. He put them into rank at a certain spot of the floor. I looked at him and thought that here was a man I should know—his face, form and dress were quite familiar. I thought that he must be a country tailor who had brought in some young friends to see the pictures. After placing them in proper position he walked rapidly to the front of his portrait, then off with his hat and put himself into the attitude of the portrait. For about a minute he was as still as the painting. I stood glancing at him and the portrait alternately. When he thought that he had given fair play to the critics he made a bow to me, put on his hat, and made hurriedly to the young ladies whose united gabble by way of approbation was fluent and racy. I took off my hat, made a return bow, and watched the life of greatness as it glinted momentarily at some point of attraction among the pictures, then as rapidly at the ladies, directing them to some object worthy of their attention. The sight of Dr Chalmers connects him with art, with my start on art hopes in the meridian of life, and leaves behind him a fine flow of humanity. Few young men could be more gallant to the young ladies than this patriarchal teacher. There was health in his life. [85]

In the public sphere the relevance of his ideas continued after his death. His influence on the Charity Organisation Society and the social Christianity which grew after mid-century has been recognised by historians. [86] Chalmers' insistence on the need to reform the individual first in the locality, as the means to reforming society in general, continued to be remarkably vibrant in its appeal in both Britain and the United States. In both countries he found a ready audience in those reformers who sought the good society and who were increasingly chary of leaving its realisation to the chance workings of unrestrained *laissez-faire* capitalism on the one hand or too extensive a state-imposed regulation on the other. To Chalmers the heavenly kingdom on earth could never be forced on society. Its emergence would depend on the unpredictable, more exciting results of the individual's free will. This meant that the rôle of anyone who could influence the individual's choice and level of material expectation would be crucial. Social progress would come from conviction and action based on deep Christian belief.

Thus Chalmers' writings, with their emphasis on moral revival, individual character and district visiting, were an important influence in the development of the New York City Mission movement in the 1840s and 50s. [87] He also helped to encourage American Presbyterians to join in the expectation of social progress via religion which was sweeping religious denominations in mid-century USA. [88] Again, in the later 19th and early 20th centuries there was a remarkable revival of interest in his ideas which arose, I suspect, because contemporaries found in him some answer to their growing fears that a century of industrial and urban progress had not been matched by an equally remarkable social improvement. Here Chalmers could provide a clue with his insistence on the need to improve the quality of the population rather than direct efforts simply at a redistribution of material benefits. His conservative reaction to social change in the early 19th century could thus be turned into the conservationist urge of the early 20th century progressive.

This is why Miss Grace Chalmers Wood published in Edinburgh in 1911 *Dr Chalmers and the Poor Law*, a compilation of the writings on pauperism, with a preface by Mrs George Kerr. In 1912 she followed this with a similar volume, *The Opinions of Dr Chalmers re Political Economy and Social Reform*. Earlier, in 1900, N Masterman had edited a summary of Chalmers' views entitled *On Charity*, and followed this with another in 1912 entitled *On Poverty*. In 1912 there also appeared *Problems of Poverty—selections from the economic and social writings of Thomas Chalmers*, arranged by Henry Hunter. Wood, Kerr and Masterman were all prominent officials in the Charity Organisation Society (COS) in Scotland and England, and Hunter had been the President of the Society of Poor Law Officials in Scotland. These appeals to Chalmers were clearly part of the debate on the future of social welfare surrounding the Poor Law Commission of 1905-9, reasserting the COS's view of the necessity for curative influences on poverty directed by means of organisation and personal case-work as opposed to schemes like that of the minority report in 1909 which verged, in their opinion, on state socialism. One of the COS's foremost apologists, Helen Bosanquet, in her book *The Strength of the People, a study in social economics* (1902), specifically stressed Chalmers' insistence on the central importance of the individual's character in society as part of this argument. [89] As the importance of environmental factors in social conditions became increasingly recognised from the 1880s, the practice of the COS had appeared increasingly negative. Thus, this re-emphasis on Chalmers was both a defence and at the same time a way of enabling the COS to restate and widen its theory in more acceptable terms in a changing intellectual context. It could emphasise the positive aspects of the regeneration of the individual through individual contact and the restorative powers of the Poor Law, and free itself from its narrowly preventive reputation. [90]

In addition, proponents of the social gospel in Scotland found new relevance in Chalmers and wove his ideas into their concern for the Churches' position in modern society. J Wilson Harper, a Free Church writer on social questions, tried to reconsider Chalmers' economic thinking and link it to 20th-century social problems in *The Social Ideal and Dr Chalmers' Contribution to Christian Economics* (the Chalmers Lectures, published in 1910). From the Church of Scotland J M Lang, in his seminal *The Church and its Social Mission* (1902), referred approvingly to Chalmers several times as proof of the Church's right to be involved in social questions. So too did W M Clow, Professor of Pastoral Theology at Trinity College, Glasgow, in his *Christ and the Social Order* (1913). Similarly, David Watson, the founder of the Scottish Christian Social Union in 1901, found much of his inspiration in the native tradition of churchmanship provided by Chalmers. At one point in *Social Problems and the Church's Duty* (1908), after stressing the need to alter the economic system so as to eliminate the economic causes of poverty (a stance well in advance of groups like the COS and closer to that of R H Tawney), he goes on to draw the argument back to the Chalmers era by saying, 'no remedy for poverty will prove adequate which does not *strengthen character* . . . therefore men are turning with renewed interest to the method of dealing with poverty which is associated with the great name of Dr Chalmers—that method should be carefully studied by every student of social economics.'[91]

Chalmers' influence in the progressive movement in America among proponents of the social gospel can also be discerned.[92] Samuel L Loomis in his lectures to the Andover Theological Seminary, published as *Modern Cities and their Religious Problems* (1887), said of Chalmers' locality plans that 'scarcely a man since the days of the Apostles could have spoken with greater weight of authority upon such a theme than he.'[93] Graham Taylor, one of the first men to set up a syllabus for the systematic study of sociology in a theological institute (in the Chicago Theological Seminary), recommended him in his *Religion in Social Action* (1913).[94] Washington Gladden, president of Ohio State University, in *The Christian Pastor and the Working Church* (1898) stated his belief in the Chalmers plan of the neighbourhood church in a planned social mission.[95]

The breadth of Chalmers' 18th-century synthesis of economics, social issues and Christian morality could thus appeal over 100 years later to reformers of various hues. From the standpoint of the later 20th century too, with its experience of the powers claimed by modern states, it is possible to give a more generous acknowledgment to the claims made by Chalmers at the Disruption, viz. that the individual conscience has rights as well founded as those of the secular authority, that conscience and character are central and that no government ought to be able to claim exclusive control of the minds of the population.[96]

This essay has concentrated mainly on the earlier and interior aspects of his life because these seem to me to be important in explaining the sort of person he was. His life can be seen as a series of contradictions because the strategy he evolved of remoulding the Church of Scotland ended in disarray. The man with the general message ended as a leader of a sect. But in another sense this is simply to say he acted as a human being, as a man of his time. As a person he was essentially simple and direct. His simple-heartedness was remarked on by friend and foe alike, and it was this together with a sense of fun which endeared him to others and won their respect. Thomas Carlyle, never given to suppressing his acerbic estimates of others, especially in private conversation, confided to Ralph Waldo Emerson that 'he valued [Chalmers] as a naif, honest, eloquent man who, in these very days believed in Christianity, and tho' he himself when he heard him, had long discovered that it could not hold water, yet he liked to hear him' (1848). [97] The very grudging nature of the acknowledgment makes it all the more telling. Chalmers' tastes and friendships were moulded by, and remained according to, the fashion of his earlier days in Fife. He constantly returned to Fife for refreshment and it was the ideal which he placed against the pressures of his daily life in Glasgow, Edinburgh or the high councils of Church and State. His gift for friendship was combined with organisation and method. When a former acquaintance, the Revd George Brown of Brampton, called on him in Glasgow unexpectedly he found he had to state to the servant first whether he was calling on business or friendship before he could be admitted, for the doctor had fixed hours for each. Luckily, it was his friendship hour and so, Brown records, they spent the time in a long walk out through Glasgow Green during which Chalmers talked almost exclusively of Fife and 'the scenes of former years on which his soul delighted to dwell'. [98]

At the same time he was forceful and active to the end. Though he was warm and sincere he could be didactic in teaching what he thought was right. He expected to lead, with others following, and was particularly fearful of giving ordinary men and women too much initiative and responsibility unless it were under guidance he trusted. His attitude to the political aspirations of labouring men was grudging and restrictive. He had other faults, too, like an easily-roused temper, pride and self-esteem; and any slight, real or imagined, could lead to outbursts of warm indignation. He could hurt others by his obduracy and obstinacy, and in carrying out his ideas could also show a fair degree of rigidity and coldness. At the same time he also had his warm side, especially if his sympathy was engaged, and the breadth of his outlook could soften opponents. While acknowledging his importance some doubted his profundity. Sir Archibald Alison noted his vigour of expression allied with 'an almost infantile simplicity of manner . . . a man . . . who for good or evil forcibly turned aside the current of human thought'. Still, Alison thought, 'he had no great variety in his ideas . . . his mind was slow . . . the predominance of one idea at one time essentially impaired his usefulness.' Yet, as Cockburn noted, though his learning was less profound than varied its strength lay 'in the largeness of the fields that he cultivated.' [99] Supporters and opponents alike all seemed to find something to revere in him and all recognised his remarkable character and the force with which he pursued the practical ends of Evangelical religion.

The lasting impression one gets of him as a person from his private journals is of the depth of his inner life. He had a strong and enduring sense of the nearness of God. Throughout his life he made a continuous effort at interior spiritual formation through daily prayer. He was open to others and other traditions and was willing to treat issues from an original standpoint by working from first principles and the existing situation as he saw it without the prejudices of preconceived notions. In many ways, especially in his efforts to reconcile science and religion, he sought to Christianise the 18th-century enlightenment tradition. He was open to other religious traditions, too, and more interested in their good points than on stressing differences. [100] The Church, for him, however defined, was not an optional extra but at the same time it had to be consolidated by taking into account the diversity of a society and its historical evolution. He saw, therefore, that in religion persuasion and not coercion was the best method to be adopted.

As for his own estimate of himself he had a dispassionate view about his fame and he was remarkably free from pomposity. David Masson recalled that although his divinity lectures were one of the great attractions in the Edinburgh of his youth, Chalmers' manner in them was simple, direct and engaging with little exaggerated notion of professorial dignity. He would, Masson recalled, hurry into the lectures and just as frequently rush out again to collect something he had forgotten. Then unselfconsciously he would continue where he had left off. Though the matter was divinity it was really, Masson wrote, 'a course of Chalmers himself . . . merely to look at him day after day was a liberal education'. [101] How many of us would be pleased simply to lay claim to as much! Amid all his contradictions, and amid the many public issues in which he was embroiled, he remained to the end a human being: hesitant and self-doubting, but acting with decision according to his conscience amid the exigencies of an age packed with incident and controversy.

Notes to Chapter I

1   All studies of Chalmers' career should start with the massive life written by his son-in-law William Hanna, *Memoirs of the Life and Writings of Thomas Chalmers* (4 vols., 1849-52). Others which follow the same pattern in a condensed form are J Dodds, *Thomas Chalmers, a biographical study* (1879), N L Walker, *Thomas Chalmers, his life and its lessons* (1880), D Fraser, *Thomas Chalmers* (1881), Mrs Oliphant, *Thomas Chalmers* (1893), W G Blaikie, *Thomas Chalmers* (1896). There is also John Anderson, *Reminiscences of Dr Chalmers* (1851), the notes of a newspaper reporter. The best modern account is S J Brown, *Thomas Chalmers and the Godly Commonwealth* (1982). Also useful are Hugh Watt, *Thomas Chalmers and the Disruption* (1943), and for his social views, S Mechie, *The Church and Scottish Social Development 1780-1870* (1960).

2   Hanna, *Memoirs*, vol. I, p.338.

3   Quoted in Anderson, *Reminiscences*, p.401.

3   Henry Cockburn, *Journal 1831-1854* (2 vols., 1874), vol. II, p.258.

5   Hanna, *Memoirs*, vol. I, p.vii.

6   e.g. reminiscences of Chalmers in letters from J Miller of Monikie to W Hanna, 6 July 1847, and from David Harris to W Hanna, 24 March 1852 in Chalmers Papers (hereafter cited as *CP*), New College Library, Edinburgh, CHA 2. My thanks are due to the Librarian of New College, Mr J V Howard, for the use of this material and especially to the Manuscripts Assistant, Mrs M Butt, for her generous help.

7   Hanna, *Memoirs*, vol. II, pp.160-61; also J J Gurney, *Chalmeriana* (1853), p.105.

8   S J Brown, 'Thomas Chalmers, the Whigs and the Poor: the Kennedy Poor Law Bill of 1824', paper given at the Chalmers Colloquium held at New College, Edinburgh, on 11 May 1977. Also R M Mitchison, 'The Creation of the Disablement Rule in the Scottish Poor Law', in T C Smout (ed.), *The Search for Wealth and Stability: essays presented to M W Flinn* (1979), pp.199-217.

9   Hanna, *Memoirs*, vol. I, pp.310-11 and vol. III, pp.231ff. cp. with Gurney, *Chalmeriana*, pp.12-13. Also, I A Muirhead, 'Catholic Emancipation: Scottish Reactions in 1829 and the Debate and the Aftermath', *Innes Review*, vol. 24 (Spring and Autumn 1973). In Belfast in 1827 he said: 'It is not in the fermentation of human passions and human politics, that the lessons of heaven can be with efficacy taught—and ere these lessons shall go abroad in triumph over the length and breadth of the land, we must recall the impolicy by which we have turned a whole people into a nation of outcasts.' 'The Effect of Man's Wrath in the Agitation of Religious Controversies' in *Collected Works of Thomas Chalmers* (hereafter cited as *CW*) (25 vols., 1835-42), vol. XI, p.184.

10 cf. letters from Mrs Elizabeth Chalmers to her family in *CP*, CHA 1. Also short MS account of her family by Anne S Chalmers, loc.cit. For Miss Nicky Murray see W Chambers, *Traditions of Edinburgh* (2 vols., 1825), vol. II, pp.27-30, 116.

11 When he died in 1818 John Chalmers left only £1000, £369 of which consisted of uncollected debts, out of the sizeable amount he had inherited from his father plus a £500 jointure brought to him by his wife. (Anne Chalmers' MS. account of her family. Also the collection of legal and business letters in *CP*, CHA 1.)

12 T Chalmers to his father, 20 Sept. 1804, *CP*, CHA 3.3.

13 Barbara Chalmers to her father, 7 Nov. 1803, *CP*, CHA 1 (family letters).

14 James Chalmers to his father, 9 June 1800, *CP*, CHA 1 (family letters). James Miller to W Hanna, 6 July 1849, *CP*, CHA 2.

15 Thomas Duncan to W Hanna, 21 Jan. 1848, *CP*, CHA 2.

16 Like John Leslie and James Mylne; the latter afterwards became son-in-law of the noted Glasgow Whig, Professor John Millar, and great-uncle of the feminist reformer Fanny Wright (who had spent her formative years in Mylne's household). See Margaret Lane, *Frances Wright and the 'Great Experiment'* (1972).

17 W Godwin, *Enquiry concerning Political Justice*, (1976 edn.), p.359.

18 Watt, *Thomas Chalmers*, p.15.

19 F Voges, 'Chalmers as a Baconian', Chalmers Colloquium, New College (1977). Also *Natural Theology, CW*, vol. II, p.167: 'In the instinctive, the universal faith in Nature's constancy, we behold a promise. In the actual constancy of Nature, we behold its fulfilment. When the two are viewed in connexion, then, to be told that Nature never recedes from her constancy, is to be told that the God of Nature never recedes from his faithfulness.' cp. with Jonathan Edwards, *The Works of President Edwards in Eight Volumes* (1817-1847), vol. I, p.152.

20 David Masson, *Memories of Two Cities* (1911, compiled for *Macmillan's Magazine* 1864-65), pp.68-71.

21 See R M Young, 'Malthus and the Evolutionists: the common context of biological theory', *Past and Present*, No. 43, 1969.

22 Hanna, *Memoirs*, vol. I, p.44.

23 David Harris to W Hanna, 24 March 1852, *CP*, CHA 2.

24 Hanna, *Memoirs*, vol. I, p.32.

25 Journal, 16 Nov. 1803, 'Hear that T did not demonstrate proof 7 but gave it out to prepare'; 29 Nov. 1803, 'Heard Dr Brown say that —— is completely ignorant of surds on which subject T has laboured for 2 days. I am finishing simple equations', *CP*, CHA 6.

26 Thomas to James Chalmers, 1 and 6 April 1808; 10 Feb. 1808, 'it wants extensive circulation—emolument is not my chief object'; and 26 March 1808, 'the great point is its circulation in London.' Also 24 Feb., 29 March, 8, 15, 16, 20, 25 April, 1808, and five more in the same vein May to July 1808, *CP*, CHA 3.3, CHA 3.4.

27 *Report of the Speeches delivered . . . to Dr Chalmers* (1823) in Glasgow City Archives, T.—PM 133. The whole argument between the General Session and the Town Council can be traced in R Renwick (ed.), *Extracts from the Records of the Burgh of Glasgow*, vols. X (1915), XI

(1916), passim. For two cool reappraisals of the financial viability of the Glasgow experiment see R A Cage and E O A Checkland, 'Thomas Chalmers and Urban Poverty', *Philosophical Journal*, vol. 13, 1976, and S J Brown, 'The Disruption and Urban Poverty: Thomas Chalmers and the West Port Operation in Edinburgh 1844-47', *Records of the Scottish Church History Society*, vol. XX, 1978. Also *CP*, CHA 5.

28 Journal, 15 May 1810. Also, 20 Dec. 1811 for an entry in which he assesses himself as having a 'sanguine temperament—too impatient under suspense, too much addicted to suspicions, and too prone to indulge in plans and calculations for futurity.' *CP*, CHA 6.

29 'In these days of adventure [*c.*1802] as his acquaintance was extended and his society became more diversified the ease with which others of his contemporaries could accommodate themselves to the ordinary usages of life and the advantages which they could command by a little attention to their personal appearance and deportment affected him with rather humbling considerations which he seriously considered it incumbent upon him to remedy.' David Harris to W Hanna, 24 March 1852, *CP*, CHA 2. Disregard for his appearance seems to have been a characteristic. Masson claims that at Kilmany 'it would sometimes happen that, when he took off his hat before going to the pulpit, strings of green stuff, which he had been gathering that morning as botanical specimens, would be hanging from his hair.' Masson, *Memories*, pp.59-60.

30 Journal, 12 July 1810. Other entries in the Journal make the same points, e.g. 9 May 1810 on another showing resentment against him: 'it is only when the displeasure is expressed in such a way as to imply disrespect that I feel so exquisitely'. On 25 July 1810, when the company made him tongue-tied: 'I felt all the awkwardness of my boyish days', and 28 July 1810: '[in company] to escape bashfulness I put on a flurried rapidity of manner which is apt to overstep propriety. Should maintain more composure and not give way so much in mixed company to the idea of my inability to support myself.' On 4 Aug. 1810: 'Perfect freedom from vanity would save me those anxieties and embarrassments which the superior manner of another is apt to fill me with.' *CP*, CHA 6.

31 Thomas to James Chalmers, 4 April 1810 and 24 Dec. 1810, *CP*, CHA 3.4.

32 Thomas Chalmers to Mr Carstairs, 26 July 1810, where he speaks of 'those examples of mortality which are every year crowding so fast upon us', *CP*, CHA 3.4.

33 Journal, 25 July 1810, *CP*, CHA 6.

34 Thomas Chalmers to Mrs Coutts, 24 Oct. 1811, *CP*, CHA 3.5.

35 A continuing preoccupation with his health thereafter shows how much he had been affected by his illness.

36 Thomas Chalmers to John Honey, 2 May 1812, *CP*, CHA 2.

37 Journal, 31 Dec. 1811, *CP*, CHA 6.

38 This was partly due to his natural tendency to view society in mechanistic terms. His normal justification of his social theories, for instance, was to explain them as being due to universally operating laws in human nature, of the same kind as the laws governing scientific discoveries. The

St John's experiment was thus like Harvey's discovery of the circulation of the blood and therefore Chalmers like Harvey was not the inventor, merely the discoverer. Such an argument allowed Chalmers to claim his ideas would work anywhere regardless of whether he was present or not; e.g. *The Sufficiency of a Parochial System* (1841) in *CW*, vol. XXI, pp.144-46. This suggests why Chalmers was less inclined to sense the puzzling complexities of communities made up of individuals of varying accomplishments and none, and was more inclined to concentrate on those individualistic virtues which were needed to sustain his social experiments, viz. thrift, frugality, independence, prudence. This stemmed from his total belief in Malthus. To Karl Marx in *Das Kapital* he was a fanatical Malthusian (*'einer der fanatischsten Malthusianer'*). For other estimates of his place in the history of economic thought see R H I Palgrave, *Dictionary of Political Economy* (3 vols, 1894), vol. I, pp.255-57. J A Schumpeter, *History of Economic Analysis* (1954), p.487, where among 'some of those who also ran' his *Political Economy* is noted as 'a book of considerable importance but not easy to appraise. It presents a mixture of sound insights and technical shortcomings.' Also Schumpeter, *Economic Doctrine and Method* (1954).

39 James Miller to W Hanna, 6 July 1847. T Duncan to W Hanna, 21 Jan. 1848, *CP*, CHA 2. His eventual reaction to the revolution in France is not so surprising for by 1800 his brothers were fighting the French at sea and one of them had been killed by enemy action.

40 *Political Economy* (1832) in *CW*, vol. XIX, p.370. This and his *Christian and Civic Economy*, *CW*, vols XIV-XVI, are extended reiterations of the same theme. He viewed the 'coarse and boastful independence' of republican America with distaste, *CW*, vol. XIX, p.372.

41 Hanna, *Memoirs*, vol. II, pp.76-77, 263, 251-52, 254.

42 *CW*, vol. XIV, pp.48-49. For his fear of disorder see his sermon preached at the time of the Radical War, 'The Importance of Civil Government to Society' (1820) in *CW*, vol. VI, pp.335-77.

43 *CW*, vol. XIV, p.186.

44 Gurney, *Chalmeriana*, pp.83-84.

45 *CW*, vol. XX, pp.40-41.

46 *CW*, vol. XV, p.340.

47 *CW*, vol. XX, pp.190-91.

48 Hanna, *Memoirs*, vol. IV, pp.205-11.

49 ibid., p.425.

50 *CW*, vol. XXI, p.19.

51 He displays a similar blend of positive and negative views with regard to the other great contemporary issue of negro slavery in America. He consistently supported abolition but always maintained it had to be accomplished gradually and respect existing property rights. His insistence on the latter aspect is rather repellent and demonstrates how one part of an argument can, in his hands, take precedence and destroy the balance of the whole. *A Few Thoughts on Colonial Slavery* (1826) in *CW*, vol. XII, pp.396-408. Also G A Shepperson, 'The Free Church and American Slavery', *Scottish Historical Review*, vol. XXX, 1951, and 'Thomas Chalmers, The Free Church of Scotland and the South', *Journal of Southern History*, vol. XVII, 1951.

52 His conviction was 'now fully established that without the helping hand of government neither Christian nor common education will be fully provided for', f.n. in *CW*, vol. XIV, p.165.

53 Hanna, *Memoirs*, vol. IV, pp.301, 435-38. *North British Review*, vol. 7, May 1847 ('The Political Economy of a Famine'). R F G Holmes, *Thomas Chalmers and Ireland* (Presbyterian Historical Society of Ireland, 1980). Anderson, *Reminiscences*, p.376.

54 D Bowen, *The Idea of the Victorian Church* (1968), pp.352-53. D L Edwards, *Leaders of the English Church 1828-1978* (1978), p.195. W F Gray, 'Chalmers and Gladstone', *Records of the Scottish Church History Society*, vol. X, 1948.

55 Gurney, *Chalmeriana*, p.76.

56 Hanna, *Memoirs*, vol. IV, p.45.

57 e.g Sir A Gordon, *The Earl of Aberdeen* (1893), pp.138-43. C S Parker, *Life and Letters of Sir James Graham* (2 vols., 1907), vol. I, pp.373-81. Also J Cunningham, *The Church History of Scotland* (2nd edn., 2 vols., 1882), vol. II, pp.479-84.

58 Gordon, *Aberdeen*, p.134.

59 A H Charteris, *Life of Revd. James Robertson of Ellon* (1863), pp.82-83.

60 A Campbell to T Chalmers, 6 May 1840, *CP*, CHA 4.289.

61 Journal 1840-41, *passim*, *CP*, CHA 6.

62 ibid.

63 R Buchanan to T Chalmers, 4 Aug. 1840, *CP*, CHA 4.289.

64 Journal 1841, *passim*, *CP*, CHA 6.

65 Gordon, *Aberdeen*, p.137.

66 Wm Boswell to T Chalmers, 19 April 1840, *CP*, CHA 4.289.

67 Journal 1841, *CP*, CHA 6.

68 This comes over very clearly from his Journals for this period.

69 Cockburn, *Journal*, vol. II, pp.180-82.

70 Sir A Alison, *My Life and Writings* (2 vols., 1883), vol. I, p.463.

71 It is difficult to give precise figures of Chalmers' total income at any one period but it is significant that he was able to lay out £2000 in investments by 1825 (R Paul to T Chalmers, 15 June 1825, *CP*, CHA 4.48.) D Keir, *The House of Collins* (1952), p.148, estimates that over his lifetime he made £14000 from his writings.

72 Mechie, *Church and Scottish Social Development, passim. Diary of Sir Michael Connal* (ed. J C Gibson 1895), pp.31, 65, 203.

73 See *The Dictionary of National Biography* for Cunningham who was a member of the Clapham sect. Cunningham to T Chalmers, 10 Jan. 1818, *CP*, CHA 4.7. Also W Hanna, *Correspondence of the Late Thomas Chalmers* (1853), pp.279-86.

74 For Bosanquet see DNB. For his admiration of Chalmers' social theories, S R Bosanquet to T Chalmers, undated (?1840) and 26 Dec. 1840, *CP*, CHA 4.289.

75 e.g. C J Blomfield to T Chalmers, 17 Aug. 1830, *CP*, CHA 4.132. Also A Blomfield, *Memoir of C J Blomfield* (2 vols., 1863), vol. I, pp.233ff., where Chalmers' cautious strategy seems to be vindicated. Also W M Hetherington, Henley-on-Thames to T Chalmers, 27 Feb. 1834: '[you are] at once the "Decus et Tutamen" of the Scottish Church', *CP*, CHA 4.224.

76 Gurney, *Chalmeriana*, pp.99-100.

77 J T Paterson to T Chalmers, 21 Jan. 1823, 17 Nov. 1833, 10 Feb. 1834. *CP*, CHA 4.28, 4.211, 4.227.

78 A L Drummond, *The Kirk and the Continent* (1956), pp.200, 212, 222. W C Shanahan, *German Protestants Face the Social Question* (1954), pp.66-67, 104-5. He was admired, too, by the American peace movement, e.g. C S Henry of the Connecticut Peace Society to T Chalmers, 4 Dec. 1834: 'the brilliant position you hold in the estimation of all on this side of the ocean . . . anything from you would be well received in the United States and encourage the friends of humanity in this country. *CP*, CHA 4.224.

79 J R Poynter, *Society and Pauperism* (1969), pp.236-37.

80 Gurney, *Chalmeriana*, p.125.

81 Cockburn, *Journal*, vol. I, pp.45-6.

82 J G Lockhart's classic account is in Hanna, *Memoirs*, vol. II, pp.2-5.

83 Cockburn, *Journal*, vol. II, pp.183, 244.

84 N H Carter, *Letters from Europe* (2 vols., 1829), pp.334-35.

85 J K Hunter, *Retrospect of An Artist's Life* (1866), p.252.

86 A F Young and E T Ashton, *British Social Work in the Nineteenth Century* (1956), pp.67-80. K de Schweinitz, *England's Road to Social Security* (1943), pp.100-113, 148-50. K Woodroofe, *From Charity to Social Work in England and the United States* (1962), pp.45-47. C L Mowat, *The Charity Organisation Society 1869-1913, its ideas and work* (1961), pp.10, 70, 94. *Reports on the Elberfield System*, C-5341 (Parliamentary Papers, 1888), p.10.

87 C S Rosenberg, *Religion and the Rise of the American City* (1971), pp.260-62.

88 H R Niebuhr, *The Kingdom of God in America* (1937, reprinted 1959), p.154. For earlier examples of his contemporary impact on American Evangelicals through the *Astronomical Discourses* and the *Evidences of Christianity* see John Laird, Georgetown, to T Chalmers, 8 Aug. 1817, and J H Rice, Richmond, Virginia, to T Chalmers, 27 July 1817, *CP*, CHA 4.6. For his influence through James McCosh, President of Princeton see J D Hoeveler Jr, *James McCosh and the Scottish Intellectual Tradition* (1981), passim.

89 pp.120-42, passim. Her history of the COS, *Social Work in London 1869-1912* (1914), p.58, gives a list of books recommended by the society in 1870 and among them are several on Chalmers.

90 Mowat, *Charity Organisation Society*, pp.114-72, passim.

91 p.90. See also D Watson, *Chords of Memory* (1936); and for the theme of the Church and its social mission in this period see D J Withrington, 'The Churches in Scotland c.1870-c.1900: Towards a New Social Conscience?', *Records of the Scottish Church History Society*, vol. XIX, 1977.

92 R T Handy, *The Social Gospel in America* (1966), p.4. F D Watson, *The Charity Organisation Movement in the United States* (1922, reprinted 1971), pp.3-4, 33, 175. C H Hopkins, *The Rise of the Social Gospel in American Protestantism 1865-1915* (1940), pp.6-7: 'The writings of Thomas Chalmers were widely read in the United States. *The Christian*

and Civic Economy was afterwards considered of such value to the institutional church movement that an abridgement was edited in 1900 by Professor Charles R Henderson of the University of Chicago. Chalmers' other important work, the *Commercial Discourses*, had numerous American printings during the [first half of the] nineteenth century.'

93 pp.199-201.

94 pp.237, 273.

95 pp.450-51.

96 H J Laski, *Studies in the Problem of Sovereignty* (1917, reprinted 1968), pp.27-68. Among the many interesting points made here is this (p.65): that the Non-Intrusionists of 1843 were staking a claim to 'the essential federalism of society, the impossibility of confining sovereignty to any one of its constituent parts.'

97 *The Journals of Ralph Waldo Emerson 1820-72* (ed. W H Gilman *et al.*, 1960 to date, vol. X, p.231.

98 G Brown to W Hanna, 24 May 1848, *CP*, CHA 2.

99 Alison, *Life and Writings*, vol. I, pp.445-48. Cockburn, *Journal*, vol. II, p.180.

100 Of Roman Catholicism, for instance, he wrote: 'Should any member of that persuasion come forward with his own explanations, and give such a mitigated view of the peculiarities of Catholics, as to leave the great evangelical doctrines of faith and repentance unimpaired by them, and state that an averment of the Bible has never, in his instance, been neutralised or practically stript of its authority, by an averment of Popes or of Councils:—on what principle of candour shall the recognition of a common Christianity be withheld from him?' Preface to *The Doctrine of Christian Charity Applied to the case of Religious Differences*, *CW*, vol. XI, p.90.

101 Masson, *Memories of Two Cities*, pp.80-81.

II

Chalmers and the State

Owen Chadwick

To any Englishman who contemplates the history of Church and State in England, and thinks about the nature of Church autonomy, and the extent to which a State may or may not legitimately control or exert pressure on a Church, two names stand as symbols of rival attitudes; two men, neither of them English, and both with the Christian name Thomas: Erastus and Chalmers.

No Anglican who seriously studies the relation of Church and State can avoid asking himself the question, what he thinks of Chalmers' theory of the State, or what he thinks about what Chalmers did: which is part of a far bigger, and less easily answerable question, what kind of freedoms are so essential to a Church that to get them you must risk even the destruction of that Church? A great theme—are there moments in history when you have to kill a Church in order that it may live?

So I propose to try in this essay to do three things: first, to ask what was Chalmers' theory of the State and how it looked to government in his own day—why Chalmers, when he came to London in April-May 1838 to lecture on Church and State, was not merely a success but a sensation; second, to touch on the relation between him and the leading members of government; and third, to ask how it looks in the perspective of the 20th century.

This theme of the State was the theme on which Dr Chalmers made his biggest impact when he came to London. At his fourth lecture in London, which was in May 1838, an observer saw 'in every direction', cramming the lecture room which was in the Hanover Square Rooms, dukes, marquises, earls, viscounts, baronets, bishops and members of Parliament. It does seem extraordinary that dukes, earls and viscounts could be in such profusion in a London lecture room; and the witness, who was an American, does not tell us how he discerned the blue blood coursing underneath the cravats. Even in earliest Victorian England great landed proprietors were often like Lord Emsworth at Blandings Castle, more at home with his pig than with a lecture on political theory. We know that a member of the Royal Family was present, the soldierly Duke of Cambridge, who had lately retired from being viceroy of Hanover. He was given a place of honour, on a sofa immediately in front of the lecturer's table; and this circumstance bothered Dr Chalmers, not because the presence of royalty made him nervous, but because the Duke of Cambridge was notorious as a fidget. Since the sons of King George III were not thought likely to be learned in political philosophy, men thought it possible that the prince might not merely fidget but fidget too plainly; and Dr Chalmers was relieved when the event proved him to be extremely attentive throughout the lecture. The Duke of Cambridge had not come, however, because he knew about Chalmers. He met Dr Begg after the lecture and said to him, 'What does he teach?' Dr Begg said that he taught theology. 'Monstrous clever man,' said the Duke, 'he could teach anything.' [1]

At present I do not know of any other duke who was in that room. But when we have subtracted whatever we wish to subtract for hyperbole and exaggeration from the American's evidence, we still have to recognise that the lectures were an extraordinary success. While I have said that I know of no other dukes being present, it is nevertheless possible to identify five earls, a marquess, and five other peers as attending the second lecture.[2]

A lecturer may be a success if his matter is thin and his delivery excellent; and he may be a success, though it is much less likely, if his matter is excellent and his delivery deplorable; but he will hardly be a sensation only on content and delivery alone, even if they are perfectly married. There must be a third element, the relation of what is said to the occasion on which it is said.

Let us first of all ask what he was like to listen to.

Chalmers had an extraordinary and fascinating appearance: a large head with what a contemporary called a mathematical forehead, by which he partly meant highbrow and partly meant unusually angular. Guthrie and others talk of his strange, mysterious, fish-like eyes, and Guthrie more than once talks of his broad, German, 'Martin Luther' head. Lockhart says that at first sight it was a coarse face. He was physically rather clumsy—at least he was capable of falling frequently off a horse that no one else fell off—and rather strangely delivered these famous London lectures sitting down, his notes on a small table, though occasionally rising from his seat in excitement to deliver some magnificent paragraph where he felt moved to the depths. He stuck to notes; holding a sheaf in his left hand and pointing with the index finger of his right hand. He had tried talking without notes at all, or just using headings, and found that instead of giving him freedom and spontaneity the method gave him constraint, tying him down to feats of memory; so he abandoned the attempt and always talked from a script fully written out, though he allowed himself to use shorthand. It was thus very easy to fulfil the wishes of his hosts, that the lectures be published very soon after delivery. Gladstone heard the last of the lectures on 8 May and read the printed edition of the lectures on 4 July. They went quickly through several editions.

His voice was not melodious, nor specially strong. Yet his speech rose, without the slightest pretence, into a unique fervour. In his earlier years this fervency could so boil up that it seemed wild or uncouth; enemies said, mad. These lectures in London were not the first time that he was not just a success but a sensation. The first time he ever made a speech to the General Assembly of the Church of Scotland was in 1809. Afterwards everyone went round asking, 'Who is he?', and saying that he must be a most extraordinary person. The subject of the speech in question was not naturally emotional, being a legislative act on the augmentation of stipends.

He was a sensation at the first lecture after he became a professor of theology at Edinburgh. The lecture, we are told, was punctuated by rapturous applause; but we cannot tell how far this was due to the special circumstance that his predecessor in the chair was totally inaudible and a cause for much grumbling.

The impression of strangeness was enormously heightened, even for Scotsmen, and *a fortiori* for Englishmen, by the accent. All his life he spoke in a broad accent. Every Briton who has lectured in the United States knows what a wonderful advantage it is to be understood and yet not quite to use the language of the people; and Chalmers in London, even Chalmers in Edinburgh, gained something from this oddity, which, in his case, was the tongue of Fife.

The accent was so peculiar and the delivery so rapid that English heads could not at first understand; English ears needed attuning. One reporter in London said that he could not give a proper report because he could not follow; but something in the way this is put makes the critic suspect that the reporter had another motive for no proper report, namely that he could not get enough space in his newspaper.

J G Lockhart heard him and said, 'Never perhaps did the world possess an orator whose minutest peculiarities of gesture and voice had more power in increasing the effect of what he says.'[3] He does not say precisely what the peculiarities were; and it is certain that, although Chalmers took the closest trouble over the drafting of the matter of sermons and speeches, and although he studied the rules of speaking, he took no trouble whatever over what might be called the historic qualities in old-fashioned eloquence. That is, he did not study what Mr Harold Macmillan has told us that we ought to study: precision of gesture as a means of adding to the effect of speech. That would have been foreign to Chalmers and perhaps would have diminished his power. He overflowed, was abundant, did not simulate.

It must be borne in mind that, although the Duke of Cambridge, who spent much time in Hanover, did not know who Chalmers was, he had established something of a reputation in London.

In 1817 he visited London and preached in the Scots Church. On that occasion the crowd was so dense and immobile that William Wilberforce was forced to gain access to the church through a window, by means of a precariously-balanced plank. During the same visit, the statesman Canning was moved to tears by one of Chalmers' sermons.

In 1820 he visited various cities of England to get information about poor relief and the poor law.

In 1827 he was sounded about the Chair of Moral Philosophy at London University, which had not yet opened its doors; and it was an odd sounding, because the founding fathers of University College would not allow theology within the walls. He went (by sea) to London, partly to open his old colleague Edward Irving's new church in Regent Square, partly to enquire further about the Chair. This was the time when he visited Samuel Taylor Coleridge and, like nearly every other visitor to Coleridge in those last years, found him unintelligible.

In 1830 he twice visited London; first in the spring, invited to give evidence before the commission on the Poor; and then in the autumn, to be one of the official Scottish delegation to the coronation of King William IV. In July 1833 he came to London to preach.

On 14 July 1833 he preached a sermon in the Scottish Church in defence of religious Establishments.

Notice the date. It was the very day of John Keble's Assize Sermon at Oxford, the day and occasion which John Henry Newman ever afterwards took to mark the beginning of the Oxford Movement. The Whig government was abolishing bishoprics in Ireland without asking the Church, and talking of taking some of the Church's money for purposes nothing to do with the Church. It was a time when every member of an established Church felt himself threatened. Keble felt threatened, and talked of national apostasy. Chalmers felt threatened. But what he talked of is less certain.

He was not sure that his sermon was well received. The people did not seem roused, the Episcopalians approved, the Dissenters disliked, and one of them said to the man with the collecting bag that he ought to be paid for coming to a sermon like that instead of having to pay anything. Bishop Blomfield of London, with whom he had dined at Fulham Palace, begged him to publish. Chalmers had scruples. 'I think it better not.' [4]

Then in 1835 Oxford University gave him the honorary degree of DCL, and it is said that this was the first time that Oxford had so honoured a Presbyterian divine.

The suave Latin of the Orator's citation at Oxford explained why the University had chosen to do something so unusual. In translation, it runs as follows:

> He is kind and learned and eloquent
> he has manfully striven to help the poor

he has stoutly defended the Church of Scotland
and weightily vindicated the Church of England;
and has encouraged good relations between the Churches;
he was chosen to give one of the courses of Bridgewater lectures,
and everyone here will know with what intelligence and
abundance he fulfilled that task.

The audience gave him special applause at three points in the Latin, which they understood better than many university dons would understand it today: they applauded first at the mention of his eloquence; second at the mention of his vindication of the Church of England; and third at the mention of the Bridgewater treatise. In Scotland, probably, the work for the poor would have taken pride of place. In 1835, as conservative Oxford moved into its Tractarian phase, what mattered to them was the preacher, the Scot who defended the Church of England, and the thinker who cared to reconcile Science with Religion. During his stay in Oxford he lived in the house of Edward Burton the Regius Professor of Divinity, so soon to precipitate the first crisis of the Oxford Movement by dying and giving Lord Melbourne the chance to appoint his successor. While there, he loved to meet John Keble, whose *Christian Year* he regarded as a work of *exquisite beauty*.[5] He was very much amused at walking up and down Oxford in a doctor's gown and, despite discouragement from an Oxford friend, insisted on the extravagance of purchasing the scarlet robes and taking them home.

Yet he sensed at Oxford that all was not perfectly comfortable; that not everyone whom he met could approve his degree and that there might be those in the Episcopalian university who would object to such an honour being given to a Presbyterian. His friend Lord Elgin reports Chalmers' regret at the reserve 'which characterised, as he thought, the manner of some eminent men connected with a certain theological party, to whom he was introduced, and which prevented him touching, in conversation with them, upon topics of highest import.'[6]

Then he was in London a little later, on the business of Church Extension. He was thus famous in England as a member of the Conservative Party and defender of both English and Scottish Established Churches.

The fact was, the audience of 1838, which included one duke and some earls and lords, was a very Conservative audience. These were the years immediately after the Reform Act of 1832, and political partisanship was very strong because everyone was frightened of what their opponents might do with power. The reason why Chalmers was a sensation in his London lectures of 1838 was largely that he said very Tory-sounding things to English Tories who were excited to hear such utterances from the lips of a leading Scotsman. We know there were members of the House of Commons in Chalmers' audience. Several of them were Tories on the extreme right wing of the party. And the fascinating thing is to see how this conservative theory of the State and the Church led in time to one of the most disruptive acts in Scottish history since the Reformation, separating country tenants from their lairds and altering the social circumstances of the Scottish landscape.

Most Evangelical clergy in Scotland in the late 1830s were Conservatives, partly because of evident wooing by the Conservative Party, and partly because they were alienated by Whig policy over the ecclesiastical establishments in the Empire.

Conservative though he might be in 1833-38, and his friend Guthrie called him a furious Conservative, Chalmers was an unconventional Conservative. The praise which no one could ever deny him is that he cared about the poor with a compassion which was also the leading passion of his life. How he cared about the poor, what methods he proposed to care for the poor (some of the methods seem peculiar, and not many of them would be acceptable to the Welfare State of the 20th century), and also the practical results of the compassion, are in question. What is not in question is that he cared. His entire theory of an established Church rested on this compassion for the poor. At the Tron Church in Glasgow he learned for the first time the nature of the urban slum, and this experience conditioned the rest of his life. He saw that no voluntary system could cope. Chapels supported by their members were chapels of the middle class. They might be chapels of the lower middle class but they were not chapels of working men and they were not in the right place. No system of raising money by gifts and bazaars could ever be enough. Therefore the State must act and supply, or at least must supplement all that voluntary effort could achieve.

A lot of people said at the time that this demand for the State to act by endowing new parishes was unwise and politically imprudent. It had that air, even in those days. The perspective of the historian cannot think it so impossible. A very few years earlier, the Government gave money to the Church of Scotland to build churches; most of the grant was used to build forty churches in the Highlands and the Isles, one of them being on Iona. Only a few years after the time when everyone said that Chalmers was absurd to ask the British government for money for churches, a Conservative government under Sir Robert Peel gave money to the college of Maynooth in Ireland for the purpose of training Roman Catholic priests. So when it is said that Chalmers was a dreamer to ask for state money for his slums, it can only be meant, not that his ideas were wild because such a grant was out of the question on principle, but that it was out of the question due to the political circumstances of that moment: for example, that the prime minister was Lord Melbourne.

He was not the sort of prime minister to do anything about anything.

But then he had good reasons for doing nothing. He needed the votes of the Dissenters and the Dissenters were very vehement. They accused Chalmers of aiming, not at the good of the poor, but at the destruction of Dissent. This was very unjust to Chalmers who cared only about the poor and was friendly to Dissenters as workers in the same field. The Dissenters were not kind to Chalmers in this matter. But their unkindness, or their delusion, or their sense of justice, was a strong reason why Lord Melbourne should do nothing, which is what he always did best.

Chalmers and Melbourne came to dislike each other with an intensity rare between a divine and a politician. Chalmers was heard to say, 'I have a moral loathing of these Whigs'; and when he pronounced the word Whigs as 'Whugs' in broadest Fifeshire, they sounded abominably corrupt. [7] Melbourne talked about 'that damned fellow Chalmers' and when he was about to receive a Scottish deputation made it clear that Chalmers would not be acceptable as a member. In 1840 he even put the following utterance on paper in a letter to Fox Maule: 'I particularly dislike Dr Chalmers. I think him a madman and all madmen are also rogues.'[8] Chalmers was an enthusiast. Melbourne took towards enthusiasm the weary contempt of the 18th century just then beginning to be obsolete. 'If we are to have a prevailing religion,' he wrote in his most famous sentence, not very complimentary to the Church of England, 'let us have one that is cool, and indifferent, and such a one as we have got.'

Was the personality of Melbourne important? He was of all men the least capable of understanding what the fuss was about in Scotland because he was incapable of understanding fuss. Chalmers was rather unkind about him in a pamphlet of 1840 when he took up the charge made by Lord Aberdeen in a moment of pique that Scottish ministers were unscrupulous, and talked of Melbourne as 'laughing it off in his own characteristic way with a good-natured jeer as a thing of nought'. [9] But the verdict was more unkind than untrue; and Chalmers, however apt to state things high, commands a measure of all our sympathies when he says that 'we cannot but lament the accident, by which a question of so grave a nature and of such portentous consequences to society as the character of its most sacred functionaries, should have come even for a moment under the treatment of such hands.'

The following is a summary of Chalmers' theory of establishment, as enunciated most notably in the 1838 lectures. It is one of the simplest and most uncompromising approaches to this difficult subject that has ever been seriously presented to a government for adoption.

It is obvious, Chalmers contends, that government has a duty to encourage the spread of Christian faith throughout the land. Why is it obvious?

First, because it is in the strong interest of government that Christianity be spread.

Second, because it is obvious that no amount of voluntary effort— collections, subscriptions and bazaars—is capable of doing what is wanted; as is plain to the first eye which contemplates the unchurched slums of Glasgow and Edinburgh.

But why is it in the strong interest of government? Chalmers observed [10] that nowadays some reckon it the very perfection of enlightened patriotism in the magistrate if like Gallio he cares for none of these things. It is one of the theories of our day, he says, that government should 'as a government, be lifeless of all regard to things sacred; and, maintaining a calm and philosophical indifference to all the modes and varieties of religious belief, should refuse to entertain the question, in which of these varieties the people ought to be trained— or rather, make it wholly the affair of the people themselves, with which they have no business to intermeddle in any form.'

This, for Chalmers, is an impossibility. Government is not a mysterious impersonal machine, it is an umbrella name for a lot of people; and if they are people they have moral convictions. 'A righteous and religious monarch, or righteous and religious senators, must impress their characters on their acts; nor can we understand the distinction, or rather the disjunction, which is spoken of in these days, between Christian governors and a Christian government.' Such an idea of government is a figment of the imagination. Men cannot cease to be men merely because they get inside a debating chamber with parliamentary authority. They never behave like that. They spend public money creating schools where morality and religion will be taught. They pass laws against racial discrimination, of which the motive is not merely the desire to make the work of policemen easier. They buy pictures and open a gallery for the improvement of a nation's taste. They spend large sums of money to rescue victims of an accident, even though it might be said that the victims became victims by their own rashness. They do it merely because they feel the same moral duty that an individual feels to try to rescue a drowning man.

Now let us postulate that a government consists of men who have none of these sentiments; and, though it is an impossibility, imagine that government consists only of persons who are what Chalmers calls 'utilitarians . . . in the coarsest or merely material sense of the term'. It is still in their interest to economise in the number of policemen that will be needed; it is still their business to reduce government expenditure if they can, to lessen the number of criminals, and if it is impossible to abolish the poor, at least abolish pauperism. If you spent much more on churches you would spend less on soldiers, constables, prisons and warders. You should have an establishment not merely on the high ground of principle, but on the low ground of economics.

We are now confronted with the problem that, to establish religion, government needs to establish one religion. How does it choose the denomination? Dr Chalmers answers this hardest of questions with extraordinary ease and directness.

There are two reasons why legislators should select one denomination rather than another. The first is truth, and the second is good moral effect. From the idea of members of the House of Commons deciding on truth—an idea so revolting to our minds in the 1980s—Dr Chalmers does not shrink. He regards it as a very specious objection that by this means the floor of the chamber at Westminster will become an arena of theological wrangling; as if he demanded that members of Parliament hurry out during debates to consult the commentaries on the Epistle to the Romans or the two hundred volumes of Migne's *Patrologia Latina*. All this Chalmers thinks absurd. And it is absurd because that is the affair of the Churches and not the affair of Parliament. The only thing Parliament has to decide is between Popery and Protestantism; and Dr Chalmers had a clear idea that in this choice the Parliament of his day would not hesitate for an instant. It would hesitate neither on grounds of truth, nor on grounds of moral effect. 'In this nation of all others,' he says [11] (and the context shows that he praised England as well as Scotland) 'there is none, with the ordinary schooling of a gentleman, who could not thoroughly inform himself, and by the reading of a few weeks on this great question, so as to decide between the authority of the Bible, and the authority of Rome's apostolic church.' 'We only need a Parliament of England's best principled and best educated men.' He asked himself the question whether it can always be guaranteed that the members of Parliament will be England's best principled and best educated men, and allowed just the possibility they might not be. 'Should the disaster ever befall us, of vulgar and upstart politicians to be lords of the ascendant; should an infidel or semi-infidel government wield for a season the destinies of this mighty empire, and be willing at the shrine of their own wretched partisanship to make sacrifice of those great and hallowed institutions, which were consecrated by our ancestors to the maintenance of religious truth and religious liberty . . .' then Dr Chalmers was persuaded that within the deep feelings of the people would be enough sense of outrage to overthrow them and their plans.

Concede for a moment—he thought there was no need to concede, but for a moment concede—that Parliament is incapable of deciding between Protestantism and Popery on grounds of truth, then it can decide on its view of moral effect. He spoke of the moral and economic loss to France by the expulsion of the Huguenots; of the contrast which leaps to the eye of the traveller between the Protestant and the Catholic cantons of Switzerland; of the difference in freedom, virtue and industry between the people of Holland and the people of Spain; of the industry of northern Ireland against the beggars of southern Ireland.

You will notice a remarkable thing, remarkable even in that age; though we see the same feature in Chalmers' critic Gladstone. The theory of establishment has little to do with the beliefs of the majority of the people in any of the different parts of the United Kingdom. For most theorists the problem was to justify the establishment of the Protestant Church in Ireland where the majority of the people were Roman Catholics; they easily justified establishment in Scotland where the majority were Presbyterians or in England where the majority were Anglicans. But Chalmers felt no such difficulty. It was obvious to him, both intellectually and morally, that Roman Catholicism was an error. The government had a duty to establish a Protestant Church which would be the means of converting the Irish away from their error. And although he admitted that the established Church of Ireland was guilty of grave errors and corruptions, nevertheless he contended not merely for its rightness but for its excellence. 'The truth is,' he said, in a sentence which must have shocked some English ears if not some Scottish, 'that, among the established Churches of our empire, that of Ireland, in the vital and spiritual sense of the term, is the most prosperous of the three.' 'The hand of power may strip it of its temporalities; but we trust that its indomitable spirit in the cause of a pure and scriptural faith, will not so easily be quelled.' [12]

Chalmers' theory postulated explicitly that a common Protestantism existed; that Baptist, Congregationalist, Presbyterian, Methodist and Anglican were all 'in essence and effect' [13] teaching the same Christianity; and he thought that it would be relatively easy to reunite the Protestant denominations in a single established Church. But the basis had to be territorialism, the provision of a minister for every parish; and the Church which the government ought to back and endow was the Church with the chance of making this territorial system effective. The idea that you should choose a Church on grounds of *polity* was not at all to his liking. In 1838 some Anglicans argued that the State should choose the Church with the apostolic ministry, that is, the succession by bishops through the centuries. Chalmers regarded this as trivial as well as erroneous.

This, then, is the basis of Chalmers' theory. I am conscious as I describe it that it sounds cold and obsolete. Nevertheless, it was cheered to the echo by right-wing members of the Conservative Party in the Hanover Square Rooms. For what mere words cannot convey is the atmosphere of faith which rendered the whole series of lectures alive and attractive. His love for the poor was very evident when he talked of slums, only recently regarded as unsafe for members of the middle class to enter, but now visited by a minister, which had become places of cheerfulness and friendliness and welcome. When he speaks of the apostolic drive towards a better people and a higher morality and an enlightened education among the once illiterate areas, the lectures, and indeed the whole theory, are stamped with a deep sense of optimism: the Church moving forward powerfully into the new age on behalf of the poorest people. The lectures were not only strong because they were just what English Tories wanted to hear. They were strong because the idea of Establishment was so obviously rooted in compassion for suffering humanity.

If a government gives money to a Church to make the people moral and educated, will it want to control the Church? Will it like it if the people whose stipends it pays denounce its policy? According to Chalmers—and here at last speaks the Chalmers of the future Disruption—'There might be an entire dependence on the State in things temporal, without even the shadow of a dependence upon it in things ecclesiastical. ... The State is the dispenser of things spiritual. ... For their food and their raiment, and their sacred or even private edifices, they may be indebted to the State; but their creed, and their discipline, and their ritual, and their articles of faith, and their formularies whether of doctrine or devotion, may be altogether their own.'[14] But strangely enough—and this is 1838 with the Auchterarder case coming into the House of Lords—he hardly bothers with the question. He assumes it as an axiom that government will not interfere on the spiritual side.

Young Gladstone knew Chalmers slightly from meetings in Edinburgh and they had exchanged letters. Gladstone said more than once that he zealously attended all Chalmers' lectures in London. The recently published diary (1968 and after) does not state that he came to the first, but records all the other five. Gladstone was only in his twenties. But he had a strong sense of history, and lately under the influence of his friend James Hope and of Dante he had moved into the high Anglican theory of the Church. He found Chalmers' accent extraordinary, and his character admirable; he saw him as the noblest of all the Scots. But his mind reacted to what he heard with disgust. 'I could not stand it,' he wrote twice in his autobiographical memoranda. 'Wretched error' he called it, and referred to it as 'insufferable'. He went away, took up his pen, and started to write.

Chalmers' theory of Church and State has a worse reputation than it should because it is regarded principally as a theory so absurd that it caused Gladstone to write his first book. No one perceives that the book which Gladstone wrote is still more impracticable, and was primarily the expression of Gladstone's reaction to the discovery that Chalmers could lump all the non-Roman Catholic denominations, including the Church of England, into a common Protestantism.

In the week after the last lecture, we have a letter from Gladstone, aged 29, to Manning, the future cardinal, aged 30 [15].

> Such a jumble of church, un-church, and anti-church principles as that excellent and eloquent man Dr Chalmers has given us in his recent lectures, no human being ever heard, and it can only be compared to the state of things '*Ante mare et terras et quod tegit omnia coelum*' [Ovid, *Met*. 1. 5: Chaos, before the making of the sea and the land and the firmament].

And, a little later in the letter:

> He flogged the apostolical succession grievously, seven bishops sitting below him . . . and the Duke of Cambridge incessantly bobbing assent [so the Duke of Cambridge did fidget after all—a benevolent fidget!]; but for fear we should be annoyed he then turned round on the cathedrals plan [that is, the plan to confiscate some endowments of English cathedrals for the benefit of new parishes] and flogged it with at least equal vigour. He has a mind keenly susceptible of what is beautiful, great and good; tenacious of an idea when once grasped, and with a singular power of concentrating the whole man upon it. But unfortunately I do not believe he has ever looked in the face the real doctrine of the visible church and the apostolic succession, or has any idea what is the matter at issue. [16]

He finished the first draft of his own book—and it is a big book, of two volumes—only a little over two months later, amid all the varied duties of a member of Parliament.

The comparison between Gladstone and Chalmers is illuminating. Here were two great conservative theorists of the relation between Church and State, so conservative that their theories were obsolete even at the moment they uttered them. Each, instead of adjusting his theory to the times, saving what could be saved from the wreck and remaining an essentially conservative theorist, though forced to adapt to liberal principles, became the leader of a movement which did the very opposite of what his original theories recommended. Chalmers was involved in the creation of the Free Church on the specific ground of freedom from state control; Gladstone in the disestablishment of the Church of Ireland, the very place where his theory so strenuously defended Establishment.

When accounting for the magnitude of the calamity in Scotland, we must bear in mind that Scotland suffered two pressures simultaneously which England endured in succession. The first pressure was the Industrial Revolution, with the rapid growth of the big cities and the inability of the old system of local government and parish life to cope. In England this led to a large disruption, in the emergence of the Methodist Churches, which stepped in to fill the breaches left by the old legal framework of English Establishment.

The second pressure was the tension set up through constitutional changes of 1828-35, by which Dissenters and Roman Catholics were given full civic rights. The old established framework had to be adapted if it was to survive and the adaptation must include the abandoning of privileges hallowed by and since the Reformation. In England this failed to lead to so obvious a disruption, though there came a point when men were afraid of just such a disaster. But it led to important developments of the same kind, which affected all the later course of English history. The leaving of the Established Church by such minds as Newman, Manning, James Hope (Hope Scott of Abbotsford), William George Ward, and many another, subtly altered for a time the very nature of Anglican leadership.

These were the two political stresses of the age: the discovery of the urban slum, and the relation of new quasi-democracy to old oligarchy. The Disruption in Scotland was so divisive not because Chalmers the conservative was any more truculent or high principled than Newman the conservative or Wesley the conservative, but because Scotland had to bear the cross simultaneously of two emergencies which England endured successively.

In Scottish minds the quarrel over patronage was much the more prominent turmoil. But underneath, half concealed but influencing the entire argument, was the tension of a new industrial society, and its pouring out of new evangelical wine which was incapable of remaining within the old parish bottles. This is the half-concealed link which joins the conservative Chalmers of 1838 with the man who walked out of the established Church of Scotland almost exactly five years later.

Sir Robert Peel was once described by Gladstone[17] as 'a religious man' but 'wholly anti-church and anti-clerical, and largely undogmatic'. Peel was an Erastian. He believed that clergymen did not run churches well, and knew that laymen ran them better. Clergymen were doctrinaires, and applied theories to facts; and laymen were practical men who let facts rule their theories. He thought it a virtue if a man refused to trouble his head too much with the niceties of ecclesiastical theory. He even made a public speech, when elected Lord Rector of the University of Glasgow, in which he claimed the virtue for himself:

> When I have joined in the public worship of your church, think you
> that I have adverted to distinctions in point of form? Think you that I
> have troubled myself with questions of Church discipline or Church
> government?[18]

This was part of the immense difficulty of finding any solution. A man like Peel thought that Chalmers and his party pretended to priestly power over the just rights of the laity. He was not capable of fathoming that the source of the claim was not pretension but principle, built into Scottish history by the course of its Reformation and with roots which went back at least as far as the Geneva of Calvin's day. Peel was not capable of fathoming this because, for all his exceptional ability, he was so practical a man that he could not recognise the deep force of historical precedent on patterns of behaviour and judgments of moral principle.

This theory of the anti-clerical, that clergymen are usually the source of darkness and laymen always the source of light, carried with it an illusion very dangerous for the politicians of that day, an illusion which even into our day has affected the history of Chalmers and the Disruption. A man like Peel supposed that the laity would only go astray if the clergy led. But the power behind Chalmers was not just a majority of the ministers in the General Assembly. In the northern and western Highlands the people were more militant than their pastors. The terrible scene amid the snows of Marnoch when a minister of the Establishment was instituted to his parish shows a people offended; the revulsion of multitudes. When the 400 ministers followed Welsh and Chalmers out of the hall of the General Assembly on that dramatic day of 18 May 1843, those who came out were greeted with cheers by vast crowds waiting outside and those within encountered hissing and boos. Some ministers certainly went out because they knew that if they remained their people would desert them for Dissenting chapels. Though Melbourne mocked Chalmers as the Pope, he was no Pope. He articulated a feeling which breathed within the body of the people. In a few of the northern parishes after the Disruption there was window-breaking and even a riot or two when the new minister of the Established Church was instituted. The characteristic attitude of the anti-clerical politician prevented Peel from seeing that it is just as often men in pews who force the decisions of ministers as ministers who persuade men in pews. Some of the men who walked out on 18 May went out with bleeding hearts and without the slightest desire to go. [19]

The attitude carried another equally important illusion: that since the movement was clerical the schism would be small: 10 ministers, 40 ministers at the worst, and, when things began to look grave, only 100 or so ministers.

Lord Aberdeen was a most sympathetic man who tended to irresolution and whose ideal of life was that of the great lord amid the formalised ritual and affectionate tenantry of Haddo House. Although he comes out well from the whole argument with Chalmers, with the possible exception of an irritated little bit of vituperation in the House of Lords, nothing suggests that his endeavours had or could have had any kind of healing effect in the argument. As patron he himself witnessed with perturbation the effect of the veto principle when used, he thought unjustly, against a candidate in whom, after due enquiry, he believed; and the attempt to give presbyteries greater power against patrons might have had a chance early in the argument but had no chance by the time Aberdeen came to apply it. His strong interest in foreign affairs took his mind away from Scotland for long periods; but he was a man who at least understood and cared about the religion of the Scots and conformed to their Establishment, and this was not so common in the Parliament of that day that we can afford to treat it lightly.

Chalmers was often charged with inconsistency because of his lectures in London in 1838. The charge left him wholly unmoved. 'It is a little too much,' he wrote to Sir George Sinclair on 4 December 1841, 'that the Conservatives . . . should think that an advocacy given to the National Church, solely for the sake of its religious and moral benefits to the population, should still be continued, after they shall have converted it from an engine of Christian usefulness into a mere congeries of offices, by which to uphold the influence of patrons or the views of a worthless partisanship.' [20] He consistently maintained that he never altered his point of view. 'I shall ever regret,' he wrote in the same letter to Sinclair, 'the necessity of a separation from the State'; and the plea is certainly justified. In theory at least he never wavered. On the very last day of his life he talked with a special satisfaction of the evidence which he gave before the Sites Commission in May 1847 and how he had justly represented the position of the Free Church on Establishment.

The evidence before the Sites Commission, given in Chalmers' last month of life, was a very steady performance, and to be praised, because he was old and tired and had not come prepared for the kind of attack which he met. Sir James Graham, the Scot who stood behind Peel in the politics of the Disruption, was a member of the Commission, and not expected to ask questions because of his old friendship with Chalmers. But at one point in Chalmers' evidence he left the room and came back with a bundle of papers including various old utterances of Chalmers, especially the lectures of 1838, and proceeded to an inquisition, always with the implication that his London defence of Establishment in 1838 was contradicted by his disestablishment of half the Church of Scotland only five years later.

The witness declared himself still a great friend to the idea of Establishment; that where the right conditions prevailed there ought to be a constitutional link between Church and State; that the Free Church stood on the side of social order. 'Grant an establishment upon right principles, and if it is well worked it is the most efficient of all machinery for pervading the people with religion. . . .' He still praised the Establishment in England, though not so confidently as in 1838 because of the rise of Puseyism. Graham asked him how he could defend the Church of England in 1838 when he knew that the Queen was the head of the Church and lay patrons powerful; but Chalmers was quite unmoved, and perfectly consistent with himself. Finally Graham came to the sharpest stab of all:

> Churchmen, though holy men, are but men, and I venture to put the question to you, whether they may not endeavour, in their corporate capacity, unduly sometimes to extend their power?

Dr Chalmers replied:

> It may be so . . . but . . . we have been charged with a desire to extend our power on the one hand, and on the other hand we have been charged with giving away our power to the people. [21]

Less than three weeks later he died quietly in his sleep. He expected to the last that the Established Church would gradually die and be unable to fill its parishes, and that the Government would need to re-establish the Free Church on better conditions. The latter expectation was one which, in the long run, was not so different from what came to pass.

Now I want to make a comparison with the 20th century, because the name of Chalmers continued to appear in the British argument long after his death.

Here is what happened in the House of Commons. On 7 March 1843, when everyone knew that unless the British Government acted the Scottish Church would be split tragically into two and the Established Church would lose some of its best ministers, Fox Maule introduced his motion into the House of Commons. It was only a motion for enquiry but it had a good chance of stopping or delaying the calamity at the eleventh hour. The result was one of the best of all arguments for devolution on a domestic issue; for the motion was rejected by 241 votes to 76. If Scottish votes alone were counted, more than two to one were in favour of the motion. Most of the English members of Parliament were culpably ignorant. The sum total of their knowledge about Scotland was that they did not like what they had heard about John Knox and had the extraordinary illusion that Scottish armies made it easier for Oliver Cromwell to cut off the head of a king. The problem raised by Chalmers and his men could only be understood by people who had the understanding that comes from *feeling*: a feeling for the long history of Scotland and its Church.

Now turn to 15 December 1927. On that day the House of Commons threw out a motion giving approval to a new Prayer Book for the Church of England. This prayer book was voted for by large majorities in the constituted organs of the Church and also by a substantial majority in the House of Lords. This disaster in the modern relations between Church and State in England had a parallel with what happened in Scotland in 1843 in the sense that, if only English members had voted on what exclusively concerned the English

Church, the motion would have been passed; quite a number of those who voted against were Scots. The most influential speech against the motion was made by the member for Paisley, Rosslyn Mitchell. Anyone who now reads the words of Mitchell in *Hansard* cannot understand how the speech, which is rant, could have had such effect. The witnesses are agreed that it had a vote-swinging effect. Just as a crisis of Church and State in Scotland was produced in part by a handful of Englishmen ignorant of the Church of Scotland, so a crisis of Church and State in England was partly produced by a smaller handful of Scotsmen ignorant of the Church of England. There was evidently a case for devolution in England.

Hansard records in one of these debates a sublime speech by a Scot, the Duchess of Atholl.[22] I quote her at length because she harked back to Chalmers:

> This is not the first time that a national Church has come to Parliament asking for help in setting her house in order. Some 85 years ago the Church of Scotland came to the House of Commons and asked for an enquiry. . . . That request was refused. Parliament would not even look into the difficulties of the Church of Scotland. That action of Parliament was lamentable and culpable but at least Parliament had incurred no previous responsibility in the matter . . . ; but here as we know, what the Church [of England] asks us to accept is something which Parliament has asked the Church to do. . . . In 1843 the request of the Church of Scotland was refused, largely owing to the votes of English members, and I submit to my Scottish colleagues that it would be an honourable—indeed a glorious— revenge on their part, if tomorrow night they should help the Church of England to secure some small measure of the liberty for which the Church of Scotland so nobly fought and which we all so greatly prize.

Thirty-six Scotsmen from a nation which, thanks first to John Knox and later to Thomas Chalmers, was dedicated to the just freedom of a Church; thirty-six Scotsmen walking into a lobby in order to screw the State's vice tighter upon the Church of England.

It was 47 years from that melodrama in the House of Commons to the moment in 1974, when Parliament passed a law abandoning its claim to control the worship of the Church of England; though of course in the intervening years it was not really controlling the Church of England, which did much as it liked. During those 47 years any attempt to force a disestablishment upon England on grounds of high moral principle, like that of Chalmers, would have created more sourness than righteousness and would have damaged religion in England.

Whether discontent tends to be more muted south of the Border; or whether it was that Queen Elizabeth I was a better queen for a country to start a Protestant epoch with than Mary Queen of Scots; or whether

F

82 *The Practical and the Pious*

it was that Knox and Melville, though not more determined than Bancroft and Laud, were determined in different ways; or whether it was that the English of Chalmers' day realised that they still needed a State to complete that Reformation of medieval endowments which almost exclusively in Europe was left incomplete by the reforms of the 16th century; whatever the reason, it is hard for an Englishman not to think that Chalmers and his men were wrong because they could not wait. Legal systems are always more flexible than they look; even lawyers have hearts beneath their waistcoats of chain-mail; quietness and patience and persuasion are no less Christian virtues than is the heroic sacrifice of stipends on high principle. Admiration is due not only to some of the men who came out in 1843 but to some of the men who had the courage to remain behind and face obloquy and charges of self-interest and cowardice. As Sir Alexander Cadogan said, in the middle of the most tense moment of appeasing Hitler during the 1930s, 'What courage it takes to be a coward!'

Nevertheless, the headship of Christ is that without which churches may as well be swept aside into heaps of rubble or converted into gymnasia. In all the span of Christian history one can find no clearer demonstration of the sacred appeal to that headship, in the realm of ecclesiastical polity, than in the events of 1842-43 and the leadership of the man whom we commemorate. So a demi-semi-Erastian of nearly a century and a half later may be allowed to make up a little for the nonchalance of Lord Melbourne and the irresolution of Lord Aberdeen and the anti-clericalism of Sir Robert Peel and the naked Erastianism of Sir James Graham by looking back at Dr Chalmers with a sense of gratitude.

Notes to Chapter II

1 Hanna, *Memoirs*, vol. IV, p.40.
2 Earls of Rosebery, Harrowby, Jersey, Wicklow, Cawdor; Marquess Cholmondeley; Lords Ashley, Sandon, Wodehouse, Bexley and Teignmouth. *Morning Chronicle*, 28 April 1838.
3 *Peter's Letters to his Kinsfolk*, 3rd edn. (1819), 3, pp.265ff.
4 Hanna, *Memoirs*, vol. III, p.393.
5 Chalmers to Lady Stuart of Allanbank, 1 July 1835, in Hanna, *Memoirs*, vol. IV, pp.4-5.
6 Hanna, *Memoirs*, vol. IV, pp.6-7.
7 Guthrie, *Autobiography* (1876), p.214.
8 G I T Machin, 'The Disruption and British Politics' in *Scottish Historical Review*, vol. 51 (1972), p.27, n.4.
9 Hanna, *Memoirs*, vol. IV. p.171.
10 Chalmers, *Lectures on the Establishment and Extension of National Churches*, in *CW*, vol. XVII, pp.264-65.

11 *CW*, vol. XVII, p.296.

12 ibid., pp.305-6.

13 ibid., p.310.

14 ibid., p.197.

15 J Morley, *Life of Gladstone* (1903), vol. I, p.127.

16 For another letter of criticism, cf. Gladstone to his French friend Rio, 28 July 1838 (M C Bowe, *François Rio* [Paris, 1938], p.156): 'The lectures ... appeared to me, when considered as a whole, to tend rather to confusion than elucidation of the whole subject'.

17 J Brooke and Mary Sorenson (eds.), *W E Gladstone: Autobiographica* (1971), p.57.

18 Lady Frances Balfour, *Life of George, 4th Earl of Aberdeen* (1923), vol. II, p.46.

19 cf. D Macleod, *Memoir of Norman Macleod* (1876), vol. I, p.202.

20 Hanna, *Memoirs*, vol. IV, pp.242-43.

21 *Parliamentary Papers* (1847), xiii q. 6398.

22 *Hansard* 218/1112, 13 June 1928.

III

Chalmers as a 'Manager' of the Church, 1831-1840

Iain F Maciver

Lord Cockburn, who knew Thomas Chalmers long and fairly well, wrote a memorable eulogy into his Journal on hearing of the latter's sudden death in 1847, but his more spontaneous reaction was expressed in a private letter to Mrs Rutherfurd quoted recently in a study of Cockburn.[1] It is worth returning to one or two phrases of Cockburn's finely tuned, affectionate and perceptive tribute, revealing of Chalmers as a public man.

'He never wasted himself on little objects,' wrote Cockburn, 'nor tried to reach his ends in a little way; but aimed high, and sought no conquests but those that reason and enthusiasm, operating on the minds of masses, could achieve.' In other words, Chalmers always sought the maximum response from his congregations, from his students, from his Church and its committees over which he presided, and from the politicians with whom he had to negotiate. It was an attitude powered by burning eloquence and deep emotional commitment. Chalmers was never a negotiator in the modern sense, with maximum and minimum demands and fall-back positions. He carried the imperatives of the pulpit and the rostrum into the committee room, strove to convince absolutely by a combination of oratory and reason, and expected the response to be just as wholehearted.

With Evangelicalism Chalmers embraced a Calvinist high churchmanship embodying a continuing expectation of a ready response from the political Establishment—'the civil magistrate'—to the legitimate demands of a Reformed and national Church. However, it was a position that failed to take note of the disappearance of Scotland as an independent political entity since the heyday of the civil magistrate doctrine, its final demise as a semi-autonomous political province after 1832, and the rise of Dissent as a powerful political constituency.

The political shortcomings that made Chalmers appear to be such a wayward and unpredictable manager of the Kirk did not fail to be noted, though indulgently, by Cockburn, who wrote: 'that concentration of mind on the object of present interest, which zeal often implies, sometimes made him forget what was due to other men or matters, and has exposed him to the only doubt—that of inconsistency—to which he has ever been supposed to be liable. But this partiality of vehemence never made him long, or seriously unjust.' What lies behind these remarks is Cockburn's identification of a tendency on the part of Chalmers to invest so much emotional capital in a single cause that he was blind to its defects, and overreacted to any criticism or check with a violence that could hurt friends and foes alike. Chalmers almost always repented bitterly of such lapses, and his diaries abound with self-reproach for instances of 'unbridled utterance' or lack of charity. [2] But temperamental eruptions of this kind tended to recur at times of crisis in his career, and possibly they were inseparable from the intense single-mindedness with which he pursued his causes.

Undeniably, this was a serious weakness in a church leader and on too many occasions Chalmers showed that he could be excited or goaded into politically injudicious actions. Cockburn hinted also at a zeal that could blind him to some of the vital detail in negotiation as he placed his own over-sanguine gloss on the statements of other parties or even neglected, as during the crucial exchanges with Lord Aberdeen in 1840, to keep in touch with his own side. [3] In this kind of situation Chalmers' skills of tongue and pen, so effective in an ecclesiastical context, were of no avail in the inhospitable climate of secular politics without the additional prosaic ability to curb his enthusiasms at the right tactical moment.

It is proposed to test these general observations by examination of some situations in which Chalmers exercised influence or authority as an ecclesiastical manager. The first study is of the canvass from June to September 1831 for the vacant professorship of ecclesiastical history at Edinburgh University, then in the gift of the Crown, represented by the Whig ministry of Earl Grey. This process, in which Chalmers played a central role, shows in some detail the way in which he handled patronage, a vital part of Church management, and how he reacted to unexpected difficulties during a tortuous and protracted process of selection.

To most contemporaries the contest came to be recorded as a simple duel between the claims of the successful candidate, David Welsh, and those of John Lee, a bibliophile of obsessive appetite, but also the most learned antiquarian in the Kirk. The public issue which proved, in Cockburn's view, 'justly fatal' to Lee's cause [4] was his reluctance to give up the 'plurality' of a parish charge held in conjunction with the prospective, poorly-salaried, Chair. However, matters were more complicated than this simple summary reveals, for Dr Lee, who was well regarded by the Whig leadership in Edinburgh, was actually on the point of being invited to accept the Chair when the reaction of

Chalmers to this unwelcome news caused a precipitate retreat. Chalmers had raised what the Lord Advocate, Francis Jeffrey, called an 'antiplurality rage' with himself and other Scottish Whig chiefs, notably in correspondence with the Cabinet minister and Edinburgh MP, James Abercromby, and the influential Lord Minto. Respectful of his great prestige and wary of his new and largely undefined power as a leading spokesman of Evangelicalism, the Whigs were anxious to placate Chalmers and to avoid the possibility he threatened of a pluralist appointment raising 'a flame all over the Church of Scotland'. Abercromby feared that the anti-pluralists would form parties in the presbyteries against a weak government, and Lee's appointment was shelved when it had proceeded almost to the point of no return.[5]

Chalmers had a substitute to hand, and, given that Lee was the natural candidate, his choice was rather an imaginative one. On 22 June he urged Lord Minto to persuade the latter's parish minister and protégé, David Aitken, to stand, pledging 'that if he come forward he will have my best wishes'.[6] Aitken's surviving correspondence reveals him as an intelligent and cultivated man and a far from unworthy candidate. He had a special and unusual interest in German literature which attracted the approbation of Thomas Carlyle, who corresponded with him and made use of his large German library. Even more exceptionally for a Scots minister of this period, he had studied church history in Prussia, striking up some acquaintance in Berlin with the intellectual lions of the city, Schleiermacher, Hegel, Neander and Raumer.[7] This activity earned the imprimatur of Thomas McCrie, who praised Aitken's activity in acquiring knowledge of German theology: 'the effect of it has been to liberalise his mind . . . while at the same time it has fortified him against the Gangrene of Neology'.[8] In addition, as a well-connected Whig, there could be no political objection to his candidature.

However, Aitken proved to be a reluctant aspirant. A diffident man much preoccupied with his health, he was rather averse to leave his comfortable country parish for a poorly-endowed university chair; and he suspected that Chalmers' enthusiasm to engage him as a colleague was influenced as much by personal antipathy to Lee as by doctrinal objections to pluralism, explaining to Minto that 'he and Dr Lee don't draw well together and would consequently be uncomfortably yoked as Brother Professors obliged to come in contact which they now never do. And secondly Dr C is embarked in the plurality contest, heart and soul, and on that account is doubly loath that Lee should be appointed.'[9] If Aitken was merely an instrument of Chalmers' design to exclude Lee, he proved to be a very defective one. Anxiety about his health and the poverty of the appointment overcame his fear of Chalmers' wrath, and on 8 August, fortified by medical advice, he made a final rejection of the offer.[10]

Chalmers was outraged. Following an earlier abjuration by Aitken in July, when the government were offering only the previous incumbent's salary of £100 a year, he had lobbied strenuously and successfully for a doubling of the sum. But, according to Aitken, Chalmers had misunderstood his position on the salary, jumping with a characteristic optimism to the conclusion that Aitken would accept if £200 was offered, and estimating class fees at more than double Aitken's figure. [11] Chalmers had certainly expended much energy in vain on behalf of his man, and Aitken's tergiversations were provoking, but the temperamental force of his reaction was out of proportion to the offence. It can be explained only by public embarrassment created by his candidate's 'distressing vacillations' and by a sense of personal betrayal sharpened by Aitken's fearful avoidance of a personal meeting in Edinburgh after his decision to withdraw. [12]

The Aitken affair is a good example of how the persuasive powers of Chalmers could, in some cases, intimidate rather than inspire. In his enthusiasm to secure a congenial colleague he ignored warning signals of Aitken's financial and other misgivings, and this inability to listen closely to what others were saying, or to read nuances in their letters, was a factor that recurred in other actions as an ecclesiastical politician, notably in the Aberdeen negotiations. Pressure on a retiring introvert like Aitken could actually be counter-productive. In his lengthy apologia to Lord Minto, Aitken complained of the organisation by the 'aweful [sic] Professor' of a team of persuaders among younger churchmen of their acquaintance with the result that 'I am daily besieged with letters, all urgent and reprehensive'; and in another revealing passage he confessed to a real fear of Chalmers: 'it was from my knowledge of the Doctor's almost irresistible importunateness that I declined seeing him when I was in Edinburgh, being well aware that one out of two things must have happened, either that I would have been partly bullied partly cajolled [sic] into doing what my judgment did not approve; or that a very awkward collision of opinion would have taken place.' [13]

The charisma of Chalmers was effective on fellow enthusiasts, or on those half convinced already of the merits of his cause and willing to be swept along in his wake. But it is important to recognise the limits of his formidable persuasiveness, and to see that to some, like Aitken, he could appear overbearing and to show too much 'inability to bear contradiction'. [14] Like many men of passionate organising drive, Chalmers could raise hackles or intimidate the timid. Though he went on in September 1831 to secure the appointment of a subsequent choice of colleague, David Welsh, a portent of future bad relations with the Whigs was the reaction of one party grandee, Lord Minto, who, offended at Chalmers' treatment of his parish minister and confidant, resolved never to co-operate with him in political business again. [15]

Minto was to remain a determined enemy of Evangelical claims before the Disruption, and of the Free Church thereafter.

Any rounded picture of Chalmers as a leader of the Kirk would be distorted if full consideration were not given to his triumphs of organisation and effort. Perhaps his greatest and most personal feat of management—still very much a part of the present parish fabric of Scotland—was the Church Extension scheme, a great surge of building and fund-raising, which, though accompanied by a rising level of political and sectarian bitterness, brought in by seven years of effort what was then a massive sum of £305 000, erecting 222 new churches. Church Extension had been a desideratum in the Kirk for a decade and a half before Chalmers took firm control of the moribund Church Accommodation Committee of the General Assembly in 1834. The earlier committee had undertaken in 1818 a countrywide survey of 'deficiencies' in church provision. Dr John Inglis, the Moderate leader, had secured a limited programme, financed by the government, after much lobbying and procedural delay. As a result, 42 new 'Parliamentary' churches had been erected in the Highlands and Islands. Thereafter, the provision promised for overpopulated urbanising parishes in the Lowlands had not materialised, and the Church's campaign had stagnated until it was revived largely by the personal intervention of Chalmers. [16]

It is likely that Chalmers saw the 'principle of locality', enshrined in his widely-publicised St John's parish scheme of the previous decade, being given new life through a national Extension project that sought to combine local effort with the aid of a central fund raised by subscription to help poorer or weaker parishes. The ultimate stimulus would be provided by state grants in the form of an annual endowment of the ministers' stipends in the new missionary and territorial churches. To Chalmers the case for action was urgent and obvious. 'In advocating this cause,' he said in his manifesto, 'we need be at no loss for the materials of a most pathetic appeal to the sympathies of the truly religious. For we can tell them of the spiritual destitution of many thousands of the families of Scotland. . . . Even to the mere politician and worldly philanthropist we can address the argument, that a depraved commonalty is the teeming source of all moral and political disorder, and a fearful presage, if not speedily averted by an efficient system of Christian instruction, of a sweeping anarchy, and a great national overthrow. But it is when pleading for the claims of so many imperishable spirits that we are on our best, our firmest vantage-ground . . . of that still greater multitude, who, with an eternity wholly unprovided for, live in irreligion and die in apathy or despair.' [17] This passionate concern was sustained through illness, for Chalmers suffered a serious stroke in 1834; and he plunged courageously in June of that year into a campaign by post, undeterred by physical weakness.

The Extension campaign brought out to their fullest extent Chalmers' gifts of inspired leadership and sheer organising ability. He replaced the colourless title of 'Accommodation' with the more purposive 'Extension' on the masthead of his committee. Possibly he had absorbed lessons from the problems of his social experiment in Glasgow, for he stressed now the necessity of organising local efforts on a national scale, explaining to his key lieutenant, William Collins, the publisher, that 'what I particularly wish is to combine a wise general superintendence on the one hand with an entire and intense local feeling in each separate town and district for its own local necessities on the other.' [18] Organisation was not to be haphazard. Each synod of the Kirk should contain its group of committed extensionists to circulate literature and encourage local effort, but if a local stimulus existed it should be kept free of undue intervention and interference by the General Assembly committee. [19] Chalmers emphasised the local factor, the legacy of his poor relief experiment, again and again, [20] and was anxious to devolve local organisation ever downwards. He explained to his agent in Aberdeen that 'I think it would add much to our prosperity if you encouraged the formation of Sub-Associations in parishes, and even smaller districts than many of our parishes. . . . I presume that all connected with that locality whether by property or residence or special tie and affection of any sort, might be contributors, from guineas a year to pennies a week, for a good parochial apparatus of Church and School in the said district. Thus you deepen the culture of the soil on which we are all operating, and in proportion as you descend have the advantage of a far more intense local feeling, and greatly more numerous contributions, though individually smaller.' [21]

If put into effect, this was an effort of fund-raising and parish organisation on a novel level of intensity in most parishes, and there are echoes too of the district 'proportions' organised by Chalmers in St John's. Specifically, he also acknowledged a debt to the structure of Bible societies, with their parent organisation, town auxiliary and parish association so characteristic of evangelical endeavour in its wider context. [22] But the imaginative scale of Extension, much of its financial and administrative framework, and, above all, the great impact of its publicity and propaganda on Established Church people, was largely the product of Chalmers' own mind. Part of his flair lay in an ability to recruit able and dedicated aides. William Collins devised for his own successful Glasgow Church Accommodation Society a scheme for raising subscriptions from affluent supporters based on a fixed contribution of aid for each church built, and promoted the creation of a supplementary fund in 1838 to forestall waning enthusiasm [23]; and James Begg, a tireless propagandist for Extension, seems to have been responsible for proposing that vague ideas for sending out agents to explain the cause should be hardened into an organised scheme to 'embrace all Scotland and appoint agents to visit every Synod', with express authority and instructions from the Committee. [24]

However, the intensity of his personal immersion in the campaign took a heavy toll on Chalmers. From the summer of 1834 until the close of 1839 he remained largely preoccupied with Extension. By 1838, when the momentum of enthusiasm for fund-raising was fading and political difficulties seemed insuperable, Chalmers seems to have abandoned himself for a time to destructive emotionalism. Even Collins was moved to comment on 'the grievous and unusual state of excitement' expressed in a letter from his mentor, [25] though the resilient Chalmers rallied and later allowed himself to be teased by his old friend and kindly critic, Professor Thomas Duncan of St Andrews, in an exchange of charades:

> My whole is a Doctor whose name I won't mention
> Who has periled his fame in Scotch Kirk Extension. [26]

It is certainly true that the actions and reactions of Chalmers in his dealings with politicians displayed many of the shortcomings revealed in the Aitken affair. However, it would be unfair to him not to place on the other side of the scales the fact that during the Extension campaign period he had to deal with the weak and not infrequently vacillating Whig governments of Lord Melbourne, which, on ecclesiastical issues, were susceptible politically to pressure from 'Voluntary' anti-Establishment Dissenters bitterly hostile to the Church. In the summer of 1834 Chalmers had high hopes, thanks to statements by Lords Melbourne and Brougham, that the Whigs would be prepared to carry a measure of endowment for his projected parishes. Melbourne had admitted that 'undoubtedly it was essential that some assistance should be offered to obviate the evil' of deficient accommodation, [27] but by September, under pressure from Scottish 'Voluntaries', he had recanted his half-promise, and, without any sense of contradiction, Brougham had completely changed sides. Subsequently, the Whigs never came so near again to granting endowment, and Chalmers' relations with them—never close—deteriorated sharply.

The next year, after an initially favourable response to the government's appointment of a Royal Commission to enquire into 'Religious Instruction and Pastoral Superintendence' in Scotland, Chalmers allowed John Hope, the Tory Dean of the Faculty of Advocates, adroitly to manoeuvre him into open opposition to the government commission, and almost entire reliance on the Conservatives as the partisans of Extension in Parliament. [28] In 1836 Chalmers gave public support to his Tory friend, Campbell of Monzie, in the Argyll by-election, writing an open letter attacking the Whig government's attitude to kirk issues, and he responded in kind to

baiting from the Whig/Radical press, led by *The Scotsman*.[29]
During 1837, a general election year, relations with the Whigs reached
a nadir, summed up by Lord Belhaven, a former ally, when he wrote to
the Lord Advocate with the comment that 'you know as well as I do
that the Parsons are *our most* inveterate political enemies [sic].'[30] The
Voluntary Dissenters, who were principally Presbyterian seceders, and
able to compete on equal terms with the Established Church in the
major cities, exploited their Liberal loyalism to the full. By 1839, their
Central Board, answering the statistics of Chalmers and his committee
with counter-statistics, and parliamentary petitions with counter-
petitions, had fought the extensionists' political campaign to a
stalemate.

Regardless of major political reverses, Chalmers retained firm
control of the Extension campaign and of the Assembly throughout the
turmoil, though, as with the Glasgow experiment, his social ideology
did not lack critics. John Lee, who had close experience of a poverty-
stricken Old Town parish in Edinburgh, pointed to the existence of 'a
perpetual fluctuation of inhabitants on whom no impression could be
made',[31] and commissioned a survey to demonstrate that between 1834
and 1836 over half of the poorest tenants in his parish moved house each
year. [32] Chalmers was deeply angered at such a fundamental critique of
the social and moral potential of Extension, and assailed Lee's
'revolting view' of the 'plebeian families' of Edinburgh as 'gypsies',
seeing Lee's thesis as designed 'to prove that the parochial system in
towns was a phantom or chimera'. [33] An even worse offence in
Chalmers' eyes was the degree of identity of Lee's views with the
Kirk's Voluntary opponents, one of whom, the publisher Adam Black,
had derided Chalmers' new parishes as 'ecclesiastical parallelograms',
destined to be as utopian as Robert Owen's communes. [34]

Chalmers was determined to hold, and to hold the Church, to his
belief that a large proportion of the population remained to be
'reclaimed' in most populous working class districts, and that
unendowed churches, regardless of whether they were Established or
Dissenting—'with their high seat rents and general congregations',
excluding the poorest parishioners—showed 'all the impotency of the
voluntary system.' [35] It was very probably indignation at this blow from
within at the Extension cause which impelled Chalmers to stifle a move
in 1836 to select Lee as Moderator of the General Assembly. But Lee's
supporters included many, like David Welsh, Robert Smith Candlish
and the Moncreiffs of Tullibole, who were otherwise allies of
Chalmers' causes; and Chalmers' blackball, defensible enough on
public issues, was fairly well known to be influenced by strong personal
dislike. In 1837 Lee's friends pressed his claims on the moderatorship
to a vote in the Assembly. Dr Matthew Gardiner of Bothwell was
Chalmers' candidate in a contest which the latter saw largely as a vote

of confidence in his Extension policies, and he asserted his firm control of the Assembly by obtaining a crushing majority for Gardiner, with many Moderates deserting Lee for tactical reasons. The cost of victory was a degree of personal and political bitterness that alienated from Chalmers, until his breach with the Tories in 1840, almost all the Evangelical Whigs still sympathetic to Extension, and divided him for a time from some leading ministers of his own party. [36]

If the moderatorship controversy showed that an overwrought Chalmers could react petulantly, and with some personal unfairness, to criticism, it also showed his stubborn devotion to his policies and tireless pertinacity in their defence. He was convinced that state support of the Church's Extension was a vital touchstone of the former's support of an established religion; and in spite of maladroit political footwork he followed successfully his own instinct and ability to enthuse and hold the allegiance of the Assembly.

In this context it is worth considering the Extension campaign as a major element in the managerial education of Chalmers, and as a means of radicalising his own outlook, a process without which he might have found it much harder to contemplate a disruption of the Church in 1843. Throughout the campaign there was one immovable politico-legal obstacle blocking any thorough restructuring of the parochial system: the self-interest of the heritors or landlords on whom Scottish Conservatism was narrowly based and dependent during this period. Chalmers was slow to react to this partly subterranean but stubborn obstruction. With his own conservative leanings, he was inclined to hope that the aristocracy and upper classes would take the lead as champions of Extension. He set great store on the persuasion of magnates, writing to the Duke of Buccleuch of the political as well as moral dividends to be gathered from generous giving by the leaders of society to a scheme that would be a powerful specific 'against all moral and political disorders'. [37]

A measure of his lack of alarm at the depths of landlord opposition to any statute-based Extension unfavourable to their financial interests was Chalmers' assurance to Buccleuch that a recent act of Parliament fully protected heritors from legal burdens arising from new erections of parishes. The existing civil law favoured heritor interests, and a lawsuit (Millar versus the Heritors of Neilston, 1834) had confirmed that heritor responsibility was limited to the conservation or replacement of existing church fabrics. Another major obstacle to the fundamental redrawing of parish boundaries, so that they might correspond better to demographic change, was one of the last acts of the Scots Parliament 'anent Plantation of Kirks' (1707), which forbade any disjunction of part of an existing parish for the erection of a new one without the consent of the heritors holding three fourths of the parish valuation.[38] It is extraordinary that Chalmers showed such insouciance in 1834 at the virtual failure of the measure introduced by J C Colquhoun MP in February to regulate the legal status of new parishes created by expansion of the Kirk. In its original draft the bill had sought to repeal the final clause of the 1707 act giving heritors a veto on disjunction, but it was emasculated radically and efficiently in the House of Lords by Tory peers led by Lord Haddington. Not only was the repeal clause deleted, but the Lords made doubly sure by removing carefully all references to the new parishes becoming parochial churches in the full legal sense, only erecting them as such 'according to the provisions of the existing law'.[39]

It is plain that Chalmers was too concerned with retaining Tory goodwill to take in the full implications of such attitudes, and the Tories, through their wily and devious Kirk agent, John Hope, remained vigilant in steering him and the extensionists away from any temptation to raise endowments from landed pockets. Hope showed a significant flurry of alarm in 1835 when there appeared to be a prospect, attractive to the more radical supporters of Extension, of using the 'unexhausted teinds'—that portion of tithe not applied to parish uses which had been appropriated (quite legally) by the landed heritors—to finance endowments, and his anxiety only subsided when the Whigs declared that they would not interfere with teinds in private hands.[40]

It was a growing realisation of the apathy of the landed interest towards Extension that inexorably eroded Chalmers' confidence in them as fitting instruments of the cause. Relations between ministers and their local heritors were not infrequently uneasy, and clerical suspicion of the lairds and aristocracy ran deep. Churchmen traditionally resented the landlords' appropriation of the unexhausted teinds, and, in this context, the complaint of Matthew Gardiner to Chalmers about his local magnate can be taken as typical of ministerial prejudice. The Tory-leaning Gardiner was very far from being a radical, yet he was moved to write: 'the Duke will probably support endowments in the House of Lords, but though as Patron and Titular of the Teinds in this and several of the surrounding parishes, he has pocketed and continues to pocket thousands and thousands of the Church's money, he is not disposed to part with a shilling for her support and extension.'[41] By 1836 Chalmers was already expressing public disappointment in his report to the Assembly that 'the nobility of Scotland, with some rare exceptions may still be regarded as unbroken ground . . . the same is true of our great landed aristocracy.'[42] A year later a small group of peers and lairds was reported to have come forward to fund new churches in their localities—Buccleuch, Bute, Lord Dundas, Dundas of Arniston and Chisholm of Chisholm—but the real drive was coming from merchants and industrialists in the cities, particularly Glasgow, [43] and the most generous lairds like Forbes of Callendar, Dirom of Mount Annan and Sir Robert Abercromby were not major landowners. [44]

The Glasgow businessmen who bore so much of the financial weight of the campaign were scornful of aristocratic parsimony. Collins, after attempting in vain to recruit an expatriate group in London to head a subscription list, wrote in disgust that: 'though our Scottish noblemen have done but marvellously little as yet in Church Extension, yet I much fear they are not the persons to begin with . . . I am satisfied that if the rich conservatives in Scotland had spent one-third of the industry in building Churches as they have in electioneering they might have made Scotland *all their own*.' [45]

Events in the political field added their quota to Chalmers' disillusion. His Conservative allies took immediate alarm at the high and uncompromising tone of the Assembly's reaction in May to the Court of Session judgment in the celebrated Auchterarder case (March 1838). The Assembly resolved that the issue of lay patronage of parochial charges was a spiritual as well as a temporal matter, that the Church had an equal, co-ordinate jurisdiction with the civil court on such an issue, and that it acknowledged no temporal head on earth. Here was the first full statement of what its press enemies were to call 'Presbyterian Puseyism', and it came as an unpleasant shock to comfortably Erastian Tory politicians. Lord Aberdeen quickly reassessed his attitude, commenting that 'it is true that the question of Church extension has no necessary connexion with the Auchterarder Case; but it is impossible to deny that even the legitimate pretensions of the Church are new and startling to English ears. To claim endowments at the same moment in which they assert their independence of civil jurisdiction, I fear will not conciliate the support of many . . . disposed to be friendly.' [46]

By September of 1838 consequential actions by the Church had hardened Aberdeen's attitude. In the parish of Lethendy the local Presbytery of Dunkeld had ordained a rival presentee to that of the patron, in open defiance of the Court of Session. Aberdeen complained that the effect on Anglican opinion was bad, and that it was imprudent to push the endowment issue [47]: by March 1839 he had concluded that, excepting the highly remote possibility of action by the Whig government, the prospects for a grant were 'utterly hopeless'. [48]

Chalmers was not a man to ignore this combination of financial apathy and what he interpreted as political fickleness on the part of the landed interest and its political allies towards his cherished scheme. Deference to rank had its limits, for, as John McCaffrey has pointed out recently, Chalmers was an amalgam of conservative and radical, with a well-rooted suspicion of the beneficiaries of the *status quo*, nurtured from his turbulent early days in St Andrews. [49] The rapid cooling of

Tory enthusiasm for Extension, in reaction to the defiance of the civil courts by the Kirk majority, caused the old spirit of rebellion to blaze forth in a remarkable outburst against the aristocracy. Chalmers chose strong and familiar ground in the Assembly of 1839 to create a momentary sensation in the middle of an oration on Auchterarder when he cried out against 'the revolt of the higher classes against the scheme of Church Extension; and that because of their causeless prejudices, as I will so call them, against the character and object of our late ecclesiastical reformations. They know us not—they understand us not.'[50] William Muir, the Edinburgh minister and educationist, and a staunch Conservative, listened with horror to this outburst of 'abuse' against the nobility, reporting that Chalmers left his notes and got very heated, clenched his fists and appeared to fix his look on Lords Dalhousie and Selkirk, the former of whom then proceeded to leave the Assembly in protest, accompanied by the Marquess of Tweeddale. [51]

Contemporary critics found it all too easy to dismiss philippics of this kind from Chalmers as the products of insensate emotion, or—Muir's explanation in the case just described—as the result of the great Doctor being 'tormented . . . by the Church radicals into whose hands he has thrown himself.' [52] But as the previous narrative has shown, Chalmers had perfectly good reasons from his point of view for reacting against desertion by the landlords and the Tories, and his emotion was tempered with reason. Even before the failure of the Aberdeen negotiations, the incident is symptomatic of a major shift in Chalmers' thinking unaffected by momentary influences on him, a turning away from reliance on the old social establishment and towards his younger and more radical followers in the Assembly. Probably he realised that full endowed Extension was unattainable in the foreseeable future and that his political campaign was at an end. But the Extension scheme had been a major success in terms of organisation and scale of voluntary effort. It had given Chalmers invaluable experience in co-ordinating a national effort on a scale unknown previously in the Church, stamped his personal influence on a large religious constituency and created a machinery of fund-raising and propaganda adaptable for the struggle against the courts and the government on the issue of 'Non-Intrusion', and, even later, for the organisation of the Free Church. It has a strong claim to be regarded as the pivotal experience of Chalmers as an ecclesiastical manager.

Notes to Chapter III

1 Rutherfurd Papers, National Library of Scotland (hereafter NLS) MS. 9688, ff. 59-60, quoted by me in A S Bell (ed.), *Lord Cockburn: A Bicentenary Commemoration* (Edinburgh, 1979), p.78.

2 e.g. his journals quoted in W Hanna, *Memoirs of the Life and Writings of Thomas Chalmers* (Edinburgh, 1849-1852), vol. 3, pp.79-104.

3 Remarks of Robert Bell, Procurator of the Church, as reported by John Hope to Lord Aberdeen, Aberdeen Papers, British Library (hereafter BL) Add. MS. 43202, f. 272 (12 February 1840).

4 Cockburn Papers, NLS Adv. MS. 9.1.8., f. 51, note by Cockburn to copy of letter of Francis Jeffrey to him, 19 June 1831.

5 ibid.; Minto Papers, NLS MS. 12123, Chalmers to Lord Minto, 22 June 1831; MS. 11800, f. 129, James Abercromby to Minto, 27 June 1831.

6 Chalmers to Minto, ibid.

7 C R Sanders and K J Fielding (eds.) *The Collected Letters of Thomas and Jane Welsh Carlyle*, vol. 5 (Durham N C, 1976), pp.44-46, 59-62; Minto Papers, MS. 11801, ff. 107-8, Rev D Aitken to Minto, 19 July 1832.

8 Minto Papers, NLS MS. 12123, Dr James Russell to Minto, 30 June 1831, quoting verbatim from a testimonial by Dr Thomas McCrie.

9 ibid., MS. 11801, f. 28, Aitken to Minto, 25 July 1831.

10 ibid., ff. 37-40, 8 August 1831.

11 ibid., ff. 42-43, 11 August 1831.

12 ibid., MS. 12123, Chalmers to Minto, 9 August 1831.

13 ibid., MS. 11801, ff. 47-48, Aitken to Minto, 17 August 1831.

14 ibid., f. 51, Aitken to Minto, 24 August 1831.

15 ibid., MS. 11800, f. 139, draft letter to Abercromby, 20 August 1831.

16 cf. I F Maciver, 'The General Assembly of the Church, the State and Society in Scotland: Some Aspects of their Relationships, 1815-1843' (M Litt thesis, Edinburgh University, 1977) pp.118-52.

17 T Chalmers, *Circular on Church Accommodation* (Ediburgh, 19 June 1834).

18 Chalmers Papers (*CP*), New College Library, Edinburgh, CHA 5.10.3., Chalmers to Collins, June 1834.

19 *CP*, CHA 5.10.15., Chalmers to Principal Dewar, Aberdeen, June 1834.

20 *CP*, CHA 5.10., 11., 12., 18., to David Stow, Rev J Lorimer and Rev R Buchanan, Glasgow, June 1834.

21 *CP*, CHA 5.10.17., to Rev A L Gordon, Aberdeen, 28 June 1834.

22 *CP*, CHA 5.10.18., to Buchanan, 30 June 1834.

23 *CP*, CHA 4.248.14., W Collins to Chalmers, 28 July 1836; T Chalmers, *Report of the Committee . . . on Church Extension* (Edinburgh, 1839), p.8.

24 *CP*, CHA 4.245.51., Rev J Begg to same, 7 May 1836.

25 *CP*, CHA 4.272.43., Collins to Chalmers, 12 April 1838.

26 *CP*, CHA 4.282.25., Professor Duncan to Chalmers, 14 March 1839.

27 cf. *Hansard*, 3rd series, vol. 25, pp.363-66.

28 cf. the Aberdeen Papers, BL, Add. MS. 43202, correspondence of John Hope and Aberdeen for 1835.

29 Hanna, *Memoirs*, vol. 4, pp.25-27; *The Scotsman*, 13, 17, 27, 31 August 1836.

30 Lord Murray Papers, NLS MS. 19736, f. 36, Lord Belhaven to Murray, 6 March 1837.
31 *CP*, CHA 4.238.48., Lee to Chalmers, 20 April 1835.
32 Lee Papers, NLS MS. 3441, f. 234, R Paterson to Lee, 2 February 1837.
33 T Chalmers, *A Conference . . . On the Subject of the Moderatorship* (Glasgow, 1837), p.11.
34 A Black, *The Church its Own Enemy, Being an Answer to the Rev Dr Chalmers* (Edinburgh, 1835), p.22.
35 Minto Papers, NLS MS. 12124, Chalmers' 'Hints . . . to Her Majesty's Government', 31 July 1835.
36 D. Shaw, 'The Moderatorship Controversy in 1836 and 1837', *Records of the Scottish Church History Society*, XVII (1969-71), pp.115-29; I F Maciver, 'General Assembly', pp.40-41, 212-17.
37 *CP*, CHA 5.10.28., Chalmers to Buccleuch, 9 July 1834.
38 *Scottish Jurist*, vol. 5 (1834), pp.353-56; *Acts of the Parliament of Scotland*, vol. XI (Edinburgh, 1824), p.433.
39 *Hansard*, 3rd series, vol. 24, p.435; *Parliamentary Papers*, 1834, vol. 1, pp.629-33.
40 Aberdeen Papers, BL Add. MS. 43202, ff. 118-19, 130-31, 139-40, Hope to Aberdeen 24, 29 August, 6 October 1835; published letter of Lord John Russell to Lord Minto, 31 August 1835 in *PP* 1835, XLVII, pp.170-71.
41 *CP*, CHA 4.236.46., Rev M Gardiner to Chalmers, 25 March 1835 (on the Duke of Hamilton, who took no more proportionally than his fellow-heritors, but was the obvious local target for the writer).
42 T Chalmers, *Report of the Committee . . . on Church Extension* (Edinburgh, 1836), p.13.
43 *Report* (1837), pp.14-15.
44 *CP*, CHA 4.234.71., Mrs M Dirom and CHA 4.270.1., Sir R Abercromby to Chalmers, 10 October 1835 and 8 June 1838 respectively; *Report on Church Extension* (1838), pp.13-14.
45 *CP*, CHA 4.272.41., Collins to Chalmers, 29 March 1838.
46 Aberdeen Papers, BL Add. MS. 43202, ff. 178-79, Aberdeen to Hope, 13 June 1838.
47 ibid, ff. 196-97, 29 December 1838.
48 ibid., ff. 204-5, 5 March 1839.
49 J F McCaffrey, 'Thomas Chalmers and Social Change' in *Scottish Historical Review*, vol. LX no. 169 (April 1981), p.38.
50 T Chalmers, *Substance of a Speech Delivered in the General Assembly Respecting the Decision of the House of Lords in the Case of Auchterarder* (Glasgow, 1839), p.8.
51 New College Library, Edinburgh, MS. X.15b.3/1, Journal Letters of William Muir, p.89 (26 May 1839).
52 ibid., p.90.

G

IV
Chalmers and the Politicians
Ian A Muirhead

The unfortunate denóuement of the summer of 1840, which left Dr
Thomas Chalmers and Lord Aberdeen accusing each other openly or
by implication of the grossest ill-faith, and the subsequent publication
in 1840 and again in 1893 of correspondence which passed between
them, has in fact given a false perspective to the political scene.
Chalmers was known to his contemporaries as an inefficient political
animal; he was never a significant force in the political arena, and, so far
as concerned Scottish church affairs, Lord Aberdeen was not much
better. They provided names to conjure with at the time, but the
published correspondence which passed between them, besides being
for several months compromised by extraordinary conduct on the part
of Lord Aberdeen, was only one facet of much more general activity in
which members of Government and Opposition, the Scottish
representatives in Parliament, the Non-Intrusion Committee (of which
Chalmers was convener, and which was the body specifically charged
by the General Assembly of the Church of Scotland with the
negotiations with the Government), and last, but by no means least, the
éminence grise of John Hope, Dean of the Faculty of Advocates, were all
active. Chalmers and Aberdeen, though each made the other scapegoat
of his chagrin, were both weak personalities in the political arena, and
victims rather than manipulators.

In the summer of 1840 Chalmers had just resigned from the
chairmanships of the Non-Intrusion Committee and the Church
Extension Committee, and Lord Aberdeen, smarting from recent
events, had referred to 'a reverend gentleman, a great leader in the
Assembly, who having brought the Church into a state of jeopardy and
peril, had left it to find a way out of the difficulty as well as it could.' [1]
As John McCaffrey points out, [2] Chalmers had a constitutional
tendency to pick up causes with great enthusiasm, only to lose interest
in an equally marked way, so the comment showed insight as well as
bitterness. It will surprise no Chalmers-watcher to discover that he had
two inconsistent replies to the attack. One was that he had taken the
decision to go at least 12 months earlier, the other that he had been
forced out by the outrageous behaviour of the politicians, Lord

Aberdeen included. 'The weary struggle of six years, that we had with his political opponents for the extension of our Church, we at length gave up in utter hopelessness of any good from them. . . . The fruitless higgling of the last six months—and in which *shorter*, all the distastes and discouragements and annoyances of the *longer* period have been fully concentrated—we now fling from us.' [3]

Here we are concerned with the shorter period referred to. By the spring of 1839, the Church of Scotland's problems and her need of a working understanding with Parliament were more urgent than ever before. The Veto Act overshadowed all. Chalmers had during the preceding winter expressed himself in favour of its repeal, and its replacement by a gradual reinstatement of the Call, to be based on a series of General Assembly decisions on individual cases; but when the House of Lords issued its decision on the Auchterarder case, all hope of replacing the Veto by another process was destroyed. 'A novel interpretation of the old statutes now existed, in which the Church simply could not acquiesce.' [4] Chalmers moved in the General Assembly a motion, which he said was 'concocted by myself', though put into practical shape by others, that there be set up 'a committee for the purpose of considering in what way the privileges of a National Establishment, and the harmony between Church and State may remain unimpaired, with instructions to confer with the government of the country, if they shall see cause.' [5]

The choice of Chalmers as convener was as inevitable as it was unhappy. As events unfolded, they displayed him in the guise of a rider, most successful when he happened to wish to go in the direction already chosen by his steed, of which he was rarely in full control, and who compounded his problems by a disconcerting habit of changing seat in the saddle, sometimes facing the head and sometimes the rump of his animal.

In the first days of the Church Extension Committee, Chalmers as their convener had approached the task by 'making their appointment known' in a series of publicity measures. He brought the same approach to the work of the new committee, which had far different tasks. At the first meeting he proposed to use the parochial machinery for agitation all over Scotland; tracts, rallies, itinerating lecturers, and the importance of making matters the subject of appeal to the electors whenever occasion offered were 'eagerly stated and approved of'. Dr Muir expressed surprise; since they were appointed to confer with government and members of Parliament to settle a great Church question, he thought the proposals indecorous and improper. The Committee were thunder-struck. They began to urge, Chalmers included, that they would make no impression without agitation, and that in the current state of balance between parties, it would be useful to their cause to suggest the Church's support for whoever would aid them most. Muir argued that they could not agitate, since it was by no means agreed what 'principle' was at stake, and there was diversity of opinion about Non-Intrusion. He was told that the Church had already decided that the principle at stake was the Veto. Muir decided he could not serve on the Committee, and withdrew. [6]

Since this is Muir's version, but as recounted six months later by John Hope, and fitting neatly into the pattern which Hope was intent on impressing upon Lord Aberdeen, it is somewhat suspect. The rush into publicity is certain, however, and the weekly pamphlets were later claimed to have had a significant impact on public opinion, while individuals in the Committee did attempt interventions in elections. [7] The Committee did also approach the Government, and, acting on a suggestion from Lord Melbourne, planned a large and influential deputation to London. At first Chalmers did not intend to go, knowing that the presence of 'our Pope', as the Prime Minister called him, [8] would not be welcome, but the Committee insisted on his presence. He reported to the August Commission of Assembly on their fortunes in London, a euphoric performance describing a visit which had little if anything to show, save a marked unwillingness on the part of the politicians to make specific commitments. The one grain of comfort was an assurance that in the exercise of Crown patronage the Veto Act would be respected. [9] Chalmers had also received a personal invitation to visit Lord Aberdeen when the latter came to Scotland.

It might have seemed a promising invitation. Educated in England, but a keen and responsible improver of his Aberdeenshire estates, a regular worshipper at the parish church, who considered himself 'a kind of eldest son of the Church' [10] and had represented the Presbytery of Ellon in the General Assemblies from 1818 to 1828, Lord Aberdeen ought to have been the ideal mediator in the Church's difficulties. Acquainted with the highest political circles in the south, he was also deeply and sympathetically committed to the spiritual as well as to the material welfare of his Scottish estates and clearly had a good understanding of some of the problems of ordinary church people. He was strongly against any solution of the difficulties which would 'humble the Church'. [11] For Chalmers, for whom, as Dr McCaffrey quotes, there was 'fascination in the attention of superiors' [12] Aberdeen was to be revered both as a great Scottish nobleman and a Tory.

Nevertheless Chalmers delayed his visit. There was apparently no urgency. Yet when he did arrive at Haddo House in mid-September, the damage had been done. [13] His host had now himself become entangled in the Veto Act, and John Hope had written a pamphlet.

Aberdeen had just presented a suitable and popular young man to a vacancy at Methlick when it became known that there was a *fama* (a scandalous report) against him. Patron, presbytery and presentee acted vigorously, and after a 16-hour hearing the presentee was entirely cleared. But the fact that a *fama* had existed was regarded by some as good reason to invoke the Veto. It took Aberdeen two long personal discussions with the parishioners to talk them out of their views. He himself emerged from the experience shaken as to the Act. Chalmers 'will find me less tolerant than when we last conversed, on the subject of the Veto'. [14]

It was a double misfortune that the experience should immediately have been, as it were, driven home by John Hope's pamphlet. Lord Aberdeen had already been in the habit of corresponding with the Dean of the Faculty of Advocates, and had written to him in July asking 'if before the winter you could find an opportunity of letting me have a full discussion and inquiry with you into a matter of pressing importance—the affairs of our Church'. [15]

It might well have been a simple, reasonable and harmless request but for the man to whom it was addressed. John Hope, the Dean of Faculty, was the solitary elder who had in 1834 tabled his dissent against the Veto Act, accompanying it with 14 reasons. It was when Hope became legal adviser to the unfortunate presentee to Auchterarder that the case took on a different complexion, and the Church's problems really began. Since then he had become the consultant of all who had a cause against the current policy of the Church.

The first instalment of the manuscript of what was to be published as *The Dean of Faculty's Letter to the Lord Advocate* had reached Lord Aberdeen just before Chalmers' visit. By the end of September he had read it all: 'I must fairly say of your book—what can rarely be said of any book—that it has convinced me'. [16] Neither Chalmers, who wrote a reply to this 'mighty maze without a plan', nor many of its other opponents or of the later scholars who have discussed the pamphlet and the reply, seem to have realised how damaging it in fact was. Able as Chalmers' reply was (Professor Watt wrote: 'Few pamphlets have ever received such immediate and crushing replies'), [17] it was largely irrelevant. The pamphlet's title in itself shows the rarified atmosphere for which it was designed. *The Dean of Faculty's Letter to the Lord Advocate*: this was the speech of the great whales! The work was intended for an in-group of parliamentarians, few of whom would read it through, and fewer still of whom would be interested in, or able to comprehend, logical argument; what would come through to most of the group was the air of menace and threat emanating from the behaviour of this distant Church in the north, which required to be firmly crushed. Hope had announced that he would read no replies or rebuttals. His rôle was to be that of a quiet Cato insisting, *Carthago delenda est*; his Carthage, the Church of Scotland in her current mood of spiritual independence.

Hope's circle, among themselves, groaned at the pamphlet. 'The Dean is fearfully long, and concludes and recommences, which is provoking, ten or twelve times'—so wrote Gladstone to Sir James Graham, and the latter replied, 'I have endeavoured to read the Dean of Faculty's pamphlet, but it is tedious beyond endurance, and proceeds on the assumption that no argument is good unless it be repeated twenty times'. But even though Gladstone had not agreed with all he had read, he had got the message: 'There are few questions more threatening'. [18]

Lord Aberdeen had written, 'I have no desire for a triumph over the church . . . we are all interested in preventing their unnecessary humiliation'; and yet he immediately became Hope's accessory, encouraging the circulation of his work, and discussing which of his colleagues would read it and which could be persuaded to dip into it enough to say they had read it. [19]

Under the double influence of Aberdeen's experience of the Veto, and of his reading of the Dean's manuscript, the conversations with Chalmers were disappointing. Aberdeen had looked forward to the visit, but 'it had no result at all'. Chalmers would not be specific as to what he might concede, but perhaps it might be something along the line of giving to the Presbytery what he took from the people. They planned to meet later in Edinburgh. [20]

Before that meeting took place, the Commission of Assembly had in December deposed the recalcitrant ministers of Strathbogie, who thereupon took their sorrows to John Hope. [21] Nothing had been heard from the Government, though everyone felt that action was necessary. Chalmers, daring to suggest that the Tories might steal a march on their opponents by espousing the Church cause, found to his consternation that Aberdeen was sharply against drawing the question into party politics. There might be a crumb of comfort, however: 'It is the real welfare of the people and the salutary influence of the ministers that we are to consider, a subject far more important than party issues'. Aberdeen would 'most scrupulously abstain from everything which would have the appearance of humbling the church'. But his views against the Veto had hardened. It was but a 'crotchet' and even popular election might be better: 'much may be said for it.' However, if Patronage is to be abolished, let it not be by 'a side-wind, under Act of Assembly'. Aberdeen would not yet commit himself but 'would give a great deal to be instrumental in healing these breaches'. [22] All this was in marked contrast to a letter from Sir James Graham (30 December), full of forebodings about 'the fatal turn which this question has taken. . . . It grieves me that at a moment of great danger arising from democratic excitement, fresh and fearful impulse should be given to the movement by proceedings which receive your sanction.' [23] But, like Gladstone, Graham had also been reading the Dean's pamphlet.

Chalmers' best expectations were placed upon Lord Aberdeen. The latter had begun to turn over a private scheme of assistance; but he communicated it to John Hope, who flattered Aberdeen, while assuring him that the Church leaders would never agree, and deprecating any present intervention.

There were two forthcoming events which might help to clear the fog in which the affairs of the Church seemed to lie. Chalmers was to meet Aberdeen again, and might produce an idea of his plans [24]; and the Non-Intrusion Committee had invited the Scottish parliamentarians to a private conference on 10 January. In preparation, Chalmers submitted a draft for a possible Bill in a letter of 2 January, complaining indignantly at the same time about 'those restless and meddling and aggressive instigators who, in the shape of various legal actions, are doing all they can to obstruct our attempts', and wishing for an Act to give the Church protection 'from the fangs of the Court of Session'. [25] Aberdeen had been reading the reply to John Hope's pamphlet, and had written a day or two earlier: 'Chalmers' work made a considerable impression upon me. A great deal of it is well done.[26] The Dean made no direct reference, but did his best to counter the impression with, 'the truth is some of their leaders are perfect fanatics. . . . Last Sunday, Mr Candlish preached two most violent sermons, and his prayer *against* the encroachments of the Law gave great offence.' [27]

When Chalmers met Aberdeen at Dalmahoy on 9 January, he had another draft Bill to submit, but that meeting was probably overshadowed by the conference in Edinburgh on the following day. It is significant of the place the Dean of the Faculty had carved out for himself, that he not only contrived to be at Dalmahoy on the evening of the 10th, to hear first-hand of the 'secret' conference, but drew up there a memorandum in Lord Aberdeen's name to be circulated to the others who had been present, even suggesting to Sir George Clerk what steps he should take next. [28] One may think it strange that Aberdeen should thus leave the interpretation of the conference to be set out by one who had not been present at it, and even stranger that he permitted this in full knowledge that they disagreed as to how the conference should be interpreted. Yet the episode is not out of keeping with a lackadaisical quality in Aberdeen of which his biographers have complained and which vitiated much of his political career. [29] The Dean was active and eager. He was regarded as the detached legal expert. How far that expertise was at the service of what was almost a personal vendetta was not appreciated.

If there was ever any possibility that the conference might have produced valuable results, it was almost immediately dispelled. The 'secret' meeting was freely gossiped about, and the Dean wrote gleefully of 'a very different result than you anticipated', claiming that Aberdeen's position was being misrepresented by reports leaked by the

Church party; 'I much fear that they have endeavoured to mislead you'.[30] A press report appeared, which the Non-Intrusion Committee considered so distorting as to demand a reply, and they issued copies of a minute of the conference to those who had attended.[31] The conference disappeared under a flurry of argument about what had, or had not, been said.

In the Committee's view, what had happened was that Chalmers had read, for information only, the draft of a Bill submitted to the Lord Advocate. Then, but entirely separate from this, there had been a discussion about framing a measure in general terms 'such as should fully recognise the power of the Church courts . . . to reject a presentee on any ground whatsoever that might seem to them to render his settlement inexpedient.'[32] Since even the Committee's minute is not clear about the relationship between the two parts of the agenda, it is not surprising that there was confusion. Did the Committee imply that the draft Bill, being in the Lord Advocate's hands, was no longer negotiable at such a conference? Then for what had the conference been called? To encourage all-party sympathy for the time when the Government might bring forward the Bill? Or was it to prepare for an alternative, if the Government failed to support the Veto? Since Lord Aberdeen had no faith that the Government would ever bring in a Bill, he regarded the conference in this latter light, as also did Clerk.[33] Chalmers' conduct suggests that he was of the same mind; but was it the mind of his Committee? Their press release had been ominous, claiming that they had 'never given the slightest countenance to the idea that the Church should abandon the power of rejecting a presentee, in respect solely and exclusively of the dissent of the people'.[34]

So was there another interpretation? Could it be seen simply as political by-play, a manoeuvring of the Committee (but without any awareness on the part of its convener) by which they signalled to the Government that, if it failed to act soon, there were others whom the Committee could court?[35] Were that the case, it was clearly in the mind of the Committee members, rather than in that of the convener. It is doubtful if Chalmers was very pleased at the prospect of Whig aid for the Church of Scotland, nor did he seriously believe in it. His orientation was towards Lord Aberdeen, from whom, sooner or later, he believed they must have help. There is less and less continuity between Chalmers' correspondence and his convenership from this point. While his secretaries, Dunlop and Candlish, were indicating that anything other than an Act which recognised the *status quo* of the Veto was unacceptable, Chalmers was exploring other possibilities, even to the extent of assuring Lord Aberdeen that he believed there was agreement 'both as to the accompaniment of their dissent with reasons by the people, and as to the full power of Presbytery to sit in judgment on *the whole case*. [36] It could be argued that Aberdeen at this point took Chalmers too seriously, and the Committee not seriously enough, but he certainly did not lack warnings on both counts from John Hope. By now a deputation was in London in the interest of the draft Bill, and the militants of the Committee were optimistic of a Whig enactment which would make an honest woman out of the Assembly's Veto Act. Aberdeen wrote, 'our friends are much pressed by the political bearings of the question', [37] but he remained dubious of the results, and not only he but both Clerk and Rae were trying to make models for alternative legislation. [38] Aberdeen spoke in the Lords (6 February) stigmatising the Veto as illegal, but 'giving as much weight as I thought right to the principle of Non-Intrusion' and obtaining from Melbourne the admission that the Government still had no proposals to make. [39] On 12 February the Dean of Faculty wrote to Lord Aberdeen. He was contemptuous of proposals which Rae was making, but his choice titbit was a conversation with Bell, the procurator of the Church of Scotland, the first conversation John Hope had had with any member of the Committee since the previous Assembly. Bell was disturbed and indiscreet. 'We suspect Dr Chalmers wholly misleads Lord Aberdeen, and others, as to the views of the Committee, and writes letters we know nothing about. We do not understand things at present—we have twice thought we were misunderstood, and it must be from Dr Chalmers' letters which he had no authority to write.' [40]

If the Committee did not know what Chalmers was writing, John Hope did. This is one of the most surprising things to come to light. Since sometime in February, all Chalmers' letters to Lord Aberdeen, which he believed were private, were being passed on by the latter, together with copies of his replies, to John Hope. This applied also to the Committee's letters. Aberdeen had mild qualms of conscience. 'It is perhaps not quite fair to Chalmers, but I enclose the continuation of the correspondence which has taken place between him and myself. Of course it is intended for your perusal only, and I would wish you to keep the knowledge of its existence to yourself.' [41] The handing over of the correspondence marks a stage in a process which can be traced through the Aberdeen-Hope letters, in which Aberdeen is more and more brought under the influence of Hope. It is done subtly: by flattery, by reported gossip and anecdote, by the continual pressing of Hope's own interpretations of people, sayings, intentions and events, and occasionally by downright bludgeoning attacks on the Church. [42] At the outset, Aberdeen's views are sometimes independent, but this becomes less and less important in comparison with the actual steps which he takes.

Early in March came the scandal of the Perth election, in which Dunlop appeared, apparently officially, with test-questions for the candidates, and suggested resolutions for the local clergy. [43] Chalmers was furious, but, although he could demonstrate that no formal meeting of his Committee had authorised such action, he failed to get as whole-hearted a disavowal from the Committee as he had wished. [44] In London the effect of the intervention was to convince people that the church agitation was merely political. [45] Worse still, it effectively ruined the possibility that the Government might take Aberdeen into their confidence, and obtain his help to frame a Bill. [46]

The visit of the Committee's delegation to London had commenced with high hopes, but frustration grew; according to Buchanan, 'some adverse influence—dissenting, it is believed—has crossed their path.' [47] Whatever truth was in that rumour, there was 'adverse influence' enough and to spare in the mole-like burrowings of John Hope. Hope was confident that 'Melbourne can have no wish to let the Scotch Church run riot', [48] but at other times he panicked lest, while Aberdeen delayed, the Government might produce a scheme which gave too great concessions. [49] He even suggested that Lord Aberdeen might approach Melbourne with suggestions which could have no real significance, but which might inhibit the Government from taking any action at all. Lord Aberdeen wrote on 25 March, 'I have mentioned to you that I have been in familiar intercourse with several of the members of the Cabinet on this subject'. He believed the Government would end by proposing no action, and 'if this should be the result, perhaps I may have contributed to produce it'.[50] He had had 'a very full conversation' during the previous week with Lord John Russell, at the latter's request, and told him that, after the Perth election, 'it was impossible for me to stultify myself by acting with him. . . . I must keep myself perfectly free to act as I thought proper', regarding any action taken by Government with 'the same jealousy and care as any other of their measures'. In fact, he told Hope it would be necessary to deal with it either 'in the way of amendments or of rejection'. If the Government did nothing, Aberdeen thought 'it might be desirable to make some proposition to Parliament', but he claimed to be as yet undecided. He had 'not the least intention of imposing any fetters on the Courts of Law', and asked the Dean to turn his mind to 'the consideration of the best practical measures to be suggested', adding 'I have myself a project, about which I am meditating at present, and which in due time, if I can bring it to any substantial form, I will submit to you.' [51]

It is this 'project' which offers a problem. Aberdeen was involved on two fronts, on the political front both with the Government and with 'those with whom he was in the habit of acting', but also with the deputies of the Edinburgh Committee. In his letter to the Dean on 25 March he makes no mention at all of an interview on 23 March with Dr Robert Buchanan at which he had made suggestions about 'adjusting this question on the basis of a *positive call*'. Buchanan wrote on the morning of 26 March, 'I have reflected much since Monday on the idea your Lordship threw out. . . .' It was a new approach for Lord Aberdeen, but one which had in the past occupied Chalmers, and now appealed strongly to Buchanan on every ground: ancient usage, simplicity, getting rid of 'dissent without reasons' and securing what the Church really required without giving 'a party triumph'. [52] It would 'have been more satisfactory to the Church than even the Veto itself.' [53]

This proposal, it now seemed, was the way ahead, for the deputies' long-awaited interview with Lord John Russell merely brought the sad comment that the Government had 'kept us waiting eight months to tell us they will do nothing.' [54] The deputies saw Lord Aberdeen again, after the Goverment's refusal, and apparently found him still of the same mind and willing to give them his authority to consult their Committee on their return to Edinburgh. [55] If this is the meeting referred to by the Editor of the Chalmers-Aberdeen Letters, it took place on 30 March. [56] On 4 April the Edinburgh Committee met, and their 'cordial approval' was formally sent to Lord Aberdeen on 6 April. [57] The 'intrinsic excellence of the scheme' [58] made a general appeal, and even years later, when he wrote his history of the events, Buchanan recorded his judgment that, had Lord Aberdeen adhered to this proposal, 'there would in all probability have been no occasion to write this history'. [59]

Tragically, Lord Aberdeen had already changed his mind, and on the day on which the Committee were warmly approving his suggestions he was writing to Chalmers in these terms: 'For some time I regarded this project with favour and was very desirous of carrying it into effect. Further examination and reflection have convinced me that it would be quite impracticable, and I have therefore abandoned it.' It is perhaps a commentary on the ambiguities of the situation in which he had placed himself that he would not himself write to the deputies. Chalmers was asked to inform Dunlop and Buchanan. [60] It was on 31 March they had left him, assured that he was willing to have them convey his suggestions to the Committee. The Editor of his letters remarks, 'Lord Aberdeen did not form his resolution to propose any measure until the following day, and only after communication with those with whom he was in the habit of acting.' [61] Was Lord Aberdeen still acting in good faith with the deputies when he announced his intentions on 30 March, and did he change his mind between that date and 4 April when he wrote to Chalmers? And who was the prime instrument in replacing his proposal with the scheme which he ultimately put forward?

Though Aberdeen did not mention his meeting with the delegates of the Committee to the Dean of Faculty, it is highly improbable that the Dean remained in ignorance of it. His letters to Lord Aberdeen, however, keep insisting on a different course of events. The decision that Aberdeen propose a Bill had, in the Dean's account, been taken long before and was only delayed because the Government's decision was delayed. [62] Hope is also at pains to reassure Lord Aberdeen that the measure which he is proposing implies no change of mind on his part, nothing which he had not adopted 'long ago', since 'the very views which you at present propose to act upon' had been expressed to the Dean in the previous autumn and had 'matured and strengthened' by January: 'there is not one part of it which I should not find in your own letters, long before you gave your notice,—I do not think any one part of it in substance, effect, or probable operation.' [63] The proposal about the 'positive call' which had delighted Buchanan, and roused hopes in the Edinburgh Committee, was as though it had never existed.

It is an interesting scene. Aberdeen had always professed to resist any suggestion of making political profit out of the embarrassment of the Church of Scotland, but whatever he imagined about this, and whatever he imagined about his own freedom of decision, the last days of the Edinburgh deputation in London and their sequel display him very much in the rôle of puppet to stronger personalities. All that is left for him to do is leave Chalmers to break the news in Scotland; and when the Committee, unaware of how far the climate has changed, seek information about what he now includes in his measure he brusquely throws them overboard, having 'resolved not to act in concert with them. . . . I declined therefore to show them any draft of a Bill. . . . They already know perfectly well the principle on which I was disposed to proceed.' Only a small concession was left: they might if they wished make suggestions. [64]

With Lord Aberdeen now committed, one can trace the Dean of Faculty's concern turning to the activities of Clerk and Rae, whose communications the Committee were inclined to regard as 'more congenial' than those of Lord Aberdeen. He urges that Lord Aberdeen should warn them to keep clear of Chalmers and his Committee, pointing out that 'neither of them are as guarded as your Lordship, nor as fully up to the subject', [65] though perhaps the real intent is to pre-empt any possibility that they might put forward a solution on their own account. Aberdeen was not unaware of the extent to which the Dean was now involved in what he proposed to do, giving a half-hearted warning that 'we must take care to avoid the impression . . . of your directing the affair too much', [66] but the Dean's interventions are clear in the correspondence. The commentary on events continues: the Committee are 'a good deal paralysed . . . in part disarmed by the wise resolution of not communicating with them'; their problem is, 'If Parliament will not give us the Veto, are we to go on?' 'If so, what next?' is a question which has never been put. [67] The correspondents continually discuss Chalmers' correspondence with Aberdeen: 'flummery letters', says the Dean [68]; 'he strains my admissions beyond what anything I said will bear,' comments Lord Aberdeen, though he keeps on hoping for Chalmers' support. You will not get it, is the reply, for Chalmers 'will sacrifice everything to the vanity of a flash speech in the Assembly'. [69] Aberdeen is given advice on the kind of speech he ought to make in presenting his Bill, is supplied with notes on 'topics' and advised that he consult his 'venerable and honourable friend' the Archbishop of Canterbury. He is all the time receiving assurances as to his success: 'you will prevail—my confidence increases every day'. [70] When one knows what Aberdeen was doing with Chalmers' letters it is ironic to read the Dean's story of how Rae had written to a certain Mr Thomson, who had sent his letter to Chalmers, 'not very handsomely, Rae thought'. [71] The drafting of the Bill went on. The preamble was extended: 'I own—it may be little self-complacency,—I think the extended recital comes to be very strong, and very satisfactory, and very mighty against the Church', [72] but all the while the Dean is reassuring Aberdeen that the Bill is really *his,* and that these have always been his views 'without the suggestion, or devise of any scheme whatsoever from me'. [73]

It is in keeping with the Dean of Faculty's view of the entire subordination of the Church, that throughout this period its leaders are effectively left in total ignorance of the contents of a Bill which, if it were to become law, would control the Church's affairs. Again and again he returns to the thought, 'the more ignorance the Committee are kept in, the more they are made to feel that you are independent of them', and 'others are thus taught to feel that this Committee are neither thought omnipotent, safe, nor prudent'. [74] There is, however, another side to this policy of isolation. The Dean distrusted Aberdeen's own contacts. 'The more you tell me, the more I see to *wonder at in what is said to you,* and therefore I urge the more, for the success of your object, do not show the Bill to any of them'. [75] Lord Aberdeen could not be trusted to keep to his adviser's line, unless the latter could make sure of his isolation. Thus a casual remark on 23 April, 'before the Bill is actually introduced, I may probably show it to Hamilton or Buchanan', [76] brings vehement warnings, 'I would *very anxiously tender my strong advice* not to show the Bill, even in the strictest confidence, either to Hamilton or Buchanan'—and, by a curious coincidence, the Dean finds that family business now demands his presence in the south! [77] Aberdeen did show the Bill to Hamilton and Buchanan, as he had intended, and they offered some amendments which they thought not inconsistent with the Bill [78] and which Aberdeen was not himself unwilling to grant. Had he done so, his biographer, Sir Arthur Gordon, thought the question might have been settled for the time being, and the Disruption averted or reduced to very small proportions. [79] But by this time the Dean of Faculty had arrived and 'denounced the amendments, partly as carrying out covertly the popular veto and partly as compromising Lord Aberdeen's position of independence'. [80] The changes had not been made when Lord Aberdeen read his Bill for the first time in the House of Lords on 5 May. That evening he wrote to Chalmers, 'I believe that the peace of the Church is at this moment in your hands; for although from the accident of birth and social position, I have had the means of proposing this measure to the Legislature, it will depend on you, whether it is to receive life and efficacy.'[81] He was wrong on both counts. He had 'the means of proposing this measure' by the courtesy and machinations of John Hope, Dean of the Faculty of Advocates, who had already written that he had 'taken special care that no one should suspect me from what I say. I do not mean even to Rae or Clerk to allude to the origin of the Bill!'[82]

As for Chalmers, he too was no less a victim of circumstances over which he had no control. But he never knew (though he may have suspected) the real betrayer. He had believed that his correspondence with Lord Aberdeen was private and significant. It was neither. He had no knowledge of the depth of the infiltration of the Dean of Faculty into Lord Aberdeen's counsels. The two victims snarled and spat at each other. But Aberdeen could hardly plead that he was misled by Chalmers' mis-statements. He was well aware that Chalmers was vacillating and out of rapport with his Committee, and he used for the basis of his Bill only what the Dean of Faculty provided.

And the Dean of Faculty himself? He was the mole, the indefatigable burrower in the dark, the extent of whose labourings have only come to the light of day over 140 years later.

Note on Sources

The basis of this essay is a privately-printed volume, containing over 400 letters from and to Lord Aberdeen. The letters have been arranged chronologically, but to achieve this, early letters which came to light when the material was partially printed were inserted in their chronological place, and the pagination was expanded with letters of the alphabet. For example, material added after page 130 is numbered 130a, 130b and so on up to 130dd.

In the prefatory note to his life of his father, the Earl of Aberdeen, Sir Arthur Gordon records that the publication of Lord Aberdeen's correspondence was 'a duty entrusted to me by the terms of my father's will' (Sir Arthur Gordon, *The Earl of Aberdeen* (1893), p. ix). This no doubt explains the origin of the volume, but there is a curious anonymity about the result. Two copies of the volume are known to me, one in King's College Library, Aberdeen, and the other in the National Library, Edinburgh. They are in precisely similar binding, lack a title page, and on the spine have the inscription, 'Selections,

1836-1846'. This may partly explain the circumstance that this large and important collection has remained so long unknown and unused by Chalmers scholars.

It is cited in the Notes as L (Letters), with page, date of letter and names of sender and recipient, though in the case of many letters exchanged between Lord Aberdeen and John Hope, Dean of the Faculty of Advocates, the recipient only is named.

I am most grateful to the Special Collections Department of Aberdeen University Library for a lengthy loan of their copy of the Letters which made this essay possible.

My thanks also are due to Mrs Butt, archivist of the Chalmers Collection in New College Library, Edinburgh, and to the staff of that library, of the Scottish Record Office and of the National Library of Scotland for help, and access to materials in their charge.

Notes to Chapter IV

1 W Hanna, *Memoirs of the Life and Writings of Thomas Chalmers, DD, LLD* (4 vols., 1849-52), vol. IV, p.170.
2 John McCaffrey, 'The Life of Thomas Chalmers', supra.
3 Hanna, *Memoirs*, vol. IV, p.173.
4 H Watt, *Thomas Chalmers and the Disruption* (1943), p.177.
5 ibid., pp.177, 178-79.
6 L pp. 76d-76e. To Lord Aberdeen, 19 March 1840: Dr Muir, minister of St Stephen's, Edinburgh, was a respected leader of the Church of Scotland. He had been one of a deputation to Lord Melbourne, representing the Church's case, and was generally seen as taking position midway between the intransigent 'Moderates' and the high-flying Non-Intrusionists.
7 Compare the intervention in the Perth Election, L pp. 62f-62h.
8 L p.16. To the Dean of Faculty, 31 July 1839.
9 Hanna, *Memoirs*, vol. IV, p.122.
10 L p.18. To the Dean of Faculty, 5 Sept. 1839.
11 L p.25. To the Dean of Faculty, 14 Dec. 1839. 'However rash and infatuated their conduct in some respects may have been, I can have no pleasure in their humiliation.'
12 McCaffrey, supra.
13 On 31 July Lord Aberdeen had told the Dean of Faculty, 'I expect a visit before long'. L p.16.
14 L p.20. To the Dean of Faculty, 12 Sept. 1839.
15 L p.16. To the Dean of Faculty, 31 July 1839.
16 L p.22. To the Dean of Faculty, 1 Oct. 1839. Part of the MS. had been in Lord Aberdeen's hands by 12 September. L p.20.
17 Watt, op.cit., p.196.
18 C S Parker, *Life and Letters of Sir James Graham, 1792-1861* (1907), vol. I, pp.374-75. I am grateful to Dr McCaffrey for this reference.
19 L p.23. To the Dean of Faculty, 1 Oct. 1839.

20 L pp.20-21. To the Dean of Faculty, 17 Sept. 1839.

21 Watt, op.cit., pp.210-11.

22 *The Correspondence between Dr Chalmers and the Earl of Aberdeen in the years 1839 and 1840* (Edinburgh, 1893), pp.16-18, Lord Aberdeen to Thomas Chalmers, 31 Dec. 1839. This is missing from L.

23 Chalmers Papers, New College Library, Edinburgh (*CP*), CHA 4.282.63. Sir James Graham to Thomas Chalmers, 30 Dec. 1839.

24 L p.28. To the Dean of Faculty, 2 Jan. 1840.

25 L pp.29-31. Thomas Chalmers to Lord Aberdeen, 2 Jan. 1840.

26 L pp.26-27. To the Dean of Faculty, 23 Dec. 1839.

27 L pp.27-28. To Lord Aberdeen, 26 Dec. 1839.

28 See the Clerk of Penicuik MSS. in Scottish Record Office. Sir George Clerk of Penicuik (1787-1867), MP for Midlothian, 1812-1832, then for a variety of English constituencies. He held various governmental posts, including secretary of the Treasury and vice-president of the Board of Trade. He was deputy-Lieutenant of Midlothian, president of the Zoological Society and chairman of the Royal Academy of Music. Grand uncle of James Clark Maxwell, the distinguished scientist.

29 L Iremonger, *Lord Aberdeen* (1978), p.138, speaks of 'constitutional apathy and irresolution'.

30 L p.31. To Lord Aberdeen, 13 Jan. 1840.

31 L pp.32-32b. Candlish and Dunlop to Lord Aberdeen, 14 Jan. 1840.

32 L p.32a.

33 L pp.35-38. Lord Aberdeen to Candlish and Dunlop, 20 Jan. 1840. See also Sir George Clerk to Thomas Chalmers, 21 Jan. 1840, *CP*, CHA 4.290.1.

34 L pp.32-33.

35 L p.32b. To Lord Aberdeen, 15 Jan. 1840. According to the Dean of Faculty, 'Rae . . . soon saw that the meeting was intended . . . for political objects'. Rae in fact seems to have suspected it was to test if Aberdeen and the others would accept the Veto.

36 L p.43. Thomas Chalmers to Lord Aberdeen, 27 Jan. 1840.

37 L p.53. To the Dean of Faculty, 7 Feb. 1840.

38 *CP*, CHA 4.290.5. Sir George Clerk to Thomas Chalmers, 7 Feb. 1840. Sir William Rae (1769-1842) was MP for several Scottish and English constituencies from 1819 onwards. More than once he was Lord Advocate (prosecuting in 1820 in the treason trials of Hardie and others); spoke in favour of Catholic Emancipation in 1829; brought in a Bill for the appointment of criminal juries by ballot. Rae was a friend of Sir Walter Scott, and introduced the Bill for erection of a monument to him in Edinburgh. Hope comments that Candlish had 'a strong touch of *craze* in his mind at present'.

39 L p.53. To the Dean of Faculty, 7 Feb. 1840.

40 L p.54. To Lord Aberdeen, 12 Feb. 1840.

41 L p.62e. To the Dean of Faculty, 29 Feb. 1840. On 18 February, the Dean referred to 'two parcels of letters and answers which you have been good enough to send me to read.' L p.58.

42 For the bludgeon in action, see L p.76g and the following pages. To Lord Aberdeen, 21 March 1840.

43 L pp.62f-62h. To Lord Aberdeen, 2 March 1840.

44 L p.75. Thomas Chalmers to Lord Aberdeen, 12 March 1840.
45 L pp.65-67. Lord Aberdeen to Thomas Chalmers, 10 March 1840.
46 L p.68f. To the Dean of Faculty, 11 March 1840.
47 Hanna, *Memoirs*, vol. IV, p.152.
48 L p.76f. To Lord Aberdeen, 19 March 1840.
49 L p.76c. To Lord Aberdeen, 17 March 1840.
50 L p.77. To the Dean of Faculty, 25 March 1840.
51 L p.78.
52 L p.79. Buchanan to Lord Aberdeen, 26 March 1840.
53 Robert Buchanan, *The Ten Years' Conflict* (1849), vol. II, p.173.
54 Hanna, *Memoirs*, vol. IV, p.152.
55 Buchanan, op.cit., vol. II, p.173.
56 L p.80 note.
57 Buchanan, op.cit., vol. II, p.172.
58 L p.82. Buchanan to Lord Aberdeen, 7 April 1840.
59 Buchanan, op.cit., vol. II, p.173.
60 L p.80. Lord Aberdeen to Thomas Chalmers, 4 April 1840.
61 L p.80 note.
62 L p.88. To Lord Aberdeen, 14 April 1840. 'The delay of the Government
    has allowed too many of the Assembly elections to be over before your line
    could be taken. . . . If your notice had been made three weeks sooner, you
    would have had a complete change.'
63 L p.112k. To Lord Aberdeen, 23 April 1840.
64 L p.84. To the Dean of Faculty, 9 April 1840.
65 L p.86b. To Lord Aberdeen, 13 April 1840. In the same letter he writes, I
    'beg of you to urge emphatically on Clerk and Rae *not* to put themselves
    into communication, either with Chalmers *individually*, which is useless,
    or with the Committee', and again, 'this may appear a most presumptuous
    suggestion in regard to such men as Clerk and Rae for me to make.
    Nevertheless I am most anxious for you shortly, but emphatically to beg
    of them to keep themselves clear. . . .' Later the Dean developed a
    different tactic, consulting them and appearing to involve them
    confidentially in the preparation of Aberdeen's Bill, but referring to them
    rather contemptuously in his letters to Lord Aberdeen. Compare L
    pp.109-112c. To Aberdeen, 20 April 1840.
66 L p.86c. To the Dean of Faculty, 15 April 1840. He had referred to 'your
    draft with a few slight alterations' in a letter of 9 April, L p.85.
67 L pp.87, 90. To Lord Aberdeen, 14 April 1840.
68 ibid., p.88.
69 ibid., p.87.
70 L p.107. See the letter of 14 April, two letters of 16 April, and 18 April.
71 L p.111. To Lord Aberdeen, 20 April 1840.
72 L p.112b. To Lord Aberdeen, 20 April 1840.
73 L p.112k. To Lord Aberdeen, 23 April 1840.
74 L pp.93-94. To Lord Aberdeen, 14 April 1840.
75 L p.112p. To Lord Aberdeen, 25 April 1840.
76 L p.112j. To the Dean, 23 April 1840.
77 L p.112o. To Lord Aberdeen, 25 April 1840. KCLP 112U. To Lord
    Aberdeen, 27 April 1840. The Dean was on 'family business' settling his
    sons in boarding school. Gordon, p.134.

H

78 Hamilton and Buchanan, the deputies of the Edinburgh Committee, saw
    Aberdeen on 31 April, and Buchanan wrote his comments the following
    day. L pp.112r-112s. They wrote a joint letter the following day, warning
    Lord Aberdeen that the Bill as it stood would fail to win the approval of
    the General Assembly, but that, if the modifications which they had
    suggested were adopted, there was 'every reason to hope for a satisfactory
    outcome.' L pp.112s-112u.
79 Gordon, *Aberdeen*, p.133.
80 ibid., p.134. Gordon's opinion of the Dean of Faculty was not flattering.
    'Thoroughly self-confident, and possessing that influence which a strong,
    narrow mind of a positively overbearing type often exerts over a mind of
    much higher quality, in which self-distrust and humility are leading
    characteristics.' His judgment is illumined when one reads the
    correspondence which was at his disposal.
81 L p.113. Lord Aberdeen to Thomas Chalmers, 5 May 1840.
82 L p.96. To Lord Aberdeen, 15 April 1840.

V

Chalmers and Poor Relief: An Incidental Sideline?

Mary T Furgol

Thomas Chalmers' name is linked with many different aspects of ecclesiastical thought and development in the 19th century. He was also concerned with social issues, particularly poor relief. This latter concern was related to his ecclesiastical interests, and in making an assessment of his work in the field of poverty it is necessary to examine the exact nature of that link. In both his written works on the subject, and his practical experiment in St John's parish in Glasgow (1819-1837),[1] he showed himself as having a great interest in the problem of poverty and a desire to implement his theories and demonstrate his solution. When analysing the ideas of any man, it is tempting to read into his early writings and actions a blueprint for all his later work. The problem with this approach is that it can hide more than it reveals, and in the case of Chalmers it may be more illuminating to focus on each development and experience of his earlier life and look at these as units in themselves. This is not to say that one cannot also look at the continuity in Chalmers: at elements which were constant and called into play whenever he was faced with a situation relating to poverty and its relief. At the same time, it is only as one comes to analyse these separate situations that a pattern begins to emerge as a whole. The present study follows that approach in examining the 15 years prior to Chalmers' removal to Glasgow in 1815.

When Chalmers became assistant to Mr Elliot, the minister of Cavers, near Hawick, in 1801, it would appear that he was primarily concerned with mathematics, chemistry and botany. This is not to say that he intended to ignore any ministerial obligations and tasks; rather, his view was that, since he conceived of these tasks as being very few and undemanding, he would have plenty of time to pursue other, more fascinating interests once his duties had been completed. His great aim at this point was to become a mathematics professor, and he saw nothing in his ministerial position which might prevent this. Thus, he confidently wrote to his father after moving to Cavers: 'I have been now two Sundays at Cavers, and find the labours of my office sufficiently easy.'[2] This attitude towards his rôle as a minister led Chalmers to write in 1805 that often-quoted assessment of the life of a clergyman:

115

after the satisfactory discharge of his parish duties, a minister may
enjoy five days in the week of uninterrupted leisure, for the prosecution
of any science in which his taste may dispose him to engage.[3]

In other words, Chalmers saw his intellectual studies and interests as
being necessary to overcome what might otherwise have been the
tedium of his 'undemanding' ministerial tasks. Accordingly, he filled
his time with his studies, and also became assistant to the mathematics
professor at St Andrews, Professor Vilant, during the session 1802-3.
In the summer of 1803, he moved to Kilmany and at the same time
started up three independent mathematics classes in St Andrews.
Thus, at the beginning of his first full ministerial charge, Chalmers was
indeed spending only two days a week in his parish, and insisting that
this was adequate to fulfil his pastoral duties.

Part of a minister's duties in the early 19th century was the operation
of the system of poor relief which centred on the parish as the
administrative unit; the kirk session, of which he was the moderator,
and the local heritors (landowners) were legally in charge of the raising
and distribution of funds, the main source of which was still the
voluntary church-door collections. If the collections were insufficient
for the needs of the area they might be increased by a voluntary or
compulsory assessment on the heritors. [4] Therefore, the parish minister
was directly involved with the daily administration of the system.

His biographer, Hanna, emphasises how Chalmers was forcibly
struck by the apparent difference between more regulated Scottish
rural parishes like Cavers and Kilmany and the squalor and lower
moral standards to be found in towns like Hawick, infected by an
approximation to the 'English' system, or, as he had been informed by
his brother-in-law, Robert Morton, to be found in the south of
England. Hanna also describes Chalmers' conclusion that the
difference was a direct result of the different types of poor relief
systems. The 'English' assessment system, which made people more
dependent on charity, was encouraging vice and duplicity since its
promise of constant legal funding provided a licence to squander any
resources one had in the sure knowledge that no one would go hungry.
In contrast, that system of relief which was provided out of the
voluntary contributions of church-goers, and was as yet more typical in
Scotland, appeared to Chalmers as the vital factor in fostering
communities where the people were more honest, independent and
morally upright, as was the case in Cavers and Kilmany. [5]

Hanna's widely used description of Chalmers' experiences at this
stage in poor relief makes brief reference to the influence of Malthus on
Chalmers' thinking, but more work needs to be done on this. Since
Chalmers considered himself at this period as being very much an
intellectual, his academic studies were clearly crucial; the essential
thing in understanding his early outlook on poverty is his interest in

political economy and his reading of Smith and Malthus. As early as 1801, his former mathematics teacher at St Andrews, Dr James Brown, wrote a letter of recommendation in which he stated that Chalmers 'is at present with genius and ability investigating some of the difficult and interesting subjects of Philosophy and Political Economy'. [6]

The impact of these investigations may be seen in Chalmers' first book, published in 1808, *An Enquiry into the Extent and Stability of National Resources.* This is largely concerned with the economic state of Britain during the Napoleonic Wars, and Chalmers apparently considered it a vital contribution towards increasing morale in Britain and pointing the way to victory abroad. (He was consequently disappointed by its lack of success.) [7] In this study, Chalmers made his first printed statements about poverty, statements which reveal the impact of Malthus in particular.

The main argument in the book revolves around the idea that the amount of disposable wealth in a country is not dependent on its trade or industry, but rather on its *agricultural production.* The latter determines the size of population, and trade and industry are only financed by the money remaining from the sale of agricultural products once the population has been fed, clothed, and housed. Chalmers deduced from this that the amount thereafter spent on 'luxury' goods (i.e. industrial goods) would remain static as long as agricultural production was maintained at the same level. If, however, one industry did go out of production (as was happening in Britain due to concentration on materials necessary for warfare) then all that would happen would be that another, more necessary industry would take its place. The reason for this lay in the 'fact' that the total amount of disposable wealth in the country was constant (i.e. the people who profited from the land were still producing the same amount, and therefore had the same total amount of money to spend). The only difference was that it would now be spent on other commodities (or, in war, given in taxation to the Government to spend on industrial goods). This led Chalmers to conclude that very little hardship would ever accompany the collapse of any industry, and indeed nothing would affect a nation's economy except its level of agricultural production. From this, he proceeded to deduce that there must be practically no hardship or poverty in Britain since over the past few decades its population had kept pace with its food production to the extent that a large amount of money was left over that could be spent on industry. Therefore, he asked:

> where, from one end of the island to the other, is there a single man in ordinary health, that may not earn the subsistence of a labourer, or a single neighbourhood that languishes for want of employment? [8]

This abstract, 'logical' approach, based on the inevitability of the laws of economics, was to be typical of Chalmers, and his confidence in the indisputability of his argument exemplifies the type of thinking which led him later on in life to take up many causes in a very intransigent way. In this particular case, his basic contention, that the level of agricultural production and population increase were linked, led him to agree with Malthus' conclusion that any poverty problem that did exist could not be solved simply by doling out large sums of money:

> Mr Malthus, in his inestimable treatise on population, has proved that it is beyond the power of legal institutions to administer effectual relief to the poverty and wretchedness of the lower orders. The only way in which poverty can be prevented, is by increasing the proportion betwixt the food of a country and the population that subsists upon it. Now, the poor laws of England serve to aggravate the mischief which they are intended to alleviate: they hold out a delusive promise of relief to the unfortunate; they encourage habits of improvidence; they offer a security to every marriage, however imprudent . . . they serve rather to increase the proportion betwixt the people and the food; they make the situation of the poor more desperate than ever. [9]

It would be true to say, then, that at this stage of Chalmers' reflections on poverty his ideas were largely conditioned by his own experience of the still prevailing voluntary system of poor relief in Scotland, and given intellectual authority by his own studies on political economy and his conviction of the truth of Malthus' findings. Experience and study together led him to conclude that poor relief and morality were linked: the system of relief was capable not only of degrading people morally by making them dependent on others and so rendering them lazy and dissolute, but also, in consequence, of making them even poorer as they were encouraged to squander their relief in the confident expectation of receiving more.

His reason for blaming the system—i.e. of legal assessment as opposed to voluntary charity—and not, say, the different types of economy in these areas, was still vague and ill defined. The compulsory system would always produce regrettable results because, like Malthus, he contended that there was some automatic basic response which induced people who were aware of a potentially inexhaustible source of relief to take advantage of 'all they could get'. For the moment, however, he stopped there, and did not attempt to analyse this basic response in any way. He simply accepted that it was so, and that under this system poverty could actually be the result of immorality encouraged by the system itself.

Thus, Chalmers' interest in poor relief in these first eight years of his ministry was very much a general one. He had set ideas on the subject, but there is no evidence so far of his distinctive zeal for it, nor his particular view of its solution. Rather, it seems that at this stage the question of poverty was an incidental one as far as he was concerned, his main interest being taken up rather with the wider study of political economy and mathematics. Hanna can be misleading, therefore, when he says that as early as 1808 Chalmers' later theories were taking definite shape, using as evidence a sermon in which Chalmers stated that:

> It is in the power of charity to corrupt its object; it may tempt him to indolence; it may nourish the meanness and depravity of his character; it may lead him to hate exertion, and to resign without a sigh the dignity of independence. It could easily be proved that if charity were carried to its utmost extent, it would unhinge the constitution of society. . . . Every man would repose on the beneficence of another . . . the country would present the nauseating spectacle of sloth and beggary and corruption.[10]

True, Chalmers' later theories on poor relief never contradicted these assertions; but simply to quote them as proof that he had such ideas at an early stage is of little help in elucidating why he felt it necessary to develop a more detailed theory, or in distinguishing those particular aspects of his theory which were to give it a distinctive stamp, peculiar to Chalmers himself.

In order fully to appreciate the subsequent development of Chalmers' ideas on poverty, it is vital that the religious experiences of the next stage in his life (1810-15) be not ignored, since they affected him profoundly and influenced his outlook on society as a whole. There does not appear to have been one obvious turning-point which completely changed him overnight, but it is clear from his letters and diaries of these years that by 1812 he had a radically different view of religion generally, and of the personal relationship with God, than he had had in 1809. In this sense it could indeed be said that he had undergone a 'conversion', a turning away from the past, and a reorientation of his outlook to the future.

The details of this significant period in Chalmers' life have often been related.[11] The important point to grasp here is that it resulted in his reassessing his position as a Christian minister to the point where he perceived that the commitment to Christ which he now wished to make would entail a very different approach to the cares of his parish. The latter were no longer identifiable duties which, once executed, marked the end of his ministerial rôle and the start of any other pursuit he wanted to follow. Rather, he came to see them as demanding a total dedication to his people and their needs. His main desires came to be to safeguard his own faith by prayer and study, and to evangelise those in his care. Thus, by mid-1811, he had radically changed his former opinion and was asserting that:

> The truth is that a minister, if he gives his whole heart to the business, finds employment for every moment of his existence, and I am every day getting more in love with my professional duties—and more penetrated with a deeper sense of their importance. [12]

He now prayed: 'Let me give my whole strength to the conversion and edification of my people'. [13]

The practical result of these changes in Chalmers' view of his function as a minister was a new approach to his parochial work. As John Roxborogh has pointed out, [14] he now paid far more attention to his parishioners: he spent his time visiting and praying with people, establishing schools for the young of his parish in his own house where they could be taught the Scriptures, and encouraging the formation of the Kilmany Bible Society as an auxiliary branch of the British and Foreign Bible Society. He finally abandoned his study of mathematics, [15] and also his dream of becoming a mathematics professor.

The main point here is that, as Chalmers became increasingly concerned with the spiritual welfare of his parishioners and with all that might affect it, so his concern with poor relief appears to have increased. This latter concern, however, was still essentially a general one which, like all other aspects of his thinking, had to be reassessed on Chalmers' new scale of priorities, to be examined in the light of his now over-riding concern for the preaching of the gospel. In other words, an intensive analysis of poverty and its relief was still missing in these years, and it is necessary to realise this if one is to understand the frame of mind in which he left his parish of Kilmany in 1815 to take up his charge in the Tron parish in Glasgow. What one finds is that as Chalmers' fame as an evangelical preacher began to grow he received an increasing number of invitations to preach for various Bible and charitable societies, and these invitations appear to have been an incentive to him to formulate more precisely his ideas on the place of charity in the Christian's list of priorities.

Chalmers' concern with Christianity and the nature of charity is shown in his sermons between 1810 and 1815. In a sermon preached before the Dundee Missionary Society on 26 October 1812—the main point of which was to exhort his listeners to spread the Gospel by funding both the Bible Society and the Missionary Society, and not to look on them as rival causes—Chalmers explained his evangelical premises thus:

> Those to whom Christ is precious, will long that others should taste of that preciousness. Those who have buried all their anxieties and all their terrors in the sufficiency of the atonement, will long that the knowledge of a remedy so effectual should be carried round the globe. [16]

Given this tendency in Chalmers' thoughts and in his preaching, the sermon he preached for the Society for the Relief of the Destitute Sick, in Edinburgh on 18 April 1813, reads as if he were driven by the very nature of the institution to which he was preaching to assess its basic aims and to assign them a place in his overall Christian perspective. He was not afraid to proclaim his conclusion:

> The main impulse of his [the Christian's] benevolence, lies in furnishing the poor with the means of enjoying the bread of life which came down from heaven, and in introducing them to the knowledge of these Scriptures which are the power of God unto salvation to every one who believeth. [17]

In the same way, when challenged by the contention that such societies as the Bible Society were diverting into their own coffers charity which would otherwise have been given to the poor, Chalmers was provoked to reply that even if this were proved to be true:

> we do not hesitate to affirm, that, it is better for the poor to be worse fed and worse clothed, than that they should be left ignorant of those Scriptures, which are able to make them wise unto salvation through the faith that is in Christ Jesus. [18]

In other words, these years saw Chalmers reaching a stage in his process of reasoning, the logic of which was to him irrefutable: everything must be made subordinate to the ultimate aim of the true Christian, to draw closer to God and to draw others closer with him, and this involves man's temporal needs being made subordinate to his spiritual ones.

Apart from this relegation of the material welfare of man to a secondary position, much in Chalmers' general outlook on poverty was carried over from his earlier years into this period. For example, in his speech at the institution of the Fife and Kinross Bible Society, printed in January 1813 in the *Edinburgh Christian Instructor* (the Evangelical mouthpiece), he spoke against providing Bibles to the Scottish people free of charge. Unlike their English counterparts, he maintained, the Scots were used to buying their own Bibles, and if these were given away free they would be devalued:

> the habit of purchasing is extinguished, and this society of ours, like the institution of the poor rates, leaves the people of the land in greater want, and poverty, and nakedness than ever. [19]

That is, Chalmers still used the argument that a regular, official source of poor relief (as of Bibles) would break down people's independence and so worsen the situation it had set out to improve, and his concurrence in Malthus' view of the detrimental effects of the assessment system remained unchanged. He also still believed, as he had asserted in his sermon of 1808, that charity could corrupt:

The hungry expectations of the poor will ever keep pace with the assessments of the wealthy; and their eye will be averted from the exertion of their own industry, as the only right source of comfort and independence.[20]

What is obvious from these writings is not that Chalmers had greatly developed his ideas in themselves, but that he was now asserting them more loudly and more frequently, and with greater authority. Most significantly, he was now giving scriptural backing for his statements, using his new emphasis on the Christian message of salvation and the Word of God not only to relegate man's material needs to a subordinate position, but also to lend a new authority to his previous ideas on poverty. Thus he used such texts as 1 Timothy 5:8: 'If any provide not for his own, and specially for those of his own house, he hath denied the faith, and is worse than an infidel'[21]; 2 Thessalonians 3:10-12: 'If a man will not work, he shall not eat'[22]; Psalm 41:1: 'Blessed is he who considers the poor'[23]; and Acts 20:35: 'It is more blessed to give than to receive'.[24]

In other words, Chalmers' renewed reading of Scripture in these years appears to have confirmed his earlier ideas about the necessity of great care being taken when relieving want because of the danger of making people more dependent and dissolute through indiscriminate help, and of the vital need to exhort them to maintain their independence and hence their uprightness of character. There was now an added dimension to all of this, however. The fact that the problem of poverty and its relief, and the wider issue of man's material needs in general, could be linked with Chalmers' new-found evangelical convictions had given the whole question greater prominence in his thoughts and writings. Charity, as a *Christian* virtue, needed greater definition; and so he came to the conclusion that the greatest charity we could show our fellow-man was to bring the Gospel message of salvation to him.

In addition to this scriptural confirmation of earlier views and this more precise definition of charity, there was a third element emerging in the later years at Kilmany. Chalmers was beginning to develop a more detailed plan for the actual solution of the problem of poverty. His earlier agreement with Malthus on the nature of the problem, and also on the general idea that Scotland had kept to the better, voluntary system because of her supposedly better-educated and more God-fearing people, was giving way to a less inhibited assertion of his evangelical ideas. Again basing himself on Scripture, Chalmers now spoke of the only possible solution as being to reform the character of the poor. They would then cease to be in want or to squander their earnings on drink, and become sober and upright citizens.

It is important to realise that in all of this Chalmers was not in fact saying that there was no room for personal alms-giving on the part of the individual Christian. On the contrary, the true Christian would do his utmost to help those around him, even though his first priority must be their spiritual welfare. Such institutions as Bible Societies would not detract from the gross amount of poor funds, since those who were interested in them would also be the people who paid most attention to the material needs of their neighbours, though always treating those needs with a proper sense of proportion. Moreover, the fact that they put spiritual concerns first would actually lessen the problem of material want, for once people had received and understood the Gospel message, they would live a full Christian life, becoming reformed, self-reliant characters who would not descend into a position where they needed material help. [25]

These developments in Chalmers' thinking on poor relief give an insight into his frame of mind when he left Kilmany in 1815 and they show that he had still not come to a fully thought-out analysis of the nature of poverty or its solution. As yet, there was no sign of a detailed application of his views on human nature and on human responses to need and suffering—views which provide an analysis of human emotions akin to what today would appear in a psychological treatise. [26] The clear-cut distinctions he was later to make between relieving *poverty* and ridding society of *poor relief* were not as yet defined in his mind. [27] In other words, the question of poor relief was still an incidental side-line to Chalmers at this period. It had been brought under the scrutiny of his deepened insights into the ministerial rôle and had been modified accordingly, but as yet there was no attempt on his part to develop a particular theory of the nature of the subject, no great awareness of the need to do so, and no highly detailed plan of action to cope with the problem.

The main reason why the poor relief issue was not in the forefront at this time is simply the fact that there was little need for it to be so. Having arrived at the conclusion that his main function was to do God's will as a minister of His Word, Chalmers found that he had plenty of time and opportunity to do this in Kilmany. The economic position of his parishioners, who made few demands on his time as an agent of poor relief distribution, did not threaten the full undertaking of his ministerial responsibilities. This becomes clear when one examines his practical experiences in poor relief between 1810 and 1815.

As has already been stated, Kilmany was a small rural parish, with a population of about 750, [28] and its poor relief system was based on the voluntary church-door collections. In Chalmers' diaries and letters after 1810 there are several references to his involvement in the distribution of relief. This personal involvement is in itself important (later on, in Glasgow, he was to come out against the minister having any part in the administration of relief). In his diaries, from March 1810 to July 1815, there are 37 references to Chalmers personally giving sessional relief, meeting the heritors to discuss the poor, writing letters to ask for the support of the relatives of paupers, and on occasion giving his own money to beggars. They show how Chalmers at this stage believed his ideas should work out in practice, and running through them all is his general idea about the necessity for care when administering charity, care to ensure the validity of the need, and the worth of the person:

> 17 July, 1811: A beggar called to whom I gave one penny after much hesitation. I should not give so much in cases of uncertainty.

> 14 October, 1811: [Chalmers often visited a Janet Grieve, who was very ill, but he suspected the family thought that he was going to pay the doctor's bill] I conceive them able to pay it. I think myself right in not making the offer. The object of my kindness should not be to secure their good opinion by coming up to their expectations, but to do them good.

> 17 August, 1813: . . . gave hastily 5/- to an application which I afterwards saw reason to suspect the goodness of the claim. I feel regret and anxiety. The thing is past and it is of the Lord. [29]

These entries reveal how Chalmers was striving to put into practice his convictions that people should be encouraged to be as independent as possible, that if relief were given it should be minimal, and that it must at all costs be made obvious that no regular official relief system could be automatically depended upon in the event of a simple plea for help. Moreover, a letter written to William Johnson of Lathisk at this time reveals two more aspects of his ideas being put into practice: that friends and relatives should be called upon to respond in a spirit of Christian charity, and that any relief given should only be in cases of extreme and *deserving* want. Chalmers had already written to ask help for a family at Rathillet who were distantly related to Johnson, and had received £10 for them from him. He was now writing to give Johnson his findings as to their circumstances. He had discovered that their position of hardship was the result of debts contracted in 'the very severe years of 1799 and 1800'.[30] He had obviously compiled a list of these debts, and concluded that:

> it is creditable to them that they were all incurred in the purchase of necessaries—and at a time when with the pressures of a numerous family—it was next to impossible to carry on the expenses of a family upon the mere wages of labour.[31]

By 1811 the family had only four dependent children, and seemingly assured him that if their remaining debts were cleared they would be able to survive independently. They also promised never to fall into debt again, and if they were under pressure to apply to him first. He consequently asked Johnson to clear the debts:

> The only return that I can offer you for your generosity is security that it will not be abused by the grateful family in whose behalf you have exercised it, and I give it as my opinion of them, that if they were once fairly out of their embarrassments, they would not run wantonly into debt in the improper confidence that you were always in readiness to step forward and discharge it. [32]

Johnson must have been convinced by all of this, since two days later Chalmers recorded in his diary that he had received £7 10s. [33] from him (the remaining debts had amounted to £7 9s. 3½d.).

Chalmers appears to have sustained this method of dealing with poverty, and its underlying premises, up to the time he left Kilmany. This can be seen from an entry in the Kilmany parochial register for 12 August 1814. Here it was recorded that over the previous two years Chalmers had received 15 guineas for the poor of the parish from Mr Thimson of Charellon, which Chalmers had been:

> distributing among them regularly from the Session money. In this way he relieved many who felt a reluctance to a present . . . and he conceives that by keeping up this principle of delicacy among those who were on the very verge of sessional relief they have been kept off from being a permanent burden on the Session. For the same reason he thought it advisable in some cases whenever the money of the session was given away not to put down the names of the receivers in the session book but to state to the deserving and undeserving poor. [34]

It is clear that, at this stage in his experience of poverty, Chalmers was willing to be personally and directly involved in the various schemes of a relatively stable and prosperous agricultural parish to ensure the material as well as the spiritual well-being of its inhabitants. He recognised these schemes as operating essentially on a very personal and individual basis, admitting of economic fluctuations outwith people's control but also taking into account the degree to which they had drawn upon their own resources to remedy their situation before asking for help.

The main products of the second part of Chalmers' ministry in Kilmany were thus his evangelical zeal, his review of his ideas on Christian charity as the result of a revitalised Christian outlook, and his experience of how comparatively easy it was to implement his convictions concerning both the pastoral oversight of his parishioners and the safeguarding of their Christian principles by a carefully controlled administration of poor relief. This comparatively safe countenancing of relief in a small rural parish and at a time of relative agricultural prosperity was to be challenged in the increasingly industrialised economy of Chalmers' Glasgow parishes, which would result in yet another modification of his ideas.

On 26 November 1814 Chalmers heard that he had been elected by Glasgow Town Council as successor to the Revd Dr Stevenson MacGill in the Tron Church, Glasgow. [35] Exactly two weeks later he wrote to the Council accepting the situation. [36] The intervening fortnight was one in which he debated this decision in his diaries and letters, and also prayed about it. The main worry weighing on his mind against moving to Glasgow was his fear of the large number of extra-ministerial tasks he knew would be expected of a city minister. Used to the relatively quiet country life of Kilmany, where his recently-found enthusiasm for a complete dedication to his ministerial rôle had first found expression, he seems to have had a premonition that all this might disappear once he was immersed in a large city parish. [37] The increased number of duties to be done and social calls to be paid, the charity and school boards of which he would be a member, and the altogether more obviously secular life of a large city, all constituted a threat.

The process whereby Chalmers arrived at a decision about Glasgow is described in Hanna's biography, where he quotes some of the letters Chalmers wrote to his Glasgow friends at this time. The total effect of these is to convey the impression that Chalmers had a very definite plan of action to combat the evils of city life, a plan which he would put into operation once he moved to Glasgow:

> I know of instances where a clergyman has been called from the country to town for his talent at preaching; and when he got there, they so be-laboured him with the drudgery of their institutions, that they smothered and extinguished the very talent for which they had adopted him. The purity and independence of the clerical office are not sufficiently respected in great towns. . . . He comes among them a clergyman, and they make a mere churchwarden of him. . . . It shall be my unceasing endeavour to get all the work shifted upon the laymen. [38]

It was in fact reminiscent of his former reading of political economy and Adam Smith's theory of the division of labour, [39] but gave no hint of the detailed scheme he was to evolve later for the creation of deacons (an order of laymen) to cope with the poor relief aspect of a clergyman's more temporal tasks. Nor was there any indication that he anticipated having to develop a complex theory on poverty and its relief in a large city.

Another letter, written during this fortnight and not quoted by Hanna, gives a more revealing insight into Chalmers' acceptance of the Glasgow appointment. He had written on 4 December 1814 to the Revd Dr Robert Balfour (1779-1818) about his decision. Balfour, himself an Evangelical, was the minister of St Paul's parish in Glasgow. In his letter Chalmers asked for reassurance that he would be able to cope with the extra tasks, and still have time for his own studies and for his more properly clerical tasks. Balfour replied on 7 December 1814, when he detailed the various extra duties Chalmers had been alarmed at, and went on to upbraid Chalmers for hesitating on their account, since he rather saw them as opportunities for coming into contact with the people and for acquiring a position of usefulness and even of influence in the administration of the city:

> I know that a scientific mind like yours, values time by opportunities of study and discovery, and that a mind like yours, now risen by the power of God beyond the regions of mere science, and the utmost reach of philosophy, to the sublime heights of spiritual and substantial reality, and to the solemn boundless prospects of eternity, cannot easily descend to inferior attentions and pursuits. Yet my dear friend while we aspire to the highest enjoyments of heaven, may we not be preparing ourselves for the highest mansions there by filling our place here, with its proper claims and with all the variety of creation, which these may justly demand. [40]

That this letter was instrumental in Chalmers' final decision to accept the Tron Church may be seen in his diary entry on 10 December 1814: 'Got a satisfactory answer from Dr Balfour, and have sent off my letter of concurrence to the Glasgow Magistrates.' [41]

These letters and Chalmers' diary entries indicate that his decision to leave Kilmany was influenced mainly by a desire to carry out God's will, to continue on the course set out for him since 1810 of which Balfour's letter reminded him, and to bring the evangelical message to bear upon the harassments of city life. Although he had thought out what he would do if the latter became altogether too burdensome—i.e. enlist the help of the laity—he did not as yet conduct any rigorous enquiry into poor relief in Glasgow, or see any necessity for doing so. That was to lie in the future.

The main point of this paper has been to show that Chalmers went to Glasgow in July 1815 not as a social reformer but as an evangelical preacher, and was indeed hailed as such by its citizens. [42] Further, his ideas on poverty and its relief had been developing over the previous 15 years, conditioned by his experiences in his parish, his studies, and his conversion; but as yet they were not in any final or definite shape. His experiences had certainly reinforced many basic attitudes which were to remain unchanged, but their main impact had been to convince him of the complete primacy of the spiritual welfare of those under his charge; and it was this conviction more than anything else which determined how he would act when faced with the far more immediate and demanding problems of poverty in Glasgow. These problems were ultimately to inspire him to set down a complete scheme of poor relief after an extensive analysis of the mechanics of poverty and its relief; and it was their urgency, as well as his earlier thinking, which conditioned his final solution. He had to evolve a more detailed plan of action to combat a situation of great material need which he considered was hindering his primary object: the conversion of his parishioners.

As was said at the beginning of this paper, the development of Chalmers' thought in this area illuminates the motivation behind his social work. His often clinical approach to poverty and its relief must be seen in the light of his growing conviction that the most important thing was to safeguard the eternal welfare of men's souls. Having realised that he would not be free to concentrate on this until he had dealt with the problem of poor relief and its interference with a minister's valuable time, as well as its detrimental effects on the morals and the Christian education of the people, he therefore turned to the task of evolving a specific plan to combat the evil. The main purpose behind the plan, however, was still the religious one of bringing the Good News to the poor, and it is vital to understand this when examining his later solution of the problem of poor relief and assessing its impact and success.

Notes to Chapter V

1   After Thomas Chalmers left St John's in 1823 to take up the post of Professor of Moral Philosophy at St Andrews University the experiment continued under the direction of the elders and deacons in St John's.
2   T Chalmers to his father, 23 Dec. 1801, in Chalmers Papers, New College Library (*CP*), CHA 3.2.28.
3   T Chalmers, *Observations on a Passage in Mr Playfair's Letter* (1805), p.11.
4   According to the General Assembly Report on the Management of the Poor in Scotland, 1839, only 96 Scottish parishes levied a compulsory assessment in 1800.
5   William Hanna, *Memoirs of the Life and Writings of Thomas Chalmers* (1849-52), vol. I, pp.379-85.
6   Dr James Brown to T Chalmers, 7 Dec. 1801. *CP*, CHA 4.1.5.
7   The progress of the book may be traced in Chalmers' correspondence with his brother James in 1808. *CP* CHA 3.4.1-16.
8   T Chalmers, *An Enquiry into the Extent and Stability of National Resources* (1808), pp.27-28.
9   ibid., pp.263-64.
10 Hanna, *Memoirs*, vol. I, p.381.
11 Research has been done on this recently by W J Roxborogh, 'Thomas Chalmers and the Mission of the Church', University of Aberdeen PhD thesis, 1978.
12 T Chalmers to his brother James, 15 July 1811. *CP*, CHA 3.5.16.
13 T Chalmers' Diary, vol. II, 4 Aug. 1811. *CP*, CHA 6.1.4.
14 Roxborogh, 'Mission of the Church', pp. 92ff.
15 T Chalmers' Diary, vol. II, 16 March 1811. *CP*, CHA 6.1.4
16 T Chalmers, *The Two Great Instruments Appointed for the Propagation of the Gospel* (1812), p.23.

17 T Chalmers, *A Sermon Preached before the Society for the Relief of the Destitute Sick* (1813), p.11.
18 T Chalmers, *The Influence of Bible Societies on the Temporal Necessities of the Poor* (1814), p.6.
19 *Edinburgh Christian Instructor*, January 1813, p.65.
20 T Chalmers, *The Influence of Bible Societies*, pp.12-13.
21 ibid., p.15.
22 ibid., p.16.
23 Chalmers, *Destitute Sick*, Text for sermon.
24 Chalmers, *Influence of Bible Societies*.
25 ibid., pp.10-14.
26 T Chalmers, *The Christian and Economic Polity of a Nation* (1821), vol. I, pp.401ff.
27 ibid., vol. I, p.398.
28 T Chalmers to Mr Sommerville, 27 April 1811. *CP*, CHA 3.6.26.
29 T Chalmers' Diary, vol. II (17 July 1811), vol. III (14 Oct. 1811), vol. IV (17 Aug. 1813). *CP*, CHA 6.1.4,5,6.
30 T Chalmers to William Johnson, 25 July 1811. *CP*, CHA 3.6.40.
31 ibid.
32 ibid.
33 T Chalmers' Diary, vol. II, 27 July 1811. *CP*, CHA 6.1.4.
34 Kilmany Parochial Register, 1706-1819. New Register House, MS. OPR 437/1.
35 T Chalmers' Diary, vol. V, 26 Nov. 1814. *CP*, CHA 6.1.8.
36 ibid., 10 Dec. 1814.
37 For example, Chalmers' correspondence with Robert Balfour and Robert Tennent, 7 and 12 Dec. 1814. *CP*, CHA 4.3.7 and 4.3.64.
38 T Chalmers to Robert Tennent, 21 Nov. 1814, in Hanna, *Memoirs*, vol. I, p.445.
39 For example, T Chalmers to Mr Duncan Cowan, 21 Aug.1811. In this case Chalmers had been tutoring a young boy, Adam Pearson, and had found that, combined with his ministerial work, the teaching was too onerous. Thus he wrote to Cowan that he thought it better for individuals to concentrate on specialised tasks—in his situation, for the minister to oversee the spiritual side of parochial affairs, and for the teacher to be responsible for secular education, following the principle of the division of labour, 'one of the best principles in Political Economy.' *CP*, CHA 3.6.41.
40 Robert Balfour to T Chalmers, 7 Dec. 1814. *CP*, CHA 4.3.7.
41 T Chalmers' Diary, vol. V, 10 Dec. 1814. *CP*, CHA 6.1.8.
42 Mary T Furgol (*née* Gibbons), 'Thomas Chalmers and the City of Glasgow'; paper given at the History Students Research Conference, University of Edinburgh, May 1981. This paper will be included in the writer's forthcoming thesis.

K

VI

Chalmers and William Pulteney Alison:
A Conflict of Views on Scottish Social Policy

Olive Checkland

In 1840 when the energies of Thomas Chalmers, then Professor of Divinity in the University of Edinburgh, were directed towards the issues which were threatening to divide the Church of Scotland, William Pulteney Alison[1] published a pamphlet. It was entitled *Observations on the management of the poor in Scotland and its effects upon the health of the great towns.* In it Alison made a strong case for the imposition of an efficient and legally binding system of poor relief for Scotland. He did this on medical grounds. By so doing Alison assailed the position which Chalmers had always taken with regard to the Scottish Poor Law. How did the opposing cases arise and how should they properly be judged?

Thomas Chalmers is remembered in Scotland as a great divine who, in the first half of the 19th century, by his actions and efforts encouraged the Church of Scotland and its churchmen to undertake a more positive rôle in Scottish life. He was the principal instigator of an attempt in the Britain of the Industrial Revolution to find a solution to the problem of pauper relief. He did this by instituting in St John's parish, Glasgow, an experiment which seemed to many to offer an alternative to the English system.[2] St John's was a crowded industrial parish. There, between 1819 and 1822, Chalmers arranged that his church officials, notably his deacons, should themselves organise the parish poor relief. The person anxious for relief applied to the deacon, who made a series of enquiries regarding the petitioner, his family and his circumstances. At every stage efforts were made to encourage the applicant to help himself. All enquiries took time. Many applicants withdrew. Thus very little money was paid out to very few. Chalmers was able to claim success in that by a combination of mutual aid among the poor, plus parish charity, together with the advice and surveillance of the deacons, the parish could look after its own poor without an assessment for poor rates and without subvention from the city.

Before the Poor Law (Scotland) Amendment Act of 1845, Scottish poor relief administration differed strikingly from that of England. In Scotland, relief could not be given legally to the able-bodied for it was argued that only the orphan, the aged and the impotent were its proper

130

recipients. Relief from public funds was granted as the last resort, and then only as a supplement to other earnings, however small. In rural parishes the kirk session and the heritors (the larger landowners) were the administrators of the provision for the poor; in the burghs the responsibility lay with the magistrates and the town council. From this difference in the administrative framework evolved two distinct sub-systems, producing a degree of flexibility within the legal framework. The funds were obtained primarily by church-door collections, augmented where necessary by a legal assessment levied on the inhabitants by the heritors and kirk session in rural parishes and by the magistrates and town council in burghs.

Chalmers always made a distinction between poverty and pauperism. Although he accepted poverty as inevitable, he regarded pauperism as the worst of social evils, a morbid growth in society which had to be removed. 'A poor man is a man in want of adequate means for his own subsistence. A pauper is a man who has this want supplemented in whole or in part, out of a *legal* and *compulsory provision*' (italics added). [3] To eliminate pauperism, sole reliance must be placed on the habits and economies of the people, the kindness of relatives, the sympathy of the wealthy for the poorer classes, and the sympathy of the poor for one another.

Poor relief should stem from a voluntary source, not from a legal assessment. Chalmers gave four reasons why he believed a system of relief based upon compulsory assessment was doomed to failure. First, people become systematically trained to expect relief as a right, thereby destroying the connection which nature has established between economy and independence and between improvidence and want. Second, neighbours and kindred of the poor lose their private sympathies and abstain from providing relief. Third, as the number of poor increases they will be less comfortably relieved, since the allowance per pauper tends to decrease. Fourth, an artificial system tends to be wasteful, both in terms of increased expenditure on paupers caused by their demands for relief as a legal right and by the increase in the number of individuals needed to administer relief. It was Chalmers' belief that every extension of the poor's fund is followed by a more than proportional increase of pauperism, and he contended that there should be no compulsory assessment, no certainty on the part of the poor that they would obtain relief, and no possibility of the numbers in receipt of relief being infinitely augmented.

But the return to a voluntary system was only one half of Chalmers' plan to eliminate pauperism. He believed that education was the fundamental need of the lower orders, transcending in importance and, indeed, cancelling out the need for most poor relief. Education prevented pauperism from developing. Money withheld from poor relief and then applied to parochial education was doubly blessed.

In expressing these views Chalmers was speaking for the silent majority of middle class Scotland who believed that it was wrong to have a system of poor relief against which the destitute could claim as of right. By refusing to impose legal assessments, the poor law administrators of Scotland's rural parishes would be able to keep the number on the pauper rolls, and the amounts paid to them, at an extremely low level, especially when compared to the English experience. Unlike England, Scotland never granted an allowance to supplement wages; little wonder then that the English Poor Law Commission in 1818 and 1834 looked at Scotland with envious eyes. [4] Indeed, Chalmers' fame and popularity in England was established during England's great debates on public relief expenditure.

Chalmers did not develop a new system of granting relief; the methods he advocated were those of traditional rural Scotland. Chalmers' innovation was to attempt to apply the legal rural system to an urban parish, one already facing all the problems of a rapidly developing urbanisation. Notwithstanding its unsuitability, the St John's experiment was popularly acclaimed in Scotland by the middle and upper classes, for it seemed to demonstrate the feasibility under urban conditions of a poor law which remained voluntary and minimal. Few doubted the validity of Chalmers' arguments.

But members of the medical profession in both Edinburgh and Glasgow were to be the exception, for some became seriously alarmed at the condition of the poor. In Glasgow there was an old and useful system of District Surgeons based at the Town's Hospital. [5] The doctors who operated it reported on the diseases and illnesses suffered by the poor referred to them by ministers and elders. The *Glasgow Medical Journal*, from its inception in 1828, provides an insight into the condition of the poor in the city. The District Surgeons' reports, published in the *Journal*, supplied a statistical table of the incidence of disease, but also often contained a written account. Some of the surgeons expressed their opinions in forthright terms. Dr Andrew Buchanan (Professor of Materia Medica in the Andersonian University in Glasgow) referred in 1830 to '*the want of food*; a cause which may destroy life by its direct agency, but much more frequently proves fatal indirectly by the innumerable diseases to which it gives rise . . . in plain language, I am of opinion, that many of the poor of this city *die of starvation.*' [6]

Many of these doctors also believed that there was a direct and demonstrable relationship between economic adversity and the incidence of disease. In 1828 Dr Weir referred to 'the exciting causes of disease' as being 'deficiency of food, clothing and fuel.' [7] Yet another, Dr Macfarlane, wrote, 'but it is obvious, that in many cases a proper supply of nourishing food will be more useful in restoring to health, than all the productions of the Pharmacopoeia.' [8]

Robert Cowan (1796-1841),[9] Professor of Medical Jurisprudence and Medical Police in the University of Glasgow from 1839 until his death in 1841, published *Vital Statistics of Glasgow* in 1838 and another volume with the same title in 1840. He also was convinced of the relationship between poverty and ill-health, writing: 'The moment, the effects of the stagnation in trade extended to the working classes, the mortality increased with fearful rapidity, aided no doubt by the season of the year, the high price of grain, and the scarcity or high price of fuel.' He wrote forcefully of 'our heaviest municipal tax—the Fever Tax',[10] emphasising that contagious fever was the 'unerring index of destitution.'[11] In direct policy terms he wrote: 'The Poor Law of Scotland ought instantly to be revised. . . . True economy and self-interest demand it; the increasing destitution pointed out by the increasing mortality shews the necessity for it and the practical precepts of Christianity urgently enjoin it.'[12] Notwithstanding the good sense of these Glasgow doctors, their writings did not attract much public attention.

But another doctor, well-placed at the centre of the Edinburgh establishment,[13] was preparing a more effective attack. This was Dr William Pulteney Alison, 'A foremost clinician of his day, respected and revered by the whole medical profession in Scotland.'[14] Alison had worked long and ardently amongst the Edinburgh poor, both in the Royal Infirmary and also in the New Town Dispensary which he had been instrumental in founding in 1815. He believed that fever spread among the poor more readily because they were underfed; he blamed the Scottish Poor Law for its failure to support them when they were in need. Convinced as he was of the validity of his case he decided to publish his opinions, although the whole of the Scottish establishment (including the General Assembly and the legal profession) approved of the *status quo*. It was a bold and courageous decision, embodied in his *Observations* of 1840.

His arguments concentrated on two main themes. Like the Glasgow doctors Alison believed that the relationship between poverty and disease had been clearly established. He used much medical evidence to prove that the poor succumbed easily to many diseases but were particularly prone to fever because of malnutrition. He moved on to an attack on the Scottish Poor Law, quoting Captain Thomson, the treasurer and manager of the Edinburgh House of Refuge, who complained: 'The grand object kept in view by almost every parish is the possibility of evading the duty of relieving the poor.'[15] Alison urged that 'the objections which are so strongly felt in this country against a compulsory provision for the poor are found . . . to be absolutely and fundamentally erroneous', and that 'in a complex state of society . . . there is no other way in which the lower ranks can be permanently preserved from an extremity of suffering.[16] He concluded that 'the idea of the poor . . . supporting themselves, without much and constant assistance from the higher ranks, is perfectly visionary and utopian', adding that 'the countries which have been most permanently successful in maintaining the destitute and dependent position of the people in comfort are those in which indigence has been long admitted as having a legal claim to relief.' [17]

Thus was mounted a direct attack not only on the old Scottish Poor Law but also on 'our present illustrious Professor of Divinity', who was of course Thomas Chalmers.

In 1840 it was nearly 20 years since Chalmers had been directly involved with the poor in St John's parish, Glasgow. He had left Glasgow for the Chair of Moral Philosophy at St Andrews in 1823 and had subsequently moved to the Chair of Divinity in Edinburgh in 1828. He continued to use the St John's parish experiment as the basis for his Poor Law philosophy and referred to his work there with enthusiasm. Within a year he responded to Alison's attack in a book entitled *On the sufficiency of the Parochial System without a poor rate, for the right management of the poor*. In this Chalmers worked over the material he had used before, repeated his account of the St John's parish experience and used both in rebuttal of Alison. He also replied to the attacks which had been made by the other medical doctors. He claimed that Christ himself had placed a limit on the claims of the hungry for free food by refusing to perform the miracle of the loaves a third time when 'he rebuked the sordid expectation' of the people. But his second argument related to the various opinions held by the medical profession as a whole, and concluded that 'there is no crying destitution whatever, on account of which any change in the existing management is called for.' [18]

The position of Chalmers was profoundly Malthusian. Revd Thomas Malthus (1766-1834) had argued that poor relief or charity paid to the able-bodied would result in larger families, and cumulative destitution. Chalmers had accepted Malthusian theory whole-heartedly many years before. He had no hesitation in conferring on Malthus 'the benediction of religion'. [19] As one commentator has opined, Chalmers 'blends the Malthusian theory into a kind of Toryism starched with Scottish sternness'. [20] But the apparent triumph of Malthusianism (which could perhaps have been seen in England in the Poor Law Amendment Act of 1834) was being increasingly challenged. For many who had accepted Malthus' ideas in theory were shocked to find, with the implementation of the New Poor Law in England, that respectable workers were often forced into the hated workhouses by unemployment. More fundamentally, the achievements of the Industrial Revolution, resulting in the unheard-of development of industry, destroyed Malthus' case which rested on the assumption of a more or less fixed technology.

Malthus' views were widely accepted in Scottish society, for they gave convenient reinforcement to that interpretation of the Scottish Poor Law which gave so little to so few. But Malthus had had his detractors in Scotland. These included Alison's father, the Revd Archibald Alison, and his two sons, Dr William Alison and his younger brother, (Sir) Archibald Alison. As early as 1808 Archibald had written an Essay on Population. [21] The position of the two brothers did not change over the years, although not until 1840 did William bring his arguments into public view. [22]

Although William Alison accepted part of Malthus' argument that it was necessary to have a 'fluctuating surplus population' [23] to supply the labour market as and when required, he believed that such labour must be preserved from 'this state of hopeless and abject destitution'. For, and this is the crux of his argument, men supported above the level of destitution were set upon a path of self-improvement: they 'gradually fall under the dominion of *artificial wants*, and form for themselves a *standard of comfort*, from which they will never willingly descend and to maintain which they will keep themselves under a degree of restraint, unknown to those of the poor who are continually struggling to obtain the first necessaries of life.' [24] Moreover, Alison concluded that 'below a certain grade of poverty the preventive check of moral restraint has no power. . . . In such circumstances men hardly look forward to the future more than animals.' [25]

Alison's case for the restructuring of the old Scottish Poor Law was an immediate success, gaining wide support. For he had a formidable ally: an economic depression swept across the country from the spring of 1841, inspiring a campaign of Chartists throughout the land. But the depression did more: it underlined the terrible poverty of a population thrown onto its own negligible resources when work failed. Government, for the first time, appalled by the disastrous situation in places like Paisley, [26] questioned the adequacy of the old Scottish Poor Law. In this Alison's 'well orchestrated campaign' had played an important part. A Royal Commission was set up on 26 January 1843 to enquire into it. The Enquiry was an important one, [27] eliciting much important information. It was followed by the Poor Law (Scotland) Amendment Act of 1845.

Chalmers, after his intervention in the Poor Law debate in 1841, made no further public comment. He was soon to be engulfed by the tragic events which led to the Disruption of 1843, after which his remaining energies went into the creation of the Free Church.

The Poor Law (Scotland) Amendment Act of 1845 could be said to embody elements of both Chalmers' and Alison's views. In line with Chalmers' thinking, the Act provided no relief for the able-bodied when unemployed. But, consistent with Alison, a new civil administrative structure was set up on which further support for the poor could be built. Each parish was required to have a Poor Law Board: each Board was given rate-raising powers, under a Central Board of Supervision. In this way a tax base was provided. Subsequent evolution also favoured Alison: over the next half-century the Scottish Poor Law could gradually become more supportive. Poor houses were built and medical relief was given on a wider scale. The gap in amount of relief paid in England and in Scotland diminished in the course of time. In 1878 the Board of Supervision reported, 'It is obvious that if a person is *really destitute* no long period would elapse before he also became disabled from want of food.'[28] This was apparently a humane interpretation of the 1845 Act and would have given Alison much satisfaction. Thus the future lay with Alison and not with Chalmers.

Yet to Alison the report of the Commissioners was disappointing and the Act did not go as far as he wished. He could not, of course, foresee the more distant future. The Commissioners seemed to him to take too little account of the sufferings of the poor, and in 1844 he published *Remarks on the report of the commissioners on the poor laws of Scotland.*[29] He hoped, by adducing evidence from a wide variety of men in Scotland concerned with the poor, to swing the Government into acceptance of far-reaching amelioration. This he failed to do. But the closing words of his 1844 book were prophetic, when he wrote: 'we may be assured that industry and independence will not be less valued when we shall cease (as cease we shall) to believe, that the only security for the maintenance of those virtues among the poor, is to leave them and their children exposed to such sufferings and sorrow, as I have taken upon me to describe and to denounce.'[30]

It is clear that Alison made a great impact with his 'masterpiece', *Observations*, in 1840. As Lord Cockburn wrote on 15 August 1845, 'I scarcely know a more striking instance of the velocity of modern change. Till very recently . . . all men and all parties concurred in admiring our Poor-Law System. . . . Dr Alison startled people by questioning all this . . . and now the whole system is extinguished in a single month by the Legislature.'[31] Like other law lords Cockburn had earlier always supported the old Scottish Poor Law system.

It is no easy matter to sum up the controversy between Chalmers and Alison, for the positions taken represent two opposing views of what the poor could expect from society. The St John's parish experiment on which Chalmers drew to formulate his social philosophy was surely wrongly conceived. For Chalmers took no real account of the fact, palpable to Alison and others, that good workmen were at the mercy of the booms and slumps of the trade cycle. Chalmers neither knew nor understood the evils of unemployment; it is hard to understand how he, living in Glasgow between 1815-1822, could have failed to appreciate so obvious a phenomenon. Chalmers was in effect helpless, locked into Malthusian theory and neo-classical economics. According to his interpretation, if any concession were made the whole fabric would disintegrate.

But Chalmers did comprehend important truths about society. He insisted on the importance of the family as the basic social unit, a source of psychic support for its members. He urged that the neighbourhood or 'locality' should become a focus for community activity; for social coherence to be effective it was necessary to work in terms of units that were manageable and which could command loyalty. He revived John Knox's idea of the deacons acting as concerned 'social workers'; by so doing he was emphasising the need for a social bond between classes, expressed in commitment. By stressing the need for the gathering of information, together with sustained contact, he presaged the need for professionalism in social work. Though these ideas were in a sense anticipated by Knox, they were of continuing value.

Alison approached the problem from a different standpoint, as a doctor committed to healing the sick. When he found that the poverty of his patients effectively prevented them from benefiting from his care, he blamed the Scottish Poor Law—though, by and large, any attack on the Poor Law indirectly attacked the Church. By raising these matters in so controversial a way, Alison focused attention on matters previously ignored and forced Scotsmen to reappraise their social policy in the light of the new conditions then prevailing in early Victorian Scotland.

Can we say it was Chalmers who stood in the way of a fuller and more timely victory for Alison? There can be little doubt that part of the responsibility could be thus assigned. With Chalmers' view still much respected, it was impossible for government to go much further in the supportive direction than it did in the 1845 Act.[32] But Chalmers was not, of course, the only influence at work. He was the spokesman for a deeply-rooted Scottish feeling that dependence of the individual and the family upon public assistance was morally wrong and socially dangerous.[33] He advocated family and neighbourhood support. It could of course be argued that his views were appropriate to that element with which he was so strongly to identify, namely the prosperous lower middle class who were the most eager supporters of the new Free Church.[34]

Notes to Chapter VI

1 William Pulteney Alison (1790-1859): in 1815 one of two physicians appointed to the New Town Dispensary, Edinburgh. 1819: Chair of Medical Jurisprudence; 1821: Chair of Institutes of Medicine (Physiology); 1842: Chair of the Practice of Medicine, all in the University of Edinburgh.

2 For a fuller account see R A Cage and E O A Checkland, 'Thomas Chalmers and urban poverty: the St John's parish experiment in Glasgow 1819-1837', *The Philosophical Journal* (Spring 1976), vol. 13, no. 1, pp.37-56.

3 T Chalmers, *The Christian and civic economy of large towns* (1823), p.397.

4 For an English interpretation see E C Tufnell's evidence, *Poor Law Commission* (1834), Appendix A, pp.2-3.

5 'The poor of this city who are unable to obtain medical aid, when under disease, are recommended by a minister or elder to the surgeon in whose district they reside, and are attended and supplied with medicine at the expense of the town's hospital, an establishment for the support of which the inhabitants submit to an annual assessment. This mode of procedure has existed in Glasgow for many years, and has been found to work so well, both as an efficient and economic plan of administering to the wants and necessities of the sick poor, that it has wholly superseded the necessity for the establishment of charitable dispensaries.' John Macfarlane (MD, Member of the Faculty of Physicians and Surgeons, Glasgow, Senior District Surgeon to the City Poor and President of the Medico-Chirurgical Society of Glasgow), 'Report on the Diseases which prevailed among the Poor of Glasgow during the Autumn of 1827', *Glasgow Medical Journal (GMJ)*, Feb. 1828, p.97. In 1816 there were 4 District Surgeons, in 1817, 5; 1818, 6; 1831, 12; 1842, 16, plus one 'extra'. Each man was responsible for those of the 'outdoor' poor in his district who applied for medical help. Burgh records suggest that the Surgeons for the Poor received a fee. The earliest figure quoted is '10 guineas per annum for each district' (1831). See also *A short account of the Town's Hospital in Glasgow* (1742); *Report for the directors of the Town's Hospital of Glasgow on the management of the City poor, the suppression of mendicity, and the principles of the plan for the New Hospital* (Glasgow, 1818); *Regulations for the Town's Hospital of Glasgow: with an introduction, containing a view of the history of the Hospital and the management of the poor* (1830).

6 *GMJ*, Nov. 1830, p.447. See also D N H Hamilton, *The Healers* (1981), p. 199.

7 *GMJ*, May 1828, p.220.

8 *GMJ*, Feb. 1828, p.98.

9 Robert Cowan was the first holder of the Regius Chair of Medical Jurisprudence and Medical Police in the University of Glasgow established in 1839. The chair is now that of Forensic Medicine. His ideas of welfare were based on those of Medical Police (see R Cowan, *Vital Statistics of Glasgow*, [1838], p.40). These concepts had come to Scotland from Germany and related to the need of the state, representing all the people, to maintain their health. Medical students were required to satisfy examiners, both in Edinburgh and Glasgow, on matters concerning medical police or, as we would now call it, public health. See G Rosen, *From medical police to social medicine; essays in the history of health care* (1974), ch. I, sect. III.

10 Had Cowan not died in 1841, two years after being appointed to his Chair, it is possible that he would have made a greater impact upon Glasgow opinion. His main works were: *Remarks suggested by the Glasgow bills of*

mortality. I. *on the mortality of children in Glasgow* (1832); *Statistics of fever and small-pox in Glasgow* (1837); *Vital Statistics of Glasgow* I. *Statistics of fever and small-pox prior to 1837,* II. *Statistics of fever for 1837,* III. *Remarks suggested by the mortality bills* (1838); *Vital Statistics of Glasgow, illustrating the sanitary conditions of the population* (1840).

11 Cowan, *Vital Statistics of Glasgow* . . . (1840). p.33.

12 ibid., p.36.

13 Hamilton, *The Healers*, pp.197-98.

14 J H F Brotherston, *The Medical Officer*, 6 June 1958, p.331. See also 'The late Dr Alison', *Edinburgh Medical Journal*, vol. LXXXVII (1859-60), pp.469-86.

15 W P Alison, *Observations* (1840), p.24.

16 ibid., p.26.

17 ibid., p.102.

18 T Chalmers, *On the Sufficiency of the Parochial System without a Poor Rate for the right management of the poor* (1841), p.262.

19 H A Boner, *Hungry generations: the nineteenth century case against Malthusianism* (New York, 1955), p.118.

20 ibid., p.118.

21 Sir A Alison, *Some account of my life and writings: an autobiography* (edited by Lady Alison, 1883), p.39.

22 Recent research has attributed to W P Alison the authorship of two articles, 'Evils of the state of Ireland' and 'Justice to Ireland—a Poor Law', *Blackwood's Edinburgh Magazine*, vol. 40 (Oct.), pp.495-514, (Dec. 1836), pp.812-31. See W E Houghton (ed.), *Wellesley Index to Victorian Periodicals 1824-1900* (1966), vol. I, pp.52-53.

23 Alison, *Observations*, p.39.

24 ibid., p.50.

25 ibid., p.49.

26 See T C Smout, 'The strange intervention of Edward Twisleton: Paisley in depression 1841-43', pp.218-42 and Rosalind Mitchison, 'The creation of the Disablement Rule in the Scottish Poor Law', pp.199-217, in T C Smout (ed.), *Search for wealth and stability* (1979).

27 On the administration and practical operation of the Poor Laws (Scotland), Royal Commission including minutes of evidence, (557) XX, (563) XXVI, (543). See also Ian Levitt and T C Smout, *The State of the Scottish Working-Class in 1843* (1979), which is based on the evidence of the Royal Commission.

28 The full quote is as follows: '*Minute of the Board of Supervision respecting Able-bodied persons out of employment.* It must be kept in view that Parochial Boards have no power to expend any of their funds in the relief of persons who are not both destitute and (wholly or partially) disabled. In considering the question of disability however, in the case of a person really destitute, the Inspector should not carry the letter of the law to the extreme, and cause delay in a doubtful case by the necessity of an appeal to the Sheriff. Moreover it is obvious that if a person is *really destitute,* no long period would elapse before he also became *disabled* from want of food. It would probably be a safe rule of practice in such cases to afford immediate relief, if the Inspector is of opinion that the Sheriff on appeal

would order it.' 34th Annual Report of the Board of Supervision for the relief of the Poor and of Public Health in Scotland 1878-79 (1879), C.2416, Appendix A, no. 7, p.16. Glasgow University Library.

29 Alison had already presented evidence to the Royal Commissioners and this he published: *Observations on the Epidemic Fever of MDCCCXLIII in Scotland and its connection with the destitute condition of the poor* (1844). On the frontispiece there is a quotation: 'The destruction of the poor is their poverty' (Proverbs X, 15). This pamphlet emphasises the interconnection between fever, poverty and malnutrition.

30 W P Alison, *Remarks on the report of the Commissioners on the Poor Laws of Scotland* (1844), p.302.

31 Henry, Lord Cockburn, *Journal of Henry Cockburn being a continuation of the memorials of his time 1831-1854* (Edinburgh 1874).

32 For a valuable detailed assessment see J F McCaffrey, 'Thomas Chalmers and social change', *The Scottish Historical Review*, vol. LXI, no. 169 (April 1981), pp.32-60.

33 Sir Walter Scott summed it up as follows: 'Helen Walker from Dalwhairn in the parish of Irongray, where after the death of her father, she continued with the unassuming piety of a Scottish peasant, to support her mother *by her own unremitted labour and privations*: a case so common, that even yet, I am proud to say, few of my country's men would shrink from that duty.' Sir Walter Scott, *The Heart of Midlothian* (1818), Introduction.

34 See A A Maclaren, *Religion and Social Class: the Disruption years in Aberdeen* (1974).

VII

Chalmers as Political Economist

Boyd Hilton

In his *History of economic analysis* Joseph Schumpeter designated Chalmers the 'McCulloch' of the Malthusian School, meaning that Chalmers had presented Malthus' ideas in more acceptable form and introduced them to a wider and 'lower-level' public, as McCulloch reputedly did for Ricardo.[1] The most important Malthusian tenets appropriated by Chalmers in this respect were population theory and underconsumptionism: the belief that population was destined to outstrip the supply of food, and the belief that a capitalist economy, even under free trade conditions, was bound to run into a series of 'general gluts' of capital and commodities. Apart from his Malthusianism, the most obvious fact about Chalmers as political economist is his rôle as a Christian apologist. Scores of churchmen in the early 19th century took it upon themselves to reconcile the fashionable new sciences with religious truth. Chalmers had previously attempted this with respect to astronomy, and as Professor of Moral Philosophy at St Andrews (1823-8) and then of Theology at Edinburgh, he tackled the most voguish of all the new sciences, political economy. The Christian reconciliation of economics became the 'favourite child of his intellect', despite the dangers of 'secular contamination' involved in such an 'earthy' field of inquiry.[2] His major contributions were the *Commercial discourses* (1820), *The Christian and civic economy of large towns* (1821-6), *On political economy in connexion with the moral state and moral prospects of society* (1832), and the *Bridgewater Treatise* of 1833. In this paper I shall attempt little more than to juxtapose these two fairly obvious aspects of Chalmers' economics, the Malthusianism and the apologetics. The argument is that Chalmers evangelicalised Malthus' political economy and that, in so doing, he propagated a version of socio-economic philosophy which was extremely influential in the first half of the 19th century.

I am not concerned here with whether Chalmers inspired or merely articulated this philosophy, but still the question 'How influential was Chalmers?' cannot be avoided. It is easy enough to record the impact of his preaching tours on devout politicians, especially if they were liberal-minded Tories of Low Church dispositions, in the two decades before the Disruption: on Canning, for example; on Peel, Binning, Vansittart, Elgin, Huskisson, and Harrowby[3]; on the undergraduate Gladstone, who had met Chalmers through his father and who in 1830 risked rustication from Christ Church in sneaking out to a Dissenting chapel to hear the great Scotsman preach.[4] It is less easy to trace direct influence on the economic policy of the period, though William Wilberforce acted as intermediary for a while in conveying Chalmers' views on taxation to Canning. For his impact generally one can appeal to the testimony of Sterling, who called him 'one of the disregarded prophets of our time', while admitting that his was 'a power quite on the heart' as distinct from the intellect.[5] Hazlitt confirms that Chalmers' *Astronomical Discourses* 'ran like "wildfire" through the country'.[6] 'His was a voice that filled the world, the English-speaking world at any rate, from end to end,' wrote F H Doyle.[7] He 'adjusted the pulpit to the exigencies of the age,' wrote W G Blaikie.[8] And so on and so on. One could cite the many Christian social philosophers in Britain and America who, themselves influential, specifically acknowledged Chalmers as their inspired prophet: Wardlaw and Weyland among his contemporaries, G H Boardman and Benjamin Gregory a little later, and John Lalor who described Chalmers as 'the man who began that baptism of political economy into Christianity, which was the main thing needful to bring about its regeneration'.[9] In this paper, however, Chalmers' importance is merely deduced, tentatively, from the extent to which ideas similar to his pervaded the 'lower level' of socio-economic debate in Parliament and in a thousand tracts and magazine articles. Professional economists (the term is applicable by 1830) were disparaging about Chalmers' contribution,[10] and it is fair to say that by 1832 the technical apparatus which he wielded as a political economist was somewhat rusty (though against this he contributed significantly to the relationship between machinery and technical progress in agriculture).[11] But there is far more of Chalmers, at least of Malthus à la Chalmers, in the mouths of backbench MPs and the pens of quarterly scribblers than there is of Ricardo, Senior, and the Mills.

Moreover, I believe that Chalmers' political economy is a much better guide than, say, Ricardo's to the economic policy of the period. It must be clear that the period c.1800-50 was, so far as government intervention is concerned, an age of free trade and *laissez-faire*,[12] but less obvious is the fact that there were two distinct models of free trade in circulation. The first and more famous was that of most professional economists: Ricardian in essentials though with some adjustments (to the value theory especially), expansionist, industrialist, cosmopolitan; it aimed at economic growth through capital accumulation and an international division of labour. Its philosophical basis was utilitarian hedonism: individuals being left to balance the pleasure of profit against the pain of labour. Thanks to Cobden and others this version of free trade became increasingly influential after about 1850. The alternative free trade model may be described as Evangelical, retributive, static or cyclical, nationalist, and essentially physiocratic, its philosophical basis being the notion of an economic *conscience*. And of this model there is no more complete exponent than Thomas Chalmers. [13] Many excellent historians of economic thought seem to have assumed that because Chalmers was a physiocrat like Malthus, and had been since his early Spencean pamphlet on the *Extent and stability of national resources* (1808), he must also have been a protectionist like Malthus, especially where agriculture was concerned. But of course he was not, and I believe that the reason why Chalmers diverged from Malthus in this respect is significant as a reflection of his Evangelical approach to political economy.

The vast majority of the Christian or devotional economists, for example Richard Whately and W F Lloyd, successive holders of the Drummond Chair of Political Economy at Oxford, adopted a natural theology approach. Political economy could be shown to explain society in such a way that a sagacious and designing Mind must be presumed to have created it. Adam Smith, with his law of markets and other instances of private vices as public virtues, was an obvious source for apologists wishing to illustrate the wit and wisdom of the Deity in this way; though in the pessimistic 19th century the old theology of evidences tended to give way to a theology of paradoxes, as natural theologians sought to explain away the apparent discrepancies in nature by showing how God wrought ultimate Good out of apparent Evil. Now Chalmers' economics too contain a good deal of this type of thing, but it was not their central message. To illustrate his particular contribution we should look at his response to the two aspects of the orthodox secular political economy which most offended Christians: the population theory, which depicted God as having maliciously invited too many mortals to nature's feast; and the profit motive, apparently central to economic man, yet so antagonistic to Christian notions of grace and other-worldliness.

The population controversy is too well known to require much rehearsal here. Malthus' prognostication of 'wars, famines, and pestilences' shattered the utilitarian, Paleyan complacency which had assumed that population increase was an indication of national contentment. The natural theologians' usual way out of this Malthusian dilemma was to argue that God must have some utilitarian purpose for such an apparent piece of malice, as it might be he had deliberately placed man in a tricky ecological condition in order to arouse man's agricultural inventiveness, encourage the use of new farming technology, and so forth. The 1800s were a time when the 'margin of cultivation' (this phrase, made famous by Ricardo, happens to be Chalmers') was being pushed up the hillsides and on to every sterile promontory in the wake of high prices and of difficulty in procuring continental supplies. But in 1815-17 this particular paradoxical solution to the population problem was refuted by Malthus himself (among others) in the law of diminishing returns, which showed how extra inputs of capital, labour and land in agriculture could not in fact yield limitless extra supplies of food. Later on, in the more optimistic 1840s to 1860s, an alternative utilitarian explanation was to prevail in the notion that God had deliberately overpeopled Britain in order that her 'excrescent population' (in Chalmers' phrase) might seek employment overseas and take with them to far-flung corners of the globe the Gospel message and the Christian civilisation. But in the interim between diminishing returns and the missionary movement such anodyne solutions seemed impossible to most thinkers. Chalmers for one thought that the emigration of excrescents could do no more than delay the problem of overpopulation, just as the exportation of commodities could merely stave off for a little while the inevitable glut of commodities.

And so apologists had to turn away from the 'positive check' of wars, famines and pestilences to the 'preventive check' of sexual restraint. This hardly figured in Malthus' scheme of things, though he had included in the second edition of his *Essay* (1803), in a belated and vain attempt to stave off charges of impiety which his first edition had aroused, 'the action of another check to population which does not come under the head either of vice or misery'. The man who, seizing on this idea, first truly reconciled population theory with Christian precept was the Evangelical bishop J B Sumner, whose *Treatise on the consistency of the principle of population with the wisdom and goodness of the Deity* (1816) seems to have been enormously influential in Anglican circles and which, according to another Christian economist, Copleston, 'beautifully developed the high moral and religious blessings which hang over Malthus' discovery'.[14] (The same message was presented in a very different theological context and probably to a different audience by the Unitarian medical reformer Thomas Southwood Smith.)[15] To quote Whately, it was not a case of God having made 'man too prolific or the earth too barren', but rather that God had made man rational and then had placed him in such an ecological trap that he would be *forced* to exercise that reason in order to escape the positive checks to the growth of his own species.[16] Natural evil was thus productive of good by stimulating human adaptation and moral 'exertion'.

So far this is squarely utilitarian and led on to the new Poor Law and the 'less-eligibility' principle. Senior, Whately, and other economists concluded, sensibly enough, that there was simply no point in systematically doling out alms to the poor since, unless one also incarcerated them in workhouses, population would quickly catch up with the new level of affluence and recreate all the old misery. This is familiar enough. What Chalmers provided was an Evangelical twist to the argument. Impending crises were an essential part of God's providential plan for regenerating and redeeming individual sinners and hence society as a whole. Just as surplus food supplies in the 18th century had led to luxurious and godless living among the poor and a consequent escalation of their numbers, so the present shortage of food, predicted by Malthus, would work a great regeneration. The existing generation of working men was peculiarly blessed, for Providence was forcing them through hunger to limit the size of their families, which without contraceptive devices meant 'elevating their minds above their passionate flesh', their faculties of reflection over their sensuality, and working a 'moral ordination' in them as a consequence.[17] For Chalmers, clearly, enchainment in the realm of necessity did not preclude the exercise of free will, but he did admit that if the poor were to respond to their opportunity aright, they must be instructed in Gospel truth. Hence the need for Christian as distinct from mere political economists, for only they could reveal how population theory linked 'the economy of outward nature' and 'the economy of human principles and passions'.

> Political economy is but one grand exemplification of the alliance, which a God of righteousness hath enlisted, between prudence and moral principle on the one hand, and physical comfort on the other. However obnoxious the modern doctrine of population, as expounded by Mr Malthus may have been, and still is, to weak and limited sentimentalists, it is the truth which of all others sheds the greatest brightness over the earthly prospects of humanity—and this in spite of the hideous, the yet sustained outcry which has risen against it. This is a pure case of adaptation, between the external nature of the world in which we live, and the moral nature of man, its chief occupier.[18]

For Chalmers it was not merely useless or self-defeating to succour paupers with indiscriminate charity, but actually vicious to do so; men must not be let off God's ecological hook by misplaced and sentimental humanity.

Chalmers believed that 'the world is so constituted that if we were morally right we should be physically happy'. Physical suffering occurs because men neglect God's laws of nature, but it is also a means to make them more obedient in future. He faced up squarely to the objection that sexual restraint ran counter to God's advice to Noah to 'increase and multiply', arguing that the present condition of excrescent population was a very different one from the immediate aftermath of the deluge. And he squarely rebutted those who pointed to Biblical injunction in order to attack his poor law policies. The Apostles, he averred, had refrained from dispensing poor rates on the grounds that

L

doing so trenched on the time that should be given to the teaching of the Word; and even Christ himself had relieved from want or hunger only twice, while in John 6:26-7 he can be seen refusing to do so. Since on the other hand he freely relieved men from disease, there was:

> a distinction which ought to be made between a charity for mere indigence, and a charity for disease. A public charity for the one tends to multiply its objects—because it enlists the human will on the side, if not of poverty, at least of the dissipation and indolence which lead to poverty. A public charity for the other will scarcely, if ever, enlist the human will on the side of disease. [19]

It was the duty of the rich to give to the poor, but every such act must be individual, spontaneous, heartfelt, not 'strained'. State poor laws and organised charity transformed beneficence from a thing of 'love' and 'gratulation' to a subject of resentment on the part of the rich, dependence on the part of the poor, and 'angry litigation' between the two. The poor, meanwhile, must be taught the vital necessity of prudence, not merely by pointing to the temporal consequences which attend indulgence (mere *political* economists could do that), but also by 'sustained evangelical tuition', or reminders of the future retribution which must *always* follow the mortal sin of licentiousness. [20]

'If prudential restraint, i.e. the *preventive check*, is disregarded,' wrote Sumner, 'who can doubt that famine, war, or epidemics will arise? just as bankruptcy will come upon a man who takes no care of his fortune.'[21] The Evangelical economists drew a parallel between the tendency of population to outstrip food supply and the tendency of capital to outstrip demand. Chalmers was ever repetitious, and there must be at least 50 references in the *Political economy* to the analogy between a 'plethora of population' and a 'supersaturation' of capital. Indeed, Chapter 4 is 'On the parallel between population and capital, both in respect of their limits and their powers of expansion'. Coleridge had diagnosed an 'over-balance of the commercial spirit' as the root of all the 19th century's evil, but had thought it capable of being counteracted by 'the spirit of State'—implying economic and moral controls as against free trade. [22] Chalmers on the other hand believed:

> in the philosophy of free trade, the essence of which consists in leaving this mechanism to its own spontaneous evolutions, [so as to reveal] a striking testimony to the superior intelligence of Him who is the author both of human nature and of human society. [23]

Of course, this left the problem of how to reconcile the notion of economic profit with Christianity. Sometimes Chalmers simply followed utilitarian consequentialists like Whately in rummaging through *Wealth of nations* to illustrate how (thanks to the market) self-interest worked for the common good, how profit-oriented middlemen insensibly rationed food supplies throughout the year, and so on. This was not, however, sufficient for the Evangelical economists, who could not simply brush aside the individual's economic *motives*, as distinct from consequences. At the core of their political economy was the search for what Chalmers called 'commercial morality', or 'spiritual discipline' in money matters. They seem to have believed that there was a 'natural' rate of economic growth, and to have shared what Keynes called Malthus' 'vague intuitions' that there was a 'natural' and therefore 'effective' demand, which production must not exceed. Accordingly, they divided business into two categories: the legitimate and the illegitimate, the moral and the vicious, rather as they distinguished, with equally mad rigidity, between poverty and pauperism. Since they could hardly condemn *all* money-making as unchristian, they picked on those who seemed to be trying to get rich too quickly, who outstripped the natural rate of progress, as well as those who were fraudulent. Where Ricardo would have used the word 'competition', Chalmers was fond of talking about 'under-selling'. Men who sought success too quickly were 'speculators', a favourite term of abuse in the earlier 19th century, and one which implied even worse things than economic immoderation, even philosophic doubt and atheism. After all, speculation was the great ingrained vice of the middle classes, even as copulation was supposed to be that of the workers.

Now of course, risk being inseparable from profit, this rigid distinction between legitimate business and speculation was absurd. But it was also fundamental. Chalmers welcomed solid commerce while denouncing 'excrescent trade' as 'the blotch and distemper of our nation'. In practice the only way to decide whether a particular item of business was legitimate was by its outcome; like rebellion, it might be presumed to have had God's blessing only if it succeeded. (There is an interesting development of this theme in Charles Reade's novel *Hard Cash* where, with business failure staring him in the face, and his soul eaten into by 'corroding debt', the once upright Richard Hardie undergoes an amazing character degeneration, and has his son certified insane and incarcerated in an asylum in order to cheat him out of his inheritance. Then suddenly, two chapters from the end, Turkish stock rise back to par, Hardie is saved financially, and also restored to virtue as he rights his previous wrong-doings.)

But how can one restrain mercantile acquisitiveness and keep business within 'the standard of the Gospel'? In *The application of Christianity to commerce* (1821) Chalmers wrote:

> An affection for riches, beyond what Christianity prescribes, is not essential to any extension of commerce that is at all valuable or legitimate; and, in opposition to the maxim, that the spirit of enterprise is the soul of commercial prosperity, do we hold, that it is

the excess of this spirit beyond the moderation of the New Testament,
which, pressing on the natural boundaries of trade, is sure, at length,
to visit every country, where it operates with the recoil of those
calamities, which, in the shape of beggared capitalists, and
unemployed operatives, and dreary intervals of bankruptcy and
alarm, are observed to follow a season of overdone speculation. [24]

These 'intervals of bankruptcy and alarm' were not altogether a matter
for dismay, however, for though Chalmers never says so explicitly, he
seems to have regarded the threat of bankruptcy (with its harsh
concomitant, imprisonment for debt) as a sort of positive check,
commensurate with pestilences, working to force businessmen into
moderation, to deter them from economic temptation, so that by
subduing the sins of the flesh-pots they might find spiritual
redemption. God had designed the trade cycle, with its periodic bouts
of bankruptcy, as deliberately as he had forged the iron law of
population. Chalmers' successors, Horace Bushnell and Edward
Bickersteth for example, shared his complacent view that, so long as
one had a stable, convertible, currency, businesses which went bust did
so deservedly, through cupidity or stupidity. Thus S J Loyd, Lord
Overstone, the guru of liberal Tory monetary policy, commented on
the business crashes of 1825, 1839 and 1847:

> Monetary pressure does not . . . convert *real* prosperity into
> embarrassment and ruin—such pressure *detects* real unsoundness and
> brings it to a crisis. It is false prosperity—undue credit and over-
> trading which alone are pinched and embarrassed by monetary
> pressure. [25]

Bankruptcies, said Overstone, raised the tone of commerce 'by
exterminating noxious weeds and destroying the seeds of spreading
mischief', and he objected strongly to 'monetarists' like Thomas
Tooke, who called for monetary management with a view to preventing
fluctuations in the economy, since this would interfere with the full free
swing of the business cycle, 'the constant rotation' of whose wheel
'nature rests upon'. [26] Fluctuations were assuredly the result, not of
erratic note issue as Drummond and Tooke believed, but of human
depravity and appetite. In all this Overstone was flying a distinctly
Chalmerserian flag.

Inevitably, Evangelicals saw business failures, not only in terms of
God's judgments on individuals, but also as a providential warning to
the nation. Many examples of this belief might be quoted, but one will
do. It comes slightly late in the day for this sort of attitude, and is an
anonymous review from an Evangelical magazine of a volume on *Life's
problems: moral, social, and psychological* (1860):

> We believe that in this speculating world, amid all these risks and
> ventures which perhaps must be entered into to make business

prosperous and to keep pace with the age, it is only a very strong religious spirit, a practical exercise of religion, that can make anyone judge acccurately between legitimate and reckless commercial speculation. . . . From the danger we are all in of taking our moral standard from the tone of the common morality of society, we are apt to forget the higher standard of the law of Christ. [But] we are every now and then recalled to a sense of the difference of these two standards by some tremendous commercial failure; in which we see that speculation has been carried so far into the region of uncertainty and risk, that trust and confidence has been abused, and the ruin of one man has involved in it that of hundreds, who trusted in him. *Now we only see this by reason of the failure of the speculation*, not from the speculation itself: had that proved successful instead of disastrous, many would not have seen the immorality at all. [27]

Moreover, so deeply did the Evangelical temper bite in the first half of the 19th century that such apocalypticism affected many who were not formally Evangelical. Even Cobbett is reported to have greeted the 1825-26 financial crisis with the apostrophe, 'Can the Unitarians still deny that there is a God?' [28] Chalmers' influence in these commercial morality matters was by no means confined to persons of his own theological persuasion.

The anonymous reviewer of *Life's problems* quoted above referred at one point to Bishop Butler in describing economic temptation as an essential part of life's 'great moral trial'. And if Chalmers' socio-economic philosophy affected many people who were not themselves Evangelicals, High Church men like Gladstone and Newman whose Evangelical origins were strong, and also Broad Church men like Whately and Arnold whose distaste for Evangelicalism was deep and sincere, then it is worth reflecting that something which all these held in common was a regard for Butler. The influence of this early 18th-century divine was transmitted to the 19th century via the Scotsmen Reid, Hutcheson, and Dugald Stewart—much as was political economy itself. But judged by the publication figures, [29] Butler's burst into prominence came in the 1820s. On the one hand, the Oxford Noetics (including Whately) had him inserted in the Greats course, where he became virtually a sacred text, a sort of supplementary revelation. On the other, Evangelicals also appropriated him, so much so that in 1825 Jerram could congratulate Bishop Daniel Wilson on the latter's edition of Butler's works, as having brought for the first time the vital Evangelical truth that had lain hidden within. [30] Very briefly, Butler like Chalmers attracted because he tried to marry a doctrine of conscience to the prevailing consequentialism of the day; and he also buttressed Evangelicalism's social message by making it possible for, say, Broad Church men to accept 'a Godly system of government by rewards and punishments' in the universe without having to subscribe to the Evangelical concomitants of hell-fire and damnation. Thus Sir

James Graham, for example, an ex-radical who had none of the Evangelical instincts of so many of his Tory colleagues, notably Peel, could nevertheless talk a similar language, as when he 'spoke much of Butler's doctrine of retribution in this world as having been sustained by the whole of his experience'. [31] Chalmers himself wrote much on Butler and subscribed firmly to the latter's view of 'the economy of redemption', and of life as 'a state of moral trial'. In just the same way had J B Sumner cited Butler in his depiction of man's 'probationary state' and spiritual examination. [32] For both men, political economy was based on the supposition of original economic sin, economic trial and temptation, and the prospect of eventual economic salvation.

Accordingly, Chalmers held it essential that governments should not thwart the dispensations of Providence by trying to prevent or alleviate business failure, any more than they should dole out alms to the poor. No wonder then that bankruptcy dominated the fevered imagination of the first half of the century: the one topic that was never mentioned in polite society. The spectre of the Marshalsea, that debtors' prison that was the workhouse of the middle classes, haunts so many of the characters in the fiction of the period—Meredith's Beauchamp, Trollope's Melmotte, Dickens' Merdle; and so often business failure is described in explicitly Malthusian terms—Merdle's spurious prosperity is a 'sorely contagious disease' and his collapse sets off an 'epidemic' of failure, while George Eliot's Bulstrode 'blights' his various clients 'like a damaged ear of corn'. In many ways the most typical tragic hero of the age was the bankrupt Walter Scott. The cyclical inevitability that, after a period of overweening inflation, each troubled bubble would be broken induced not merely fatalism among businessmen, but even a sort of glorification of purgative, atoning, failure. Chalmers' friend, the Evangelical merchant John Gladstone, could say masochistically, amid the bankruptcies of 1826, 'We shall be the better for passing through the ordeal' [33]—better, that is, for the receipt of Christian truth. The sacrificial image is here again in Chalmers:

> The accumulating policy of Dr Adam Smith will at length give way, before the doctrine that capital has its limits as well as population, and that the Christian liberality of merchants would not only secure them from the woes denounced in the Bible against those who, hasting to be rich, pierce themselves through with many sorrows, but would induce a' far more healthful state of commerce than it is possible to maintain with the distempered over-trading of the present day. [34]

Like the new Poor Law, short shrift to bankrupts was also a part of Ricardian economics, but in that case its aim was to promote growth. A short shower of bankruptcy might weed out inefficient businesses and enable the worthwhile firms to expand more confidently. Evangelical economists like Chalmers, on the other hand, aiming to restrict growth to a 'natural' level, wished to weed out not *inefficient* but *immoral* businesses. Bankruptcies would promote not growth but the fear of God among capitalists. Thus they desired the repeal of the Usury Laws, but not (like Bentham and Ricardo) in order to encourage further lending and expansion, rather because businessmen must first be tempted to overreach themselves if they were finally to achieve their commercial salvation by resisting that temptation. (Note in contrast that Richard Jones, another Christian economist but decidedly anti-Evangelical and I think anti-Butlerian, opposed repeal of the Usury Laws as 'a fearful and intricate experiment upon the moral habits . . . of the people.) [35] As William Sewell put it, the money market ought not to be suppressed, since it was 'a field of discipline for man's greatest virtue'—that is, self control. [36]

To sum up, the Chalmers school of political economy, faced with Malthusian fears of gluts, sought release not in new outlets for exports and emigration (since informal or free trade imperialism could merely palliate the problem for a while), but in the reduction of production by the application of commercial and sexual conscience. They were free traders in order to give that conscience room to develop. Keynes was therefore wrong to criticise the Malthusians for illogicality in having (correctly) diagnosed underconsumptionism but failed to prescribe public works and other types of demand management to restimulate consumption, for this of course is precisely what they were anxious not to do. Their underconsumptionism was really a theory of overproductionism, and their consistent aim was, in J S Mill's more sober and much more sceptical words, 'to inculcate in businessmen the practice of a moral restraint in reference to the pursuit of gain'.[37] It is this static, even retrogressive, vision of the economy which made free trade, for Chalmers, perfectly compatible with, and even conducive to, the preservation of a predominantly agrarian economy; and it justifies his defence of *unproductive* spending by the idle rich.

A few words should be said about the rapid decline of Chalmers' economic influence in the middle of the century. As the poor law authorities expanded their functions beyond that of being mere relievers in the last resort, and as philanthropy became increasingly organised through 'internal missions' and so on, the Chalmers ideal of a predominantly 'spiritual tuition' for the working class was eroded. More suddenly, the limited liability legislation of 1855-62, by releasing individual shareholders from the obligation to pay with *all* their worldly assets until the debts of a company had been discharged, effectively emasculated the retributive mechanism of business failure. Chalmers' economics, based on man's natural depravity and need for redemption, gave way to the more generous version of Mill, based on confidence in mercantile virtue and common sense. Thus it was that the parliamentary doyen of limited liability, Lowe, could challenge the Chalmers school in introducing the legislation: 'You must deal on the basis of confidence. Fraud and wickedness are not to be presumed in individuals.'[38] In the same way philanthropists like Sadler argued that the best way to make the poor more prudent was to treat them like adults and not like sinful children.

We can account for the limited liability revolution in several ways. In part it reflected more positive attitudes to economic growth. Instead of seeing Britain pull dangerously and recklessly ahead of the rest of the world, economists of the 1850s began to worry that rival nations were catching up. In this new climate it seemed important to encourage capital investment. The word 'speculation' began to lose its predominantly pejorative overtones, and enterprising investors took over in many people's minds from the 'rentiers' or 'creditors' as the real heroes of the economy. Limited liability also reflected more positive attitudes to social mobility, as one can see from this despairing private comment by a stalwart of the old Chalmers school, Lord Overstone: 'Joint-stock banks and limited liability companies are the order of the day, and the boldest man seems most likely to be prosperous. . . . The world is going up and downstairs, *without* laying hold of the bannister.'[39] Again, it was evident from the scandalous proliferation of failures and frauds associated with the railway booms of the 1840s and 1850s that the retributive or unlimited liability system simply was not working its promised regeneration in the land.

However, I believe that at the heart of the reaction against Chalmers was a mid-century distaste for his moral theology. As the Duke of Argyll (a neo-Chalmers individualist and also Butlerian) wrote towards the close of the century, 'the problem of limited liability cannot be probed to the bottom, without taking into account a thousand considerations, which concern metaphysics, jurisprudence, politics, morals, and even religion'.[40] Writers like Chalmers and Thomas Nolan[41] who believed in the *fever of speculation* as a vital part of the *economy of redemption* were also men who held to a literal interpretation of the doctrines of Atonement, Eternal Punishment, Vicarious Sacrifice, Substitutionary Punishment, and the like. Defenders of this Evangelical *scheme of salvation* invariably adopted the Calvinist terminology of likening sin to a debt which was owed to God; God would have to exact his recompense in return but—by analogy with Christ's atonement—did not care who precisely repaid the debt so long as it was repaid by someone. Some, like Gladstone, regretting the later 19th-century decline in the literal interpretation of the Atonement, blamed the use of commercial terminology for turning people against it[42]; but as the homiletic and Chalmerserian novelist Frances Power Cobbe wrote:

The 'scheme of redemption', beset at every step with moral and philosophical difficulties to other men, seems to the evangelical the perfection of Divine ingenuity. Its resemblance to a human commercial transaction strikes *him* as the most natural instead of the most offensive thing in the world. [43]

At all events, whereas Chalmers and Overstone had not, in the last analysis, minded all that much whether business crashes eliminated the morally bad capitalists or not (though on the whole they thought they did), since bankrupts could be regarded as sacrificial offerings atoning for the sins of a crazy commercial world, the reformers of the 1850s were determined to abandon such hangovers of the old 'flogging theology' (to use R H Hutton's phrase). They abandoned Chalmers' political economy when they enacted that, in future, the blood of bankrupts should be only sprinkled, and not spilt.

In a sense one could interpret limited liability as the middle classes opting out of the capitalist system at the point where it stood to damage themselves. Until then they had been able to rationalise their relative prosperity by arguing that it was they who carried the capitalist system on their backs, as it were, by risking the terrible losses and shame incurred in business crashes. With that justification gone, many capitalists in the later 19th century followed Mill in admitting that the rich had a positive responsibility to improve materially the condition of the poor, with or without spiritual effort by the latter. And without wishing to make Chalmers' political economy seem more glibly symmetrical than it was, again an analogy may be drawn between the treatment of business failure and the treatment of poverty. Chalmers' view that upper-class charity must always be spontaneous, the product of what he called 'free-will offerings', and not of legislative injunction or mere routine dutifulness, meant of course that it was the upper classes who were being put to the test spiritually. While the poor were, relatively speaking, spiritually superior, being less subjected to corroding temptation, the rich knew that unless they could truly have faith (and alms-giving was of course a temporal indication that one might have found such a thing), then they faced an eternal workhouse, namely hell. This too was a sort of spiritual justification of privilege. And so when, in the middle decades of the century, [44] fashionable theologians abandoned the doctrine of a literal and endless hell-fire, they too were opting out of the capitalist-spiritual system adumbrated by Chalmers; they were, in fact, limiting the liability of sin.

The reformers of the 1850s were able to argue that, by allowing capitalists to associate how they would, with or without limited liability, they were in line with the doctrine of free trade; in the same way working men should be allowed to associate freely in trade unions. But to the Chalmerserians, of whom Overstone was now the most prominent, limited liability had as much to do with free trade 'as with the tides'. The reformers thought it was unnatural that enormous pains and penalties and liabilities should hang over the trembling speculator; to Chalmerserians, believing implicitly in providential judgments as in wars, famines and pestilences, such dangers seemed the most natural thing in the world. Both sides believed in free trade, but meant different things by it. McCulloch may have been the 'Chalmers' of the Ricardian school, but he was also a man of the earlier generation, and he lamented the enactment of limited liability with a notably Chalmerserian complaint:

> In the scheme laid down by Providence for the government of the world, there is no shifting or narrowing of responsibilities, every man being personally answerable to the utmost extent for all his actions. But the advocates of limited responsibility [i.e. liability] proclaim in their superior wisdom that the scheme of Providence may be advantageously modified, and that debts and obligations may be contracted which the debtors though they have the means, shall not be bound to discharge. [45]

For McCulloch as for Chalmers, free trade was essential in order to eliminate temporal and especially governmental interference with the economy of nature, and to restore the operation of God's own moral government, through a natural system of rewards and punishments.

Notes to Chapter VII

1 Joseph Schumpeter, *History of economic analysis* (1954), pp.487, 477.
2 W Hanna, *Memoirs of the life and writings of Thomas Chalmers* (1849-52), vol. III, pp.298-99 and 93-94.
3 See, for example, G R Gleig, 'Memoirs of Dr Chalmers', *Quarterly Review*, vol. CXI (1852), p.428, on Chalmers' visit to London with the Astronomical Sermons in 1817: 'Canning was in raptures—Sir James Mackintosh full of them. Bobus Smith . . . permitted himself to be carried away with the stream. Besides these, Wilberforce, Romilly, Huskisson, Lord Binning, Lord Elgin, Lord Harrowby, and many more of rank and influence forthwith sought him out. They formed part of his congregation wherever he preached, and vied with one another in their anxiety to do him honour in society.' See also *Memorials of the earls of Haddington*, by W Fraser (1889), vol. I, pp.321-22; Hanna, *Memoirs*, vol. III, p.161; and Wilberforce's diary: 'All the world wild about Dr Chalmers . . . Canning . . . quite melted into tears', in *The life of William Wilberforce*, by R I and S Wilberforce (1838), vol. IV, pp.324-25.
4 *Reminiscences and opinions of Sir Francis Hastings Doyle 1813-85* (1887), pp.101-2.
5 J Sterling in *The Athenaeum*, XXXI (1828), p.487.
6 W Hazlitt on 'Rev Mr Irving' in *The spirit of the age* (1825).

7 Doyle, loc.cit.

8 W G Blaikie on Chalmers in *The Dictionary of National Biography*.

9 J Lalor, *Money and morals. A book for the times* (1852), p.xvii. For a selection of later writings showing Chalmers' influence directly, see W R Greg, *Essays on social and political science* (1853), vol. I, pp.458-504; H Bushnell, 'How to be a Christian in trade' from *Sermons on living subjects* (1872), pp.243-67; Benjamin Gregory, *The thorough business man* (1871), passim; H A Boardman, *The Bible in the counting-house* (1854); G N Boardman in *Bibliotheca Sacra*, vol. XXIII, pp.73-107.

10 The best known of several dismissive reviews is G P Scrope, *Quarterly Review*, vol. XLVIII (1832); see also T P Thompson, *Westminster Review*, vol. XVII (1832).

11 M Berg, *The machinery question and the making of political economy* (1980), p.86.

12 Of course, this statement could be disputed, and has been by such historians as David Roberts and H Scott Gordon. My own position coincides with the recent analysis by Oliver MacDonagh, *Early Victorian Government 1830-70* (1977), p.9. MacDonagh was a pioneer of the argument that, *institutionally*, the welfare state has *pre*-Victorian origins, but he nevertheless recognises that c.1830-70 was an age 'of positive and aggressive individualism', and that such centralist and collectivist steps as were taken either 'slipped through unnoticed' or else had to be 'explained away as exceptions, as unusual necessities or even on occasions as subtle applications of the principle of individualism'. It may be added here that David Roberts would reject the conclusions of this paper. In *Paternalism in Early Victorian England* (1979), he defines the word 'paternalism' so widely as to include virtually every member of the upper classes that ever showed any lovingkindness towards, and concern for, the poor. Not surprisingly, this includes nearly everyone, and so Chalmers is duly numbered among the paternalists. But since Roberts has to admit that Chalmers took a *laissez-faire* attitude towards state action, believing that 'the poor should be self-reliant, should stand on their own two feet, and should not be dependent on government' (Roberts, p.42), he has perforce to comment that 'Chalmers was of course somewhat untypical'. So much for Sterling's 'prophet of the age'! Also Roberts' remark, p.31, that 'There was in Chalmers' Scottish Calvinism an individualism that *verged on* the philosophy of self-help later developed by Samuel Smiles' (my italics) strikes me as a serious understatement.

13 But see the comments about S J Loyd, Lord Overstone. See note 25.

14 E Copleston, *A second letter to Robert Peel on the causes of the increase of pauperism and on the poor laws* (1819), p.23.

15 T Southwood Smith, *The Divine Government* (1816), 5th edn. (1866), pp.75-108.

16 R Whately, *Introductory lectures on political economy* (1831), pp.164-66.

17 T Chalmers, 'The political economy of the Bible', *The North British Review*, vol. II (1845), p.40.

18 T Chalmers, *On the power wisdom and goodness of God as manifested in the adaptation of external nature to the moral and intellectual constitution of man* (1833), vol. II, p.49; T Chalmers, *The Christian and civic economy of large towns*, vol. I (1821), pp.3-24.

19 Chalmers, 'The Political economy of the Bible', p.47.

20 ibid., pp.8-17.

21 J B Sumner, *A treatise on the records of the creation, and on the moral attributes of the Creator; with particular reference to the Jewish history, and to the consistency of the principle of population with the wisdom and goodness of the Deity* (1816), vol. II, p.166.

22 S T Coleridge, *Lay sermons*, edited by R J White (1972), pp.169-70, 202-8, 223, 228.

23 Chalmers, 'The Political economy of the Bible', p.29.

24 T Chalmers, *The application of Christianity to commerce* (1820), pp.iii-vi.

25 Overstone to G W Norman, 4 Nov. 1856, and Overstone to G C Lewis, 6 Nov. 1856, *The correspondence of Lord Overstone*, edited by D P O'Brien (1971), vol. II, pp.678-82.

26 ibid.

27 Anonymous review in *The Ecclesiastic and Theologian*, vol. XXII (1860), pp.261-64.

28 See Lord Granville to Canning, 14 Feb. 1856, *Life of Lord Granville*, by Lord E Fitzmaurice (1905), vol. I, pp.164-65.

29 See J D Yule, 'The impact of science on British religious thought in the second quarter of the nineteenth century', Cambridge University PhD thesis (1976), pp.165-67.

30 C Jerram to D Wilson (?1825), *The life of Daniel Wilson*, by J Bateman (1860), vol. I, p.162.

31 See *The Gladstone diaries*, edited by M R D Foot and H C G Matthew, vol. III (1974), p.557.

32 J B Sumner, op.cit., pt. iii, ch. II.

33 John Gladstone to Robertson, 12 Jan. 1826, quoted in S G Checkland, *The Gladstones* (1971), p.155.

34 Chalmers, 'The political economy of the Bible', p.52.

35 Richard Jones, *Reasons against the repeal of the usury laws* (1825), p.3.

36 W Sewell, *Christian politics* (1844), pp.226ff.

37 J S Mill, *Principles of political economy* (1848), 1909 edn., p.557 (bk. III, ch. xiv).

38 Robert Lowe in House of Commons, 1 Feb. 1856, *Hansard's Parliamentary Debates*, 3rd series, cxl. 124.

39 Overstone to Norman, 24 Oct. 1863, *Correspondence of Overstone*, vol. III, p.1017.

40 Duke of Argyll, *The unseen foundations of society* (1892), p.557.

41 T Nolan, 'The fever of monetary speculation', *Twelve Lent lectures on 'the signs of the times' for the year 1858* (1858), pp.87-94; T Nolan, *The vicarious sacrifice of Christ, the only foundation for the sinner's hope, the only motive to the Christian's holiness* (1860).

42 W Gladstone, 'True and false conceptions of the Atonement', *The Nineteenth Century*, vol. XXXVI (1894), pp.317-31.

43 Frances Power Cobbe, *Broken Lights* (1864), p.37.

44 And rather earlier, of course, in Scotland.

45 J R McCulloch, article on company law and limited liability in *Encyclopaedia Britannica* (1861).

VIII

Chalmers' Thinking Habits:
Some Lessons from his Theology

Friedhelm Voges

To the majority of people, Thomas Chalmers is a figure of social and political rather than theological interest. His social activities were strongly influenced by the fact that he was a minister of the Church, but he is usually referred to as a churchman rather than as a thinker in the philosophical or theological field. Yet Chalmers himself valued his theological contribution much more highly. When his strength began to fail him near the end of his life, he left the business of the Free Church and concentrated on his theological teaching at New College. At the same time, he finished his *Institutes of Theology*. In his *Collected Works*, the social and political volumes are outnumbered by those dealing with philosophy and theology.

This paper makes no attempt to 'rediscover' Chalmers as a major theological thinker. He remains a figure of his own time, and even then his contribution was respectable rather than outstanding. His theological convictions and philosophical premises were, however, an integral part of his thinking. It is unlikely that he left them behind when he entered into his social ventures. What then is the relationship betwen the two sides of his thinking?

This is not the same as asking about Chalmers' motivation. That he was looking to restore the Christian Scotland of old, that he wanted to raise the working classes at least in a moral sense and that he was moved by a genuine Christian love especially for the common people: these are facts easily gathered out of the *Memoirs* compiled by W Hanna. His theoretical and his practical work alike were meant to further these great aims. At least in the practical field, Chalmers' limitations are fairly obvious; they are dealt with elsewhere in this volume. But where is the root of these limitations? How did Chalmers come, for instance, to regard the assimilation of a town to a country parish as possible—even after his experiment had had to be discontinued? A closer look at his thinking habits as shown in his philosophical and theological works can help to explain why he so stoutly adhered to some of his favourite notions. Indeed, it is the main suggestion of this paper that Chalmers' shortcomings in the social field can be linked to certain failings in his theology.

157

In the second of his *Commercial Discourses*, Chalmers maintained the connection between Christianity and 'the world' in these terms: 'It is false, that the principle of Christian sanctification possesses no influence over the familiarities of civil and ordinary life. It is altogether false, that godliness is a virtue of such a lofty and monastic order, as to hold its dominion only over the solemnities of worship or over the solitudes of prayer and spiritual contemplation. . . . There is nothing that meets us too homely to be beyond the reach of obtaining, from its influence, the stamp of something celestial. It offers to take the whole man under its ascendancy, and to subordinate all his movements.'[1] No serious Christian could disagree. But the question must be asked whether Chalmers succeeded in applying this maxim to his own processes of thought, whether he did not stick to certain assumptions without allowing the 'celestial stamp' to reach them. Chalmers frequently insisted that 'the humbling truth of their own depravity' was to be 'habitually presented to the notice and proposed to the conviction of fallen creatures.' 'This is a truth which may be recognised and read in every exhibition of unrenewed nature.'[2] Surely the knowledge of such depravity should have affected not only Chalmers' theology, but also his practical outlook? Much in nature was plainly 'unrenewed'. Should this not have tempered the optimism which Chalmers took to his schemes?

It seems possible to identify three problematic aspects of his theology that can help to explain his reactions.

1. Before his conversion Chalmers' theology centred mainly on God the Father, whose majesty had been important to him ever since the 'mental elysium' of his student days, when 'the one idea, which ministered to my soul all its rapture was the magnificence of the Godhead.'[3] This orientation was probably strengthened when, as an undergraduate, Chalmers became closely acquainted with the Common Sense philosophy. In 18th-century fashion, God was again the Father and the Creator, who had given man those salutary 'natural' instincts that Reid and his followers appealed to. It must have been at this stage that Chalmers learned to view the world as basically harmonious. Among the early writings, his *Enquiry into National Resources* (1808) gives the clearest evidence of how this belief in harmony carried over into quite practical matters. Given goodwill all round—something Chalmers saw as realistic—there could be no problems at all in managing the economy.

Then came the conversion, and Chalmers was a changed person. It is worth enquiring how his old and his new faith agreed with each other. The leading element now was 'a total, an unreserved, and a secure dependence on Christ the Saviour',[4] a characteristic phrase from Chalmers' diary of 1811. But there was no easy harmony between this new focus on Christology and the earlier emphasis on 'the magnificence of the Godhead'. It is hardly a coincidence that, even at the end of his life, the chapter on the Trinity is only an appendix in the *Institutes of Theology*. Chalmers does not appear to have devoted much attention to the relationship of Father and Son.

He does of course have very clear views regarding their respective rôles in the 'scheme of salvation'. Christ is 'the PRICE of our deliverance', [5] who atoned for our sins and also brought positive righteousness that can be imputed to the sinner. Christ thus set right the relationship between God and the individual. But his rôle seems to go no further than that. In his dealings with the rest of the creation, God is seen only as God the Father, who can apparently be understood quite apart from the love that he showed in Christ.

The main evidence for this criticism comes from that department of Chalmers' Natural Theology which seeks to produce evidence for the excellence of God's moral government. Chalmers is not content with the ordinary proof for the existence of God out of 'those collocations, which bespeak a designing cause'. [6] From man's 'mental constitution'— which he mostly viewed in line with the Common Sense tradition of moral philosophy—he attempts to produce 'the most full and unambiguous demonstrations, which nature hath anywhere given us, both of the benevolence and the righteousness of God.' [7] From a survey of human life, Chalmers wants to show that God not only created man but also, by intending man to be good, displayed his own moral characteristics. Such an undertaking sounds innocent enough, but it is hard to square with Chalmers' own convictions about human depravity. For it is from human life or the human constitution that the evidence for the divine excellence will have to come. On the basis of a human condition broken by sin, such proof would be hard to carry through.

The difficulty remains even though Chalmers points to the rôle of the conscience in giving man a certain power of knowing right and wrong, so that he can be held responsible for his actions. This theology of conscience, often emphasised, also enables Chalmers to give some credit to virtuous human behaviour and thereby saves him from that temptation of evangelical theology: the beating down of all human endeavour. He is very conscious of the difference between actual sin, which need not be present, and that 'estrangement of the heart from God' which is 'the decisive factor' in man's depravity. [8] With the help of his conscience, man may well avoid actual trespasses and also know about his condition. Recognising conscience allows Chalmers the conclusion that there may well be enough of God's good gifts left in man to say something about him who gave them. The proof of God's moral attributes would thus, on Chalmers' terms, be possible.

But that proof would have to look different from what Chalmers is actually presenting. His task would be to survey a broken world in order to discover the purpose it had before it was broken. Over long stretches of his *Natural Theology*, Chalmers appears not even to realise that this world and man in particular may be broken. Only towards the very end of the book does the tone change, for now Chalmers has to show that Natural Theology leaves certain questions unanswered. But his talk of 'that dilemma in which the world is involved' [9] comes only after long passages that show no trace of that dilemma.

For instance, Chalmers 'cannot imagine a more decisive indication of His favour being on the side of moral good, and His displeasure against moral evil, than that . . . virtue and happiness on the one side, vice and wretchedness on the other, should be so intimately and inseparably applied. Such sequences or laws of nature as these, speak as distinctly the character of him who established them, as any laws of jurisprudence would the character of the monarch by whom they were enacted.' [10] In making such claims, Chalmers is speaking of the real world: 'There can be little doubt of such being the actual economy of the world, such the existing arrangement of its law and its sequences—that virtue and happiness are very closely associated.' [11] Elsewhere, Chalmers can talk with great knowledge about the conditions he had encountered in Glasgow. He was also aware of the sufferings involved in, for example, the slave-trade, where virtue and great misery could be associated. How then are such statements to be explained?

It seems reasonable to assume that pre-conversion ideas about the harmoniousness of the world are coming to the surface. It may well be that Chalmers gets carried away on to a path that he ought to have left in 1810. Old, trusted and therefore unchecked notions seem to retain their place. It might not be too much to say that Chalmers' conversion did not extend to certain parts of his thinking, even of his theological thinking. New insights were added, but their relationship to the old ones remained strangely unexplored.

Unless he is dealing explicitly with the 'scheme of salvation', Chalmers prefers to see the Lord as the one who gives, not as the one who takes away. In the Natural Theology, the disturbing question of the *malum physicum* is only too quickly disposed of: 'There are, it is true, sufferings purely physical, which belong to the sentient nature—as the maladies of infant disease, and the accidental inflictions, wherewith the material frame is sometimes agonised. Still it will be found that the vast amount of human wretchedness can be directly referred to the waywardness and morbid state of the human will—to the character of man and not to the condition which he occupies.' [12] This may well be so, and Chalmers is quite justified in concentrating on those sufferings which are caused by man. Physical ills do exist, however; yet with the above-quoted sentence Chalmers has brushed them aside. One could be forgiven for the suspicion that he tries to get away from this problem because it is not easily squared with his notion of a harmonious world.

The same sort of argument also appears in the famous *Astronomical Discourses*, and David Cairns has pointed out how Chalmers really goes too far in his claim that God's government of the world leaves no space at all for criticism. [13] If it were otherwise, 'should we not see some traces of neglect, or of carelessness in His management? . . . Now, point out a single mark of God being thus oppressed.' [14]

The conclusion seems hard to escape that Chalmers can, over long stretches, forget what he had learned through his conversion. If he has been credited with a Pascalian insight into the human dilemma, [15] this would only seem to apply to some of his writings, namely when he is on expressly theological ground and deals with the 'scheme of salvation'. But when Chalmers talks about God the Creator, he seems to forget about God the Mediator, who—on his own insistence—came into this world because of human sin. God's maintaining of the world can therefore be seen quite apart from his concern about its salvation. It is then hardly a coincidence that, in the *Institutes*, the Trinity is only treated in an appendix. The persons of the Trinity are seen as separate, and the relationship between them comes only as an afterthought.

2. In seeking out those 'laws of nature' that 'speak as distinctly the character of him who established them, as any laws of jurisprudence would the character of the monarch by whom they were enacted', Chalmers gives us unique insights into his likes and dislikes. In order to make his point, he must give more than a simple description of reality. He must look at a particular 'collocation' of things from a certain angle; and the choice of standpoint—vantage point would have been Chalmers' term—is usually revealing. Thus Chalmers claims divine sanction not only for such feelings as compassion or the sense of property; he even invests the workings of the old Scottish system of poor relief with divine authority. On the first two points, public opinion of the time would probably have followed him, but on the question of poor relief its agreement became ever more doubtful. By 1845, when the Scottish Poor Law Amendment Act was passed, opponents like Chalmers were obviously in the minority. The voice of the old system could hardly have spoken very distinctly by then.

The theological argument developed from the poor relief question is as follows. Chalmers sees the old system as an application of 'nature's strong and urgent and general affections [which] may be regarded as an impressive while experimental demonstration for the matchless wisdom of nature's God.' [16] Among these affections, he counts friendship, patriotism and, in particular, the 'ties which bind together into a domestic community, as if by a sort of certain peculiar attraction, all of the same kindred and the same blood.' [17] The English system of pauperism, however, 'hath, by the most pernicious of all bribery, relaxed the ties and obligations of mutual friendship. . . . Had the

M

beautiful arrangement of nature not been disturbed, the relative affections which she herself has implanted would have been found strong enough.'[18] By instituting this system, English statesmen have traversed 'the processes of a better mechanism instituted by the wisdom of God.'[19]

It is now clear why Chalmers so resolutely refused to change his position on poor relief. Any other system could not have had the divine blessing. It seems equally clear that Chalmers had a powerful tendency to see things as natural and thus God-given that were really the products of human activity at a certain time and place. So the practical weakness is also a theological one. Chalmers never seems to ask whether he has interpreted God's will correctly. He is ready to trust the evidence of his senses and his sympathies to an astonishing degree. Like a whole generation of Scottish students, he had been encouraged to do so by the philosophy of Common Sense, but few people went as far as Chalmers. The Common Sense thinkers showed great disdain for all 'scepticism'. But with regard to his own judgment, Chalmers might have done well to be rather more sceptical. Dealing with poor relief in the context of Natural Theology, his harmonistic view again prevails, and he never asks whether human weakness might not enter into the operation even of the 'natural' scheme of poor relief.

3. It is well known that Chalmers always showed a keen interest in mathematics, chemistry and related subjects such as astronomy. This interest was strongest in his youth, but even in his last decade Chalmers lectured on the subject of heat to the Mechanics Institute in Greenock. Dealing with these subjects left its mark. Chalmers is ever asking for 'evidence'—factual evidence that will stand up to the criticism of the sceptics. In the social field, he thought he had furnished such evidence through the St John's experiment, and he persisted in this conviction even after the scheme had had to be abandoned. 'My experiment has been made and given forth its indelible lesson, although my experimentalists have been disheartened and frightened away.'[20] In theology, the search for evidence features prominently in his apologetics, and he finds such evidence, first in the facts of biblical revelation—authenticated by miracles—later in the 'experimental evidence' of minds and hearts influenced by the gospel. He frequently invokes the spirit of Bacon and Newton against people whose reasoning seems to stand on uncertain grounds. 'It is the glory of Lord Bacon's philosophy . . . to have disciplined the minds of its votaries into an entire submission to evidence—to have trained them up in a kind of steady coldness to all the splendour and magnificence of theory and taught them to follow, with an unfaltering step, wherever the sure, though humble path of experiment may lead them.'[21]

Being used to such ways of thinking, Chalmers displays a refreshing freedom in his dealings with the theological tradition in which he had grown up. He frequently criticises a 'fierce and flaming orthodoxy' [22] that he saw following its own rules and habits rather than those of Scripture. The arrangement of the material in his *Institutes* is radically different from that approach. Chalmers sets out to follow the natural order of human inquiry into religious questions, and he starts with those doctrines 'which meet the anxieties of the spirit in quest of peace with God.' [23] This is also the area where it is least difficult to find 'evidence'. As his next step, Chalmers treats those articles 'which guide the disciple's way along the progressive holiness that qualifies him for the pleasures and companionship of Paradise.' And only then come those 'higher and transcendental themes which sublime the contemplation both of the saint and of the scholar.' [24] Implied in such an order of things is a challenging of theological convention that should not be overlooked when Chalmers' achievements are counted, though it was not a 'fierce', but a faded 'orthodoxy' that he challenged.

It is unlikely that the Baconian way of thinking influenced only the way in which Chalmers arranged his materials. One would also expect an influence on the content of his thinking. Though it is difficult to prove the extent of such influence, a few suggestions can be made. Consider the nature of the scientific approach. It tries first of all to get a clear identification of the elements involved in any given problem. In algebra, for example, 'a "means" a' and is clearly defined as such. In chemistry, a substance is either pure or impure. The scientist can attain considerable precision, even though in modern science there are new problems in this area. In Chalmers' age, no doubts existed. Scientists knew what they were talking about.

In the social field, problems are much less easily identified. There is usually an interaction of factors that makes it difficult to single out cause and effect with certainty. Yet the temptation to do so must always be there, and if one wants to speak with any clarity, some simplification is even necessary. Being used to the scientific approach, Chalmers probably fell for this temptation quite easily. His readiness to propose easy solutions for social problems, particularly poor relief, may well have its root here. He concentrated on one aspect of the problem and then had very sanguine hopes about the prospects of success. Taking his Baconian stance, he had repeatedly warned against 'lofty theories', but it seems as if he did not escape this temptation himself.

The same tendency can also be seen in his theology. Chalmers had very clear views about God and Christ and about individual man as a sinner. Indeed, according to Chalmers man possesses a 'moral mechanism'—described in some detail in his *Moral Philosophy*—and in God's scheme of salvation for man he can admire the 'exquisite skilfulness of the whole contrivance.' [25] The use of such terms is hardly a coincidence, and it points to a rather mechanistic mode of thinking. A contrivance presupposes component parts, of which presumably man with his moral mechanism is one. Even God himself is bound by his own rules. 'The Character of the Deity,' Chalmers assures us, 'will sustain no mutilation by any one act in the moral administration of the Deity, and unless the truth and the holiness and the justice and the other perfections of God give their full consent to the exercise of His mercy, then the exercise is impossible.' [26] Thus, even the Christ event had to follow certain rules. God could not, by an exercise of his power, have healed the breach 'by a simple act of remission.' God 'has other attributes than those of mere power. And in virtue of them, He has chosen to conduct the administration of His government on certain great and unchangeable principles.' [27] 'A mere act of general mercy would have unhinged the whole system of the divine economy among man.' [28] God's revelation of his love in Christ is just one aspect of the divine character beside others. There is thus even some reason for the small regard that Chalmers had for the Trinitarian dogma.

Analogous to this concept of God is Chalmers' view of the world, which he saw as a framework of causal chains, unalterably bound together by God. In the sceptical period of his youth, Chalmers had found peace through thinking about the 'constancy of nature' as something firm that he could take as a stepping stone for his reasoning. This belief remains firmly in evidence and shows itself, for instance, in what Chalmers has to say about the efficacy of prayer. Given a constant, unchangeable world, this was not an easy question, but Chalmers finds an answer: 'Prayer may obtain its fulfilment without any visible reversal of the constancies of nature—provided that its first effect is upon some latent and interior spring of the mechanism.' [29]

The world—just like man—can thus be seen as a mechanism and the God to whom this world belongs appears in the same light. At this point, Chalmers' grounding in the Baconian approach and his familiarity with science have questionable consequences. They helped him to look at the technical side of theology with a fresh eye but the nature of neither God nor man can really be grasped in terms of 'mechanics'.

It must be said in Chalmers' defence that he is also capable of other tones. His piety is very Bible-oriented, and the effects of his Bible reading are noticeable not only in semi-private writings such as the *Horae,* but also in the *Institutes.* Indeed, he sometimes almost contradicts himself, because he makes strong claims on the strength of ⟨ ne and then of another biblical quotation. But time and time again, the 'mechanism' of his approach comes to the fore, and though the modern Christian may well read individual passages with profit, this can hardly be said about Chalmers' system as a whole.

If Chalmers could be unduly optimistic—the first point of this paper—he could also be prone to see matters as too easily definable. Both habits of his thinking can be shown in his theology as well as in questions of poor relief and economics. Of course there is also a strength in this approach: where Chalmers moved into immediate action, a greater realist might well have hesitated. At the same time, the consequences of such activity were not all happy ones, as is shown elsewhere in the present volume. This particular paper has tried to show that for a better understanding of Chalmers it is helpful to take all aspects of his thinking into consideration. He was a churchman and theologian at heart, and what he did and thought in the field of churchmanship and theology would seem important, if not essential, for an adequate understanding of his endeavours.

Notes to Chapter VIII

1 *Collected Works of Thomas Chalmers (CW)* (25 vols., 1835-42), vol. VI, p.51.
2 *CW*, vol. VIII, p.10.
3 W Hanna, *Memoirs of the Life and Writings of Thomas Chalmers* (1849), vol. I, p.17.
4 ibid., p.225.
5 T Chalmers, *Institutes of Theology* (1856) in *Select Works*, vol. VII, p.475 (Chalmers' capitals).
6 ibid., p.85. cf *CW*, vol. I, pp.259ff.
7 *CW*, vol. I, p.289.
8 *CW*, vol. VIII, p.303.
9 *CW*, vol. II, p.406.
10 *CW*, vol. II, p.27.
11 *CW*, vol. II, p.122.
12 *CW*, vol. II, p.219.
13 D Cairns, 'Thomas Chalmers' Astronomical Discourses: A Study in Natural Theology?', *Scottish Journal of Theology*, vol. IX (1956), pp.417f.
14 *CW*, vol. VII, p.78.
15 D F Rice, 'The Theology of Thomas Chalmers', Drew University PhD thesis, 1966.
16 *CW*, vol. II, p.67.
17 *CW*, vol. II, p.61.
18 *CW*, vol. II, p.68
19 ibid.
20 T Chalmers, *The Sufficiency of a Parochial System without a Poor Rate, for the Right Management of the Poor* (1841), p.129.
21 T Chalmers, *The Evidence and Authority of the Christian Revelation* (1814).
22 *Institutes*, vol. I, p.428.
23 *Institutes*, vol. I, p.7
24 ibid.
25 *Moral Philosophy* in *Select Works*, vol. XII, *Institutes*, vol. I, p.511.
26 *CW*, vol. X, p.318, cf. *CW*, vol. VIII, pp.130f.
27 *CW*, vol. IX, pp.242f.
28 *Institutes*, vol. I, p.494.
29 *Institutes*, vol. II, p.337 (*Select Works*, vol. VIII).

IX

Chalmers and the Church:
Theology and Mission

Henry R Sefton

When one considers how deeply Thomas Chalmers felt and how
prolifically he wrote about the Church's position in society, it comes as
a surprise to discover that his considerable literary output contains no
systematic theology of the Church and that his divinity lectures never
got as far as dealing with the subject. My aim in what follows is to
survey Chalmers' many and various occasional lectures and sermons
and to deduce therefrom his doctrine of the Church, its nature and its
mission to the world.

Among the most notable of the occasional lectures was the series
which he was invited to deliver by the Christian Influence Society.
This was a group composed mainly of laymen who were concerned
about the assaults currently being made on the position of the Church
of England. The Duke of Wellington, speaking in 1838, put it thus:
'The real question is Church or no Church; and the majority of the
House of Commons—a small majority it is true, but still a
majority—are practically against it.' [1] Wellington's fears were
exaggerated, perhaps, but John Keble had already denounced the
national apostasy [2] of applying surplus ecclesiastical revenue in Ireland
to other than ecclesiastical objects, and many shared Welllington's
forebodings about the future of the Church of England. [3]

Chalmers delivered his lectures on 'The Establishment and
Extension of National Churches' in London between 25 April and 12
May 1838 before 'all-ticket' and distinguished audiences, and the *Sun*
and the *Globe* newspapers made sure that their message reached a wider
public. [4] In these lectures he made it clear that there were certain views
of the Church which he did not hold.

Chalmers urged the Church of England to 'come down from all that is
transcendental or mysterious in her pretensions' and quit 'the plea of
her exclusive apostolical derivation.' [5] He clearly had no sympathy with
the views of Keble, Newman, Pusey and their associates in the Oxford
Movement. W E Gladstone, who had a considerable respect for
Chalmers, was in the audience, as were no fewer than seven bishops,
and he was deeply pained by this 'flogging' of the apostolical
succession. Gladstone's well-known comment to Manning (referred to

by Professor Chadwick in his article)—'Such a jumble of church, un-church, and anti-church principles as that excellent and eloquent man Dr Chalmers has given us in his recent lectures, no human being has ever heard. . . . I do not believe he has ever looked in the face the real doctrine of the visible church and the apostolical succession'[6]—shows quite clearly that Chalmers never envisaged the problems of defining the Church in such terms. The two men came from quite different historical traditions. The evidence which Chalmers gave nine years later to a House of Commons committee indicates that his views had not changed. He describes the 'inroads of Puseyism in the Church of England' as 'a very great corruption'. Recalling his lectures of 1838, he remarks: 'I advocated the Church of England as a good machine, but which required to be mended: and indeed I ventured to say so, and suggested that they should rid themselves of the figment of apostolical succession.'[7] In his view, 'there is marvellously little of express enactment in Scripture for an ecclesiastical constitution.' Apostolic succession is 'more in the shape of an indeterminate or discretionary question' and to be decided by considerations of expediency. Expediency, however, is to be understood in the context of 'what makes most for the prosperity of religion in the world, for the extension and the glory of our Redeemer's Kingdom.'[8] His description of the Church of England as 'a good machine' is thus typical of his practical, rather than mystical, view of the Church. Rightly established, the Church is 'the most efficient of all machinery for pervading the people with religion.'[9]

Writing to his old friend and fellow-student, Bishop Strachan of Toronto, Chalmers gave this account of his position: 'We are steering on the middle path between Puseyism on the one hand and Voluntaryism on the other. I do not say that we will succeed, but it is my firm belief that if we do not, National Establishments of Christianity will and ought to be put down, not for a perpetuity, but till that period when the Kingdoms of the earth shall become the Kingdoms of our Lord and Saviour Jesus Christ.'[10] Chalmers is at pains to answer those who see in national establishments of Christianity a 'distrust in the efficacy of divine grace':

> A machinery is not the less essential upon earth, that the impellent force which guides and animates its movements is from Heaven. There is nothing in this to disparage or do away with the paramount necessity of a spiritual influence.

In his London lectures Chalmers set out to vindicate religious establishments in opposition to the Voluntary System and 'what has been termed the System of Free Trade in Christianity.'[11]

This was no new concern for Chalmers. As far back as 1817 he had taken issue with Adam Smith's views that religious instruction should be left to the pure operation of demand and supply, like any article of ordinary merchandise. In the appendix subjoined to his sermon on the death of Princess Charlotte, Chalmers had pointed out that 'the appetite for religious instruction is neither so strong nor so universal as to secure such an effective demand for it. Had the people been left in this matter to themselves, there would, in point of fact, have been large tracts of country without a place of worship, and without a minister.' [12]

Voluntaryism received powerful support in Scotland from a sermon preached in April 1829 by the Revd Andrew Marshall, a Secession minister in Kirkintilloch. Chalmers was not mentioned in the sermon but Marshall attempted to deal with the argument that 'unless we send the gospel to men they will never seek it'. He saw this not as a justification for a national Establishment but as a challenge to voluntary generosity. [13] Chalmers clearly had this sermon in mind when in the following month he preached before the Society for the Daughters of the Clergy in St George's, Edinburgh, for his theme was a vigorous defence of religious Establishments. In the London lectures, also, he was concerned to contest the sufficiency of the voluntary principle. He pointed out that 'after a century of perfect freedom for the enterprise and the utmost strenuousness in the prosecution of it' voluntaryism in Scotland had 'left without the blessings of a gospel ministration half-a-million who ought to have been church-goers.' Furthermore those who attended the meeting-houses were not the poorest in the community, upon whom 'the evils of our ecclesiastical destitution have principally fallen.' [14] By contrast he defined Establishment, in his sermon before the daughters of the clergy, as 'a universal home mission'. Since the days of Constantine its object had been 'not to extend Christianity into ulterior spaces but thoroughly to fill up the space that had been already occupied.' [15]

This conception of Establishment found its outworking in Chalmers' emphasis on the need for a territorial ministry and his efforts on behalf of Church Extension. The system of territorial Establishment by which 'the clergyman has a certain geographical district, whether in town or country, assigned to him' seemed to Chalmers to be 'the only one by which the mass of a community can be out and out pervaded':

> It may not introduce Christianity within the precincts of every family; but it brings the overtures of Christianity or of Christian instruction to the door of every family. The lessons of the Gospel are brought by it to every door; and our experience is, that, when once brought thus far, in the vast majority of instances an entry is permitted and so these lessons are carried by it across almost every threshold. It is our further experience, that, when this system of aggression on the households of a newly assigned parish is kept up and perpetuated by the clergyman—not only does it secure a private ministration to the inmates on a week-day; but these inmates are at length evoked by it

into the act, which in time ripens into the habit, of attendance on the public ministrations of the Sabbath. [16]

In a pamphlet published in 1835 Chalmers explained his preference for the title 'Church Extension' rather than 'Church Accommodation'. The enterprise was concerned not only with the building of new churches but also with the vicinity for whose good the new church was intended. The object was to provide a church near enough and with seat rents low enough to benefit the families by whom it was surrounded. The district to be served had to be small enough and its families few enough to be 'thoroughly pervaded by the week-day attentions of a clergyman.' It was not intended to build churches in general but rather 'to plant territorial churches in those places where we judge that they are wanted.' [17]

While still a professor at St Andrews, Chalmers set out his attitude to Establishment and the Church in Scotland:

> I have no veneration for the Church of Scotland merely *quasi* an Establishment, but I have the utmost veneration for it *quasi* an instrument of Christian good; and I do think, that with the means and resources of an Establishment she can do more, and does more, for the religious interests of Scotland than is done by the activity of all the Dissenters put together. I think it a high object to uphold the Church of Scotland, but only because of its subserviency to the still higher object of upholding the Christianity of our land. [18]

But Chalmers' horizons were never limited to Scotland. As early as 1812 he commended the work of the Dundee Missionary Society in a sermon which when printed ran to four editions. In this he made the then comparatively novel point that the dominical comand 'Go ye therefore and teach all nations' means that a great part of the task has devolved on us, for it is not yet accomplished. [19]

In the anniversary sermon preached in 1814 before the Society in Scotland for Propagating Christian Knowledge he defended the utility of missions and pointed out the absurdity of the current prejudice against the name of missionary:

> Convert the Preacher into a Missionary, and all you have done is merely to graft upon the man's preaching the circumstance of locomotion. How comes it that the talent and the eloquence and the principle, which appeared so respectable in your eyes, so long as they stood still, lose all their respectability as soon as they begin to move? [20]

In 1825 (his second session as Professor of Moral Philosophy in the University) Chalmers was elected president of the St Andrews Missionary Society and held this position until he left for Edinburgh in 1828. He also gave considerable support to the Students' Missionary Society, [21] and six of his students offered themselves for missionary service. [22] The most notable of these was Alexander Duff, the first missionary sent out by the General Assembly of the Church of Scotland. Chalmers preached at Duff's ordination in 1829, [23] and until he took up the work of church extension was an active member of the Assembly's foreign missions committee.

When Duff returned to India in 1839 after an extended furlough spent raising funds for overseas work Chalmers preached at a special farewell service. In his address he was at pains to point out that there was no necessary conflict between the committees he and Duff respectively represented:

> We are both alike free of those jealousies which are sometimes felt between one philanthropic society and another. . . . It is true, in fact, that our two causes, our two committees, might work into each other's hands. Should the first take the precedency, and traverse for collections the whole of Scotland, the second would only find the ground more softened and prepared for an abundant produce to itself. . . . The success of the first will be the best security or guarantee for the success of the second—they will grow with each other's growth—they will strengthen with each other's strength. [24]

Among the many missionary societies [25] before which Chalmers preached was the Glasgow Auxiliary of the Hibernian Society for establishing schools and circulating the Holy Scriptures in Ireland. His sermon, preached in 1818, applies the doctrine of Christian charity to the case of religious differences and more particularly those between Roman Catholic and Protestant. He does not hesitate to comment on the errors of popery but suggests that these errors may not be confined to Catholics. The doctrine of transubstantiation may be monstrous on the ground of its absurdity or its impiety:

> But in the sacraments of our own country, is there no crucifying of the Lord afresh? Is there none of that which gives the doctrine of transubstantiation all its malignant influence on the hearts and lives of its proselytes? Is there no mysterious virtue annexed to the elements of this ordinance . . . does the conscience of no communicant solace itself by the mere performance of the outward act, and suffer him to go back with a more reposing security to the follies and vices and indulgences of the world? [26]

Chalmers commends the wider distribution of the Bible, the ability to read it and the lessons the Scriptures impart as 'enlightening the prejudices and . . . aiding the frailties to which, as the children of one common humanity, we are all liable':

> You Catholics have justly reproached us with our manifold and never-ending varieties; but here is a book, the influence of which is throwing all these differences into the background, and bringing forward those great and substantial points of agreement, which lead us to recognise the man of another creed to be essentially a

Christian,—and we want to widen this circle of fellowship, that we may be permitted to live in the exercise of one faith and one charity along with you. [27]

In the same spirit Chalmers made an impassioned appeal on behalf of the political emancipation of Roman Catholics in a memorable public meeting held in Edinburgh in March 1829. [28] He declared: 'In this emancipation of Papists I see for Protestants a still greater and more glorious emancipation.' The laws intended to disable Catholics had in fact disabled Protestants for more than a century: 'They were meant to serve as a barrier of defence for Protestants *against* the encroachments of Popery; and they have turned out a barrier of defence *for* Papists against the encroachments of Protestantism. . . . Had we been suffered to mingle more extensively with our Catholic fellow-subjects, and to company with them in the walks of civil and political business, there would at this day have been the transfusion of another feeling, the breath of another spirit amongst them; nor should we have beheld as now the impracticable countenance, the resolute and unyielding attitude of an aggrieved and outcast population.' [29]

Chalmers, however, would not have approved of the disestablishment of the Church of Ireland. In his London lectures he roundly asserted: 'The remedy is not to abolish the Protestant Establishment of Ireland, but rightly to patronise it.' The failure of the Church of Ireland lay not in 'the magnitude of those revenues, which the wayward politicians of our day are now labouring so hard to reduce, if not to annihilate' but in the quality of many of those who had been presented to the livings and in their reluctance to make the Establishment 'a great home mission'.[30]

Two questions should be asked when a government is to select one denomination of Christianity for the national religion. The first is, 'What is truth?' and the second, 'What is the most effectual regimen for training the successive generations of a country in the virtues of good citizenship, and so as shall be likeliest to ensure for the commonwealth the blessings of a moral and religious population?' On neither count has Chalmers any fear for 'our own Protestantism'. [31]

Chalmers also considers the problems which confront a government in selecting one of the evangelical Protestant denominations to be the national Establishment. The territorial principle, upon which he sets so great store, makes it necessary that only one denomination should be established. He concedes that it 'may be difficult to allege, and still more to vindicate, the superiority of any one of these denominations to all the rest.' [32] This, however, does not justify a delay in making a selection:

The moral well-being of the nation is not to stand at abeyance, till an adjustment shall have been made among controversies not yet determined, and perhaps indeterminable. . . . Enough for

> government that it has taken a scriptural church into its service; and vindication for its not taking more, that its work can be better done by one such servant than by several. [33]

Chalmers turns to the argument that questions such unequal treatment of the denominations when the difference between them is so insignificant, and replies: 'When the difference is so insignificant, why keep up that difference at all?' He has little time for those who speak of the sin of schism 'in language far too strong for any sympathy or even comprehension of ours.' He will not describe other denominations as being unapostolical and has no use for the bigots within the Establishment who would unchristianise the Dissenters. But he is unable to see why the majority of English Nonconformists who are so near in theology to the Establishment continue to stand without its pale. For Chalmers the mission and purpose of the Church demand an end to such divisions:

> Only by an undivided church, only by the ministers of one denomination can a community be out and out pervaded, or a territory be filled up and thoroughly overtaken with the lessons of the gospel. Tell, whether it is of greater consequence that minor differences be upholden, or that the universal Christian education of our families shall be provided for. [34]

The essence of Chalmers' idea of the Church is surely to be found here. It may have been over-simplified, and on the surface mechanistic; but it was a view to which he was impelled by his urgent conviction that nothing in the life of the Church was more important than that it should proclaim the Gospel to every community and to the entire world.

Notes to Chapter IX

1 W Hanna, *Memoirs of the Life and Writings of Thomas Chalmers* (4 vols., 1849-52), vol. IV, p.35.
2 J Keble in his famous Assize Sermon at Oxford in 1833.
3 e.g. Thomas Arnold, writing in 1832: 'The Church as it now stands, no human power can save.'
4 Hanna, *Memoirs*, vol. IV, p.39.
5 *Collected Works of Thomas Chalmers* (*CW*) (25 vols., 1835-42), vol. XVIII, p.352.
6 J Morley, *Life of Gladstone* (1903), vol. I, pp.171f.
7 Hanna, *Memoirs*, vol. IV, pp.599f.
8 *CW*, vol. XI, pp.439f.
9 Hanna, *Memoirs*, vol. IV, p.598.
10 W Hanna (ed.), *A Selection from the Correspondence of Thomas Chalmers* (1853), p.361.

11 *CW*, vol. XVII, pp.187, 191, 194.
12 *CW*, vol. XI, p.46.
13 A Marshall, *Ecclesiastical Establishments Considered* (1829), pp.41f.
14 *CW*, vol. XVII, pp.274, 273.
15 *CW*, vol. XI, pp.445f.
16 *CW*, vol. XVII, pp.312, 333f.
17 *CW*, vol. XVIII, pp.108, 110-13.
18 Hanna, *Memoirs*, vol. III, p.109.
19 *CW*, vol. XI, pp.328f.
20 *CW*, vol. XI, pp.228f.
21 W Orme, *Memoir of John Urquhart (1869), pp.70, 286f.*
22 W John Roxborogh, 'Thomas Chalmers and the mission of the Church with special reference to the rise of the missionary movement in Scotland' (Aberdeen University PhD thesis, 1978), pp.339-50.
23 G Smith, *The Life of Alexander Duff* (1879), vol. I, p.53.
24 Chalmers, *Posthumous Works* (1849), vol. VI, pp.450-52.
25 Dr Roxborogh records invitations from the Scottish Missionary Society, the Perthshire Missionary Society, the Edinburgh auxiliary of the London Missionary Society, the London committee of the Society in Scotland for the Propagation of Christian Knowledge and the St Andrews Missionary Society during Chalmers' first two years in Edinburgh, though not all were accepted. op.cit. p.353.
26 *CW*, vol. XI, pp.103f.
27 ibid., p.111.
28 There is a vivid, and at times amusing, account of this meeting in James Dodds, *Thomas Chalmers: A Biographical Study* (1879), pp.199-210.
29 Hanna, *Memoirs*, vol. III, pp.235, 237.
30 *CW*, vol. XVII, pp.305, 302f.
31 ibid., p.293.
32 ibid., p.343.
33 ibid., pp.344, 349.
34 ibid., p.353.

X

Chalmers' Theology of Mission
John Roxborogh

Chalmers as a theologian

Despite his almost 20 years as a professor of theology, his undoubted popularity as a teacher and the written legacy of his *Institutes of Theology*,[1] Chalmers is little remembered as a theologian.[2] Moreover, although he was deeply involved in the issues which changed the face of the Church in his lifetime, his extensive lectures on theology never dealt explicitly with the nature of the Church or the theological basis of its mission. Nevertheless Chalmers does have significance as a theologian, and one has little difficulty in determining what his underlying theological convictions were and what he considered the purpose of the Church to be.

For Chalmers, the essential tasks of the Church were to propagate its message concerning the saving significance of the death of Jesus Christ and to seek to influence society in all its aspects by the inculcating of Christian values and morals. His understanding of and involvement in this mission was a product of his own pilgrimage in faith and his interaction with the social and religious issues of the day. His basic commitment arose out of his evangelical conversion early in 1811, and is reflected in his doctrine of man, his attitude to the distinctive tenets of Calvinism and his understanding of the rôle of the Church in the world.

It has been rather misleadingly suggested that if Chalmers' *Institutes* had been 'less orthodox in content or more orthodox in system' they might have better survived the passage of time.[3] In structure Chalmers' theology was modelled on that of George Hill,[4] who taught him as a student; and although he never thought of himself as anything other than orthodox, that did not mean agreeing with every detail of the Westminster Confession. Contrary to what is often assumed, Chalmers was no friend of the tradition of scholastic Calvinism which was to be exemplified by the first generation of Free Church professors at New College in the 1840s and subsequently.[5]

Following Hill, the order of Chalmers' *Institutes* is anthropocentric,[6] beginning with Natural Theology, and moving through 'the need for which the gospel remedy is provided' to the nature and extent of that remedy. Such matters as the Trinity, the Person of Christ and the doctrine of the Holy Spirit are left to a few supplementary lectures. It was a congenial pattern, following as it did a chronology of spiritual development which he himself exemplified.

Although Chalmers' approach might conceivably have led to purely individualistic concerns, he was at pains to relate his theology to every aspect of life. Were it to occupy its rightful place, he contended, it 'would be found to touch at almost every point on the nature of man, and to bear with decisive effect on the whole frame and economy of civil society.' [7] This task required flexibility and was essentially creative.

> Although the subject matter of theology is unalterably fixed . . . is there not a constant necessity for accommodating both the vindication . . . and the illustration of this subject matter to the ever-varying spirit and philosophy of the times? . . . In theology, as well as in the other sciences, there is indefinite room for novelties both of thought and expression. [8]

Chalmers' theological reading can be closely monitored from the borrowing records of St Andrews University Library as well as from his journals and correspondence. [9] Apart from his student days the most formative period was from 1811 to 1815 (after conversion and prior to moving from Kilmany to Glasgow). At Kilmany Chalmers was determined to forge his own synthesis of Moderate and Evangelical ideals, and without an appreciation of this fact it is impossible to understand the extraordinary breadth of his appeal. The English Puritans were of considerable influence, and the names of Doddridge, Baxter (above all), Alleine, Matthew Henry and John Owen recur frequently in Chalmers' papers. Wilberforce and Richard Cecil were also influential, however, and from the Scottish Moderate tradition his old friend and mentor, Samuel Charters of Wilton. [10] Jonathan Edwards was much read, but with reservations, perhaps because neat theological systems (including Calvin's) were always suspect in Chalmers' view. [11] In later years he grappled with Turretin and Ernesti and specific topics such as Hume on miracles, the problem of evil and questions of eschatology. [12] He knew nothing of Schleiermacher and little of developments in biblical criticism, but was concerned that continental theology be studied by others if not himself.[13] In his lecture room the set books were Hill, Paley and Butler and these were undoubtedly the theological and apologetic writers who meant most to him, even if he derived some of his underlying spiritual values from elsewhere.

The Bible he always considered the most important source book for Christian belief. Aware of growing challenges from science he was confident that these would not be insurmountable. Early in his ministry he found room in the first few verses of Genesis for the geologists' estimates of the age of the universe. In his enormously successful *Astronomical Discourses* he popularised Andrew Fuller's response to the incongruity of claiming cosmic significance for the life of one man in this tiny corner of a vast universe. At the end of his career he was insistent that the New College in Edinburgh should equip its students to deal competently with the questions that contemporary science was raising.

When challenged, he would state his belief in the 'plenary inspiration' of the Bible, and reject doubts concerning the historicity of the events it describes. Yet it is revealing that he could resort to allegory to find meaning in an account whose historicity he defended, and that he was careful to say that the inspiration of Scripture was 'responsible not for the thing recorded, but the truth of it.'[14]

He stood very much within the tradition of Scottish Common Sense philosophy, and this had for him its theological counterpart in the doctrine of the *imago dei*. After reading Genesis 1:26-31, he noted:

> Let me make this use of the information that God made man in his own image. Let it cure me of the scepticism which distrusts man's instinctive beliefs or perceptions. Let me recollect that in knowledge or understanding we are like unto God—and that in this light we see light. He would not practise a mockery upon us by giving us constitutional beliefs at variance with the objective reality of things. . . . We were formed in his image intellectually as well as morally.[15]

The result of the Fall may have been fatal to man's relationship with God, but it did not totally obliterate the image of God as far as man's human relationships were concerned. While there was much sin and evil in the world, there was also much virtue which the preacher was duty-bound to acknowledge as having value in this life at least, if not in the next. Chalmers was critical of 'injudicious defenders of orthodoxy' for their sweeping condemnations which were 'not merely obnoxious to the taste, but obnoxious to the understanding.'[16] The character of men in classical antiquity or in the contemporary world of business could be perfectly moral, and if so should be applauded. Depravity lay not in 'the utter destitution of all that is amiable in feeling', but simply in ungodliness.[17]

Chalmers was caught between those who objected altogether to such evangelical language, and those who felt he used it in too lenient and heterodox a manner. William Cunningham, who succeeded Chalmers as Principal of New College, took particular exception to his praise of natural virtue, and taught that 'works done before justification . . . are truly sins and deserve the displeasure and condemnation of God.' Referring to Chalmers' teaching, he disputed the 'propriety of calling anything in the character of unrenewed men *good*, absolutely or without explanation.'[18] Cunningham was mainly concerned about the danger of compromising orthodox Calvinism; Chalmers about the necessity of communicating the Gospel. He did not believe he could do this if he ignored people's own use of language and their best aspirations. This is another instance of his belief that creeds and confessions were 'out of their place . . . as magazines of truth' since they had generally come into existence as 'mere landmarks against heresy',[19] and he lamented their change of function into 'insignia' for different denominations.[20]

The *imago dei* also carried the implication that all men were equal in the sight of God. While Chalmers accepted a stratified society, and was no lover of democracy, this was a principle he constantly reiterated. As he declared at the laying of the New College foundation stone in 1846, this was the 'one quality of man' which was to be 'strenuously taught'[21] in the college. It was because it included the poor that one worked to convert and educate them. They have:

> all the capacities of human spirits . . . they have talents . . . they have
> imperishable souls . . . they are on a full level of equality with
> ourselves in all that is essential to man.[22]

Of course, this equality applied to judgment as well as to salvation. While he usually preferred to strike a more positive note, Chalmers did not shrink from portraying what he regarded as inescapable facts of life:

> Even to the most remote and unlettered tribes, men are everywhere
> the fit subjects for a judgment day. Their belief, scanty though it be,
> hath a correspondent morality which they may either observe or be
> deficient in, and so be reckoned with accordingly.[23]

While the central theme of his favourite sermon, 'Fury not in God',[24] was God's present beckoning mercy to all who would receive it, the consequences of refusal were not to be ignored:

> It makes one shudder seriously to think that there may be some here
> present whom this devouring torrent of wrath shall sweep away;
> some here present who will be drawn into the whirl of destruction,
> and forced to take their descending way through the mouth of that pit
> where the worm dieth not, and the fire is not quenched.[25]

Yet he was sympathetic to the reasons which led his friend Erskine of Linlathen into universalism,[26] and was accused of holding the same opinions himself.[27] Not all Evangelicals were cold-bloodedly confident about the eternal torments of unbelievers,[28] and Chalmers for one certainly preferred to avoid speculations.[29] He told his students that he did not want to appear as a 'stern dogmatist', but was mindful of the moral dangers of deferring repentance, since the Bible gave no warrant for believing that 'our all is not staked, and irrevocably staked, on the faith and obedience of the present life'.[30]

The question of judgment also raised the problem of being held accountable for ignorance. Byron had asserted that man was not

N

responsible for what he believed. Asked for his reaction to this opinion, Chalmers replied:

> You are not to blame if you have not found some valuable article that you had lost in an apartment of thickest darkness, but you are to blame if you might have opened the shutters or lighted a candle. [31]

He believed that:

> there was a sufficient difference between the future prospects of the heathen and those of Christian believers to justify the utmost extent and ardency of missionary exertions. [32]

Nevertheless, the heathen would be judged less severely. 'The nations of Christendom who have been plied with the offers of the gospel':

> incur a darker doom throughout eternity than the native of China, whose remoteness, while it shelters him from the light of the New Testament in this world, shelters him from the pain of its fulfilled denunciations in the next. [33]

In this Chalmers was flying in the face of the Westminster Confession [34]; and when reading of the centurion whose alms and prayers had been accepted by God before he became a Christian, [35] he prayed that 'a factitious and freezing orthodoxy' would not shut him up against the lesson of the passage. [36]

   The duty of the Christian was to prepare for heaven, [37] but this was not to cultivate an other-worldliness so much as to demonstrate the reality of faith by conduct; and 'the business of . . . sanctification' needed to be a 'daily and hourly and ever-doing business'. [38] Chalmers was only too well aware of his own shortcomings, but since heaven was 'no heaven at all but to the holy' [39] it was the more necessary to remember that 'the great end and object . . . of the Christian doctrine is not that I should believe as a Christian but that I should do as a Christian'. [40] The 'great object of the economy under which we sit' was to be restored to the image of God which had been lost. [41]

Calvinism and the universality of the Gospel offer [42]

That a high doctrine of election, such as that embodied in the Westminster Confession, can be compatible with evangelism, has often been more of a problem for those outside the Westminster tradition than those within. It needs to be remembered that logical possibilities are not always logical necessities, and that the morbid doubts of the poet William Cowper, and the anti-nomianism of James Hogg, [43] are far from typical outworkings of Calvinistic faith. While during Chalmers' lifetime examples of 'hyper-Calvinism' were to be found in Scotland, it was among the Baptists that there was most concern about it being presumptuous and unnecessary to preach the Gospel to the unconverted. [44] Those for whom the Westminster Confession was their creed knew that, whatever else it said, it noted that God in his ordinary providence used means for the achievement of his ends, however fore-ordained [45]; and Thomas Boston was among those who taught that 'calls and exhortations' were necessary since they were 'the means that God is pleased to make use of for converting his elect'. [46]

Chalmers himself was not in the least inhibited by his Calvinistic heritage in this matter, and preached salvation as a free gift offered to any who would receive it. He was highly sensitive to the barriers which theological systems placed between God's offer of salvation and the possibility of response. When a tract by Horatius Bonar was treated with suspicion because it was too 'free', Chalmers would have none of the criticism. [47] If the Gospel was not freely offered it was no good to a person like himself and he could not imagine it being of help to others. Almost the last sermon he preached was entitled 'The fulness and freeness of the gospel offer', [48] and the evening before his death he complained of those who 'unnecessarily restricted' the word 'world' as applied in Scripture to the sacrifice of Christ:

> The common way of explaining it is that it simply includes Gentiles as well as Jews. I do not like that interpretation and I think that there is one text that puts that interpretation entirely aside. . . . 'God commandeth *all men, everywhere* to repent.' . . . In the offer of the gospel we must make no limitation whatever. [49]

What concerned him in treating the question of predestination was not the difficulties of the doctrine (which he virtually ignored), but the necessity of not allowing it to inhibit the proclamation of the Gospel which had worked in his own experience. Paul found no difficulty in preaching the Gospel and at the same time believing in election, and Chalmers saw no reason to quibble with apostolic precedent. [50] As far as predestination itself (and the related question of the extent of the atonement) was concerned, he was effectively agnostic and regarded the matter as irrelevant to practical Christian life. In a conversation with the Quaker, J J Gurney, he was reported as saying:

> I believe the doctrine to be true, nevertheless, the Christian's course of duty is precisely the same as it would be if the doctrine was not true. [51]

And as one of his students took down in class, the subject should only be 'cautiously introduced into the pulpit':

> Calvinism is not to influence you . . . you have nothing to do except with what is revealed. Repent else you perish, believe in the Lord Jesus—Seek the Lord while he may be found. Cease to do evil. [52]

Chalmers could eulogise the Westminster Confession when that was called for, but his summary of its teaching is revealing:

N ✳

> The natural depravity of man; his need both of regeneration and of an atonement; the accomplishment of the one by the efficacy of a divine sacrifice, and of the other by the operation of a sanctifying spirit; the doctrine that a sinner is justified by faith, followed up . . . by the doctrine that he is judged by works; the righteousness of Christ as the alone foundation of his meritorious claim to heaven, but this followed up by his own personal righteousness as the indispensable preparation for heaven's exercises and heaven's joys; the free offer of pardon even to the chief of sinners; but this followed up by the practical calls of repentance, without which no orthodoxy can save him; the amplitude of the gospel invitations, and, in despite of all that has been unintelligently said about our gloomy and relentless Calvinism, the wide and unexplained amnesty that is held forth to every creature under heaven. [53]

Those who knew their Confession might have been puzzled at his emphasis, but his views were indicative of what was to become more widespread.

The attitudes of the Scottish presbyterian churches towards the Calvinism of the Westminster Confession altered considerably during the course of the 19th century; and it is significant that when the United Presbyterians passed a Declaratory Act in 1879 modifying the terms of subscription to the Confession, there was hardly a point covered which did not find support from Chalmers' lectures of 50 years earlier. The Free Church followed with a similar act in 1892 and the Church of Scotland in 1910. [54] The close correlation between these historic acts and Chalmers' teaching suggests that he is far more representative of the mainstream development of 19th-century Scottish theology than has hitherto been recognised.

The Church in the world

In common with Geneva, the Scottish Reformers took as the 'notes' of a true church the preaching of the Word of God, the right administration of the sacraments, and a proper exercise of discipline. [55] But for many in the Scotland of the 1830s, a true church was one which had control of its own spiritual affairs and which proved itself by its evangelistic activity. [56] It is not difficult to see the Disruption as a move to preserve both of these as *notae ecclesiae*. For Chalmers the organisation of the Church, like the organisation of theology, was subservient to the task of proclaiming the Gospel. On reading a sermon which argued that the Church was free in different times and circumstances to alter its government, worship, and discipline, since its 'institutions stand not on the strength of statute, but in that of their fitness to fulfil the great objects of her mission', [57] Chalmers felt moved to write to the author [58] agreeing that it was 'competent on mere human discretion to decide on questions of ecclesiastical regulations and polity.' [59]

Chalmers treated church government as a matter of expediency because the missionary purpose of the Church underlay all his thinking concerning its polity, independence and unity. His interest in pauperism and political economy received justification from his conviction that Christianity ought to be applied to the whole of society:

> It would be well if religion was to pervade the corporate as well as the individual body, that the day might arrive when corporate bodies were as much under the influence of religion in all their operations as pious individuals are. [60]

Here is the meeting-point of Chalmers' social and evangelistic concerns, but the relationship was not an easy one, and he did not really reconcile the fact that he would 'count the salvation of a single soul of more value than the deliverance of a whole empire from pauperism' [61] with his spending so much time attempting to achieve the latter. Nevertheless in his heavily worked phrase, 'the Christian good of Scotland', [62] he sought to convey the comprehensiveness of the Christian enterprise. He held that 'every part and every function of a commonwealth should be leavened with Christianity' [63] and prayed that 'rulers might Christianize their legislation and philosophers their systems'. [64] Both the Church as a body and Christians as individuals were called to apply themselves not only to evangelism, but to pastoral care, the problems of working-class society, the ethics of the business world, famine relief and prevention, issues of science and religion and questions raised by philosophy. He recognised that the environment of the Church must influence the Church as well as the Church its environment. Out of what was the most consistent theme in his fluid beliefs concerning eschatology he wrote:

> The kingdoms of the earth may become the kingdom of God and his Christ with the external framework of these present governments . . . . There must therefore be a way in which Christianity can accommodate itself to this framework—a mode by which it can animate all the parts and all the members of it. [65]

As frequently with Chalmers, this conviction was illustrated by his life rather than expounded by his theology. If the focus of his vision was indicated by the causes he did not get involved in—beyond the benefits of worshipful and peaceful Sundays, Sabbatarianism held few attractions, and Temperance never interested him for more than a day or two at a time—the breadth of his sympathies was shown by the encouragement he gave to others. When Hew Scott laboured in Anstruther on the seemingly thankless task of compiling his monumental *Fasti Ecclesiae Scoticanae*, it was Chalmers who said to him, 'Go on, Mr Scott, go on; the unborn will bless you, sir. It is the work I would so like to do.' [66] Behind all the diversity of his life and thought there was a single conviction, one that he had first embraced in the Kilmany manse early in 1811:

> Jesus Christ died, the just for the unjust, to bring us unto God. This is a truth, which, when all the world shall receive it, all the world will be renovated. . . . It is this doctrine which is the alone instrument of God for the moral transformation of our species.[67]

The interaction of faith with its environment is not likely to produce identical effects in different historical contexts, but the belief that this interaction ought to take place is surely of the essence of Christian faith. While aspects of Chalmers' organisational theories may still inform the practical mission of the Church, and emphases in his theology may or may not be shared by those who have come after him in the Reformed tradition, the inspiration of his insistence that personal faith cannot be contained as private religion must continue to challenge those who seek to realise the social implications of Christian commitment. And it may be that in speaking of 'the Christian good of Scotland' he provided an understanding of mission which is at once sufficiently vague and sufficiently specific to remain relevant wherever men seek to define both the breadth and the central emphasis of the Church's unending task.

Notes to Chapter X

This chapter is based on my 1979 University of Aberdeen PhD thesis, 'Thomas Chalmers and the mission of the Church with special reference to the rise of the missionary movement in Scotland'. Parts of it have been included in the 1980 Annual Lecture of the Presbyterian Historical Society of New Zealand, Dunedin, 1981.

1 T Chalmers, *Posthumous Works* (1847-49), vols. VII and VIII.
2 Nevertheless his theology has been the subject of at least two doctoral theses: W P Huie, 'The theology of Thomas Chalmers', University of Edinburgh PhD thesis, 1949, and D F Rice, 'The theology of Thomas Chalmers', Drew University PhD thesis, 1966 (copy in British Library Lending Division). See also H P Philips, 'The development of demonstrative theism in the Scottish thought of the nineteenth century', University of Edinburgh PhD thesis, 1951, pp.89-126.
3 H Watt, *Thomas Chalmers and the Disruption* (1943), p.84.
4 George Hill (1715-1819), Principal of St Mary's College, St Andrews from 1791. Chalmers used Hill's *Lectures in Divinity* as a text for his own students (Chalmers, *Posthumous Works*, vol. IX, pp.125ff.) and freely acknowledged his general indebtedness to Hill (ibid., p.xviii).
5 Notably William Cunningham (1805-1861), George Smeaton (1814-1899) and James Bannerman (1807-1868).

6 On the right order of a theological course, see Chalmers, *Posthumous Works*, vol. VII, pp.ix-xx.

7 W Hanna, *Memoirs of the Life and Writings of Thomas Chalmers* (1849-52), vol. II, p.535.

8 Chalmers, *Posthumous Works*, vol. IX, p.xv.

9 See also Chalmers' catalogue of books, Chalmers Papers, New College Library, Edinburgh (*CP*), CHA 6.2.12, 14.

10 Samuel Charters (1742-1825) of Wilton had a profound influence on Chalmers both before and after his conversion. This was totally ignored by Hanna in the *Memoirs* and subsequently by most of Chalmers' other biographers including Hugh Watt. The exceptions to this neglect are M F Conolly, *Eminent men of Fife* (1866), p.114, and (James Hamilton), *North British Review* 7 (August 1847), pp.561f.

11 Hanna, *Memoirs*, vol. I, pp.241f. Journal, 22 March 1813. S Charters to T Chalmers, 16 Feb. 1814, *CP*, CHA 4.3.

12 Theological commonplace books, *CP*, CHA 6.2.6, 7, 9.

13 Hanna, *Memoirs*, vol. III, pp.436-41. *North British Review* (February 1847), pp.271-331.

14 T Chalmers to A J Scott, 22 March 1845, W Hanna, *Letters of Thomas Erskine of Linlathen* (1878), pp.569f.

15 T Chalmers, *Posthumous Works* (1847-49), vol. I, pp.2f.

16 T Chalmers, *Works* (1836-42), vol. VI, pp.15f.

17 ibid., vol. VIII, p.174.

18 *Historical Theology*, vol. I (1960), p.553.

19 Hanna, *Memoirs*, vol. IV, p.456.

20 T Chalmers, *On the Evangelical Alliance* (1846), pp.9-17.

21 H Watt, *New College Edinburgh. A centenary history* (1946), pp.3f.

22 T Chalmers, *Churches and schools for the working classes* (1846), p.11.

23 Chalmers, *Works*, vol. I, p.76.

24 Isaiah 27:3.

25 Chalmers, *Posthumous Works*, vol. VI, p.425.

26 Hanna, *Memoirs*, vol. III, p.247. T Chalmers to Lady Elgin, 6 March 1830, W Hanna, *A Selection from the Correspondence of Thomas Chalmers* (1853), p.348. T Chalmers to J Morton, 29 Nov. 1828, ibid., p.213.

27 Anon to T Chalmers, n.d., *CP*, CHA 4.102.

28 Hannah More wrote to Wilberforce of the 'impenetrable veil' drawn over 'the awful mysteries of judgment'. 2 Sept. 1823, William Perkins Library, Duke University.

29 Chalmers, *Posthumous Works*, vol. IX, p.416. See also Chalmers, *Works*, vol. VIII, pp.310-31.

30 Chalmers, *Posthumous Works*, vol. IX, p.417. cf. also ibid., vol. V, p.9.

31 Recipient unknown, 15 March 1826, Hanna, *Correspondence*, pp.299f. There are manuscript copies at National Library of Scotland, 10997 f. 68 and St Andrews University Library MS. 2032. cf. also Chalmers, *Works*, vol. I, p.72.

32 Hanna, *Memoirs*, vol. III, p.392.

33 Chalmers, *Works*, vol. 22, p.141. This is part of a sermon examining the converse implication of the text that 'to whom much is given, of them will much be required'. See also ibid., vol. X, p.380 and vol. XIII, pp.142f.

34 Chapter 10.4. 'Of effectual calling' states that there is no prospect of non-Christians being saved 'be they ever so diligent to frame their lives according to the light of nature . . . and to assert that they may, is very pernicious and to be detested.'

35 Acts 10.

36 Chalmers, *Posthumous Works*, vol. IV, p.161. Chalmers made a similar observation when reading of the Queen of Sheba's visit to Solomon: 'even at great distances from Judea the true God was not altogether unknown'. ibid., vol. V, p.469.

37 See Chalmers' sermons, 'The necessity of a personal meetness for heaven', Chalmers, *Works*, vol. X, pp.122-32, and 'Heaven a character and not a locality', ibid., vol. VII, pp.320-38.

38 ibid., vol. XI, p.367.

39 T Chalmers to R Edie, 3 April 1819, J Baillie, *The missionary of Kilmany* (1854), p.35.

40 Chalmers, *Posthumous Works*, vol. IV, p.52.

41 ibid., vol. VI, p.2.

42 cf. ibid., vol. VIII, pp.403-13.

43 J Hogg, *The private memoirs and confessions of a justified sinner* (1824); see A L Drummond and J Bulloch, *The Scottish Church 1688-1843* (1973), pp.217f.

44 See, for example, (A Maclean), *Thoughts on the calls and invitations of the gospel* (1797).

45 Westminster Confession, ch. 5.3.

46 *Human nature in its four-fold state* (1769), p.147. See also J Walker, *The theology and theologians of Scotland* (1872), p.60.

47 T Chalmers to Mrs Dunlop, 22 Sept. 1844, Hanna, *Correspondence*, pp.514-16.

48 *The fulness and freeness of the gospel message. A sermon, preached in Hanover Presbyterian Church, Brighton, on Sunday, May 16, 1847*, Hanna, *Memoirs*, vol. IV, p.505.

49 ibid., p.512. cf. also Chalmers, *Works*, vol. XIII, pp.387f.

50 T Chalmers to E Morgan, 1 March 1827, Hanna, *Memoirs*, vol. III, pp.528f. On the doctrine of predestination, see Chalmers, *Works*, vol. IX, pp.151-75. R Watson, *Works*, vol. 7, pp.240-57.

51 A Philip, *Thomas Chalmers apostle of union* (1929), p.223. See also T Chalmers to Mrs Glasgow, 12 Oct. 1825, Hanna, *Correspondence*, p.126.

52 Notes from Dr Chalmers' lectures on theology, n.d. (c.1831), Edinburgh University Library, Dc. 7.

53 Chalmers, *Works*, vol. XI, p.155. Sermon preached on 11 May 1827, at the opening of the National Scotch Church, Regent Square, London.

54 J T Cox and D F M Macdonald (eds.), *Practice and Procedure in the Church of Scotland* (1976), pp.434-37.

55 G D Henderson (ed.), *The Scots Confession of 1560* (1960), p.75.

56 The latter point is well illustrated by the Church of Scotland's response to the Voluntary controversy in the support of church extension and overseas mission. See also Alexander Duff's address, *Missions the chief end of the Christian church* (1839).

57 W Hanna, *Letters of Thomas Erskine of Linlathen* (1878), p.569.

58 A J Scott (1805-66), formerly Irving's assistant in London and the immediate source of his charismatic beliefs. H Scott, *Fasti Ecclesiae Scoticanae*, vol. VII, pp.502f.

59 T Chalmers to A J Scott, 22 March 1845, Hanna, *Correspondence*, p.569. In 1829 Chalmers had explicitly rejected attempts to use the situation of Israel in the Old Testament as a model for the relationship of church and state. Presbytery of Edinburgh, the Catholic claims, 1 April 1829. Charles Watson papers, New College Library.

60 Notes from Dr Chalmers' lectures on theology, n.d. (c.1831), Edinburgh University Library Dc. 7, 115, p.123.

61 T Chalmers to James Brown, 30 Jan. 1819, Hanna, *Memoirs*, vol. II, pp.341f.

62 ibid., vol. IV, p.394 and elsewhere.

63 T Chalmers, *The addresses delivered at the commencement and conclusion of the first General Assembly of the Free Church of Scotland* (1843), p.7.

64 Chalmers, *Posthumous Works*, vol. V, p.417.

65 Hanna, *Memoirs*, vol. II, p.203. See also ibid., vol. IV, pp.496f.

66 Scott., *Fasti*, vol. I, p.xvi.

67 Chalmers, *Works*, vol. VI, p.261.

XI
The Chalmers Papers
Margot Butt

The large collection of papers donated by Thomas Chalmers'
descendants to New College Library in Edinburgh contains material
not only about his own life but also about his forbears and his children
and grandchildren. As well as over 700 of his own letters, it contains
14 000 letters to him from his correspondents, manuscripts of some of
his written works, the texts of his sermons (mostly in shorthand),
lectures, reports on church business and a great deal of biographical
material. The last category includes a notebook entitled *Short account of
her family* by Anne Simson Chalmers [1] which gives a lively account of
her father's family with brief character sketches of his brothers and
sisters. The correspondence includes letters from politicians such as
Peel, Gladstone, Melbourne and Brougham, and philanthropists such
as Wilberforce, Elizabeth Fry and Kay-Shuttleworth. Letters from
Evangelical ministers in Scotland naturally predominate, but Chalmers
was also in communication with many English clergymen, such as
Jabez Bunting, Charles Simeon and several bishops of the Church of
England. Less predictable are the scientists whom he met at meetings
of the British Association, and the painter Sir David Wilkie, an old
friend from Fife. Among the writers are Carlyle (with some letters from
his wife), Roget, Cockburn, Susan Ferrier, Amelia Opie and Hannah
More. Much of this material has been extensively used by researchers,
and it has formed the basis of several books, theses and articles. [2] Not all
these have been concerned with Chalmers as a church leader, as his
innovatory work in Glasgow makes him of interest to economic and
social historians. Two topics which have not yet been dealt with,
however, are the history of the papers and Chalmers' use of shorthand,
and these I propose to discuss.

Chalmers' financial capacity, so usefully exercised in fund-raising for
Church Extension and the Free Church, led to many a trial for his
publishers. A less practical man might have been content with the large
fortune they enabled him to earn from his writings, and with the rapid
spread of his ideas in Europe and America. But he was never satisfied
with the arrangements for advertising and selling his works, and all too
ready to complain of lack of zeal in these matters, which he felt as a

personal attack. Dealings with John Smith & Son in Glasgow, who published the early sermons which established his fame as a preacher, ended with a dispute which was taken to arbitration in 1819.[3] William Collins was a teacher and church worker much admired by Chalmers, who encouraged him to turn to publishing and gave him much support, including the opportunity to print Chalmers' works. It is difficult not to suspect that the quarrel with Smith was provoked in order to facilitate the transference to Collins. The latter had the longest innings of any of Chalmers' publishers, a reasonably peaceful one on the whole, conducted with great mutual respect. But storms were liable to blow up at any time and eventually, after accusing Collins of indolence and inefficiency, Chalmers transferred his publishing rights and all existing copies of his works to Oliver & Boyd in 1846.[4]

Perhaps it was to avoid the strain on his patience, as well as to preserve his time and energy for church matters, that Chalmers made over his literary affairs to William Hanna, the husband of his eldest daughter Anne, in 1841. After complaining in his journal on 15 October of that year, 'The devil is taking a great advantage of me through the medium of Mr Collins by whose neglect and inattention I have been sadly discomforted all this day', he follows this up the next day with 'Have written to Mr Hanna to undertake the business part of my authorship. It is a melancholy view of my spiritual weakness.'[5]

In a new will of 1846[6] he added four names to those of his son-in-law and his wife and constituted all six as his trustees and executors: John Mackenzie, husband of his second daughter Eliza, his brother Charles Chalmers, founder of Merchiston Castle School, and two of Charles' sons, John and Thomas.

In January 1848, six months after Chalmers' death, Hanna left Skirling, near Biggar, where he had been minister of the Free Church, and settled in the Morningside district of Edinburgh. Living with his wife Anne in the family home of Church Hill he embarked on his four-volume *Memoirs of Dr Chalmers*, which he followed with the *Correspondence* and *Posthumous Works*. He was also at this period editor of the *North British Review*. If we are to believe Anne Hanna's statement to her friend Anne Parker, later Viscountess Cardwell, her husband had made no conscious preparation for this task:

> I feel very much for him in the responsibility that lies upon him in regard to the Memoir. It will be a very difficult task, but with his diffidence I do not tell him so. You have somewhat misunderstood the preface if you think Papa requested him to undertake it. I do not believe he ever thought of such a thing being done, and he never gave any materials for it or spoke of his early life unless to relate some humorous anecdote.[7]

Materials for the biography were not lacking, however; in addition to the 14 000 letters which Chalmers had bound up in large leather volumes, facts and memories came pouring in from people who remembered him as a young man. These records were in response to requests from Thomas Duncan, Professor of Mathematics at St Andrews and lifelong friend from their student days. His own letters from Chalmers, probably the most intimate and revealing written to anyone outside his family, Duncan had unfortunately burnt.[8] John Mackenzie also took part in collecting material for the volume, and among those to whom he wrote were Sir Robert Peel, Lord Cockburn, Lord Jeffrey and Thomas Erskine.[9] For the most part the papers left by Chalmers seem to have been kept together, though John Campbell, editor of *The British Banner*, was probably not the only one to receive a memento. This took the form of a sermon in shorthand.[10] (His gratitude turned to indignation when his innocent request for a shorthand key to enable him to read it was turned down after a family conference!)

The initiative for the writing of the memoirs, and the choice of Hanna as author, may well have come from the printer Thomas Constable. He was prepared to invest a considerable sum in this enterprise, and to buy up the whole of Chalmers' literary remains for the sum of £5000. A deed to this effect was signed on 24 November 1847, in which the trustees resolved, under the powers conferred on them by Chalmers' will of 1846, 'to sell and dispose of the property or copyright of the whole works or books pamphlets and writings of every description written and composed by the said Doctor Thomas Chalmers whereof the copyright belonged to him at the time of his death, including those printed and published in his own lifetime, as well as those in manuscript and unpublished at the time of his death.' Specifically mentioned among the latter were *Horae Biblicae Quotidianae, Horae Biblicae Sabbaticae, Theological Institutes, Lectures on Butler's Analogy* and a volume of sermons or discourses hitherto unpublished. The decision as to what parts of the remaining manuscripts were to be published was to be in the hands of the trustees, 'it being however distinctly understood, that the whole manuscripts of every description left by the said Doctor Thomas Chalmers which his said Trustees and Executors may at any time hereafter consider fit for publication shall be the exclusive and absolute property of the said Thomas Constable.' The trustees also undertook that William Hanna should write a life or memoir of Chalmers, payment for which was included in the £5000, and that the copyright for this work also was to belong to Constable.[11]

This agreement caused bitter distress to the four unmarried daughters remaining at Church Hill, Grace, Margaret, Helen and Fanny, and led to a break in relations between them and the trustees, William Hanna in particular. It was after the death of her mother in January 1850 that Grace became aware that the terms of the sale included all the manuscripts remaining in the house, among which were the journals, devotional works and her father's journal letters to his daughters during his absences from home. She felt this as an invasion of privacy and as a reflection on her mother, and fought to retain the manuscripts until her death in December 1851. She does not appear to have seen the deed when she started her campaign. [12] Grace was perhaps the most remarkable of the daughters, and the one who took most closely after her father; her strong square handwriting resembled his. He wrote of her to Mrs Keith Dunlop: 'I was much gratified by your favourable opinion of my daughter Grace. Though I say it myself she is no ordinary person; and therefore it is, that she has lived beyond the sight and sympathy of ordinary minds.' [13] Her spirituality and literary ability appeared when her devotional book, *The road and the resting-place*, was published at the instigation of her sister Helen in 1864. [14] She also showed a mature appreciation of her father in the notes she took of her conversations with him at the end of his life, to which we are indebted for this description of himself: 'I've always been a kind of outlier between the practical and the pious. I have a liking for both. I can't get people with both about me so either I have the pious that look down on practicality as a secular thing, or the practical that nauseate the piety.' [15] It was not surprising that she showed some of his pugnacious spirit when it came to defending his reputation.

Hers was a rearguard action which was bound to fail, but she made some impression on Constable, who wrote to her in these conciliatory terms in December 1850:

> My proposal is, that all your father's MSS. shall be collected at Church Hill, as soon as the purposes of publication shall have been served, and shall there continue in the custody of yourself and your sisters, so long as any of you shall remain unmarried, or until death shall have removed the last survivor of you from the paternal roof; that, in the occurrence of either event, the documents in question shall come without division into the possession of Mrs Hanna, with disposition to her issue, when failing, to Mrs Mackenzie in like manner; in default of whom passing to yourself and your sisters, according to seniority. In the sad event of the extinction of your father's family, I propose that his MSS. shall become the property of the library, in connexion with the Free College in Edinburgh.
>
> You will not deem me more than reverently covetous, if I entreat that one volume of the valued MSS. be laid aside for me, that I may bequeath it to my children as a prized memorial of my connexion with the literary and domestic history of your father.' [16]

Although Grace agreed to this at the time she was clearly not satisfied, for after her death her sister Margaret asked Constable to return her letter of agreement, as it had caused her such remorse. He replied:

> It is with deep regret I learn that your late sister wrote with reluctance, and decided to withdraw, a letter which was very gratifying to me, and which I thought creditable to herself and her sisters.
>
> I am very far from admitting that I can with propriety be blamed for availing myself of a very usual provision in the sale of copyright—the more especially as by the disposition which I proposed to make, I should at once have relinquished the property of the valuable MSS. and secured their continuance in your father's family. As it does not appear, however, that I can otherwise hope to obtain a verdict even of justice in this matter, it is my intention to place the property of the MSS. in question in the hands of your father's trustees, to be disposed of as they may think fit. [17]

Meanwhile it appeared that Constable was not making the expected profits from his purchase of Chalmers' works. A new agreement between him and the trustees was signed in June 1852. It referred to a minute of January 1850 which declared that his disbursements had exceeded his receipts and arranged for a postponement of the payment of royalties for one year. In the agreement of 1852 Constable was relieved of his responsibility to pay royalties on the *Memoir* and *Correspondence* in exchange for a further sum of £5,000 to be paid in early instalments. The deed also incorporates the proposal made in his letter to Margaret, to hand over the manuscripts to the trustees while retaining the copyright and the right to make use of them. [18]

Though Grace failed in her attempt to have the papers returned to Church Hill, it was perhaps her agitation which prompted Constable's suggestion that they should ultimately find a home in the Free (now New) College. The bulk of them remained for many years in the Hanna family, the only one with descendants still living today. The next record I have found of them is in a letter of 1939 from Mr William Gemmill Hanna, who as a chartered accountant played a great part in sorting out the financial situation at the Union of Churches in 1929. He wrote to Dr Mitchell Hunter, then librarian of New College, confirming 'the gift of the correspondence, letters etc. of my great-grandfather, Dr Thomas Chalmers, which his descendants, through me, have gifted to the New College Library.' [19] He referred to Thomas Chalmers' own letters and the bound volumes of correspondence, one of which has turned up in St Andrews University Library, probably the volume which Constable was determined to keep for himself.

There had evidently been a fairly wide distribution of the papers among the Hanna descendants and Margaret and her husband William Wood, because the next donor was William Hanna's niece, Mrs Marjorie Penney, who in 1963 gave a very large donation of family letters, which extends from the latter part of the 18th century through to the early years of the present one. In her correspondence with the librarian at this time, Dr John A Lamb, she speaks of her uncle having inherited his part of the collection from Miss Grace Wood. [20] Her own papers came to her from her aunt, Jeanette Hanna and her great-aunt Mrs Blackie. She used her inheritance along with papers already in New College to write an article on Eliza Mackenzie's nursing services in the Crimean War, which was published in *Blackwood's Magazine* in May 1954.

One of the sections of Chalmers' papers which has been less intensively studied than his letters and journals is the large quantity in shorthand, which includes several hundred sermons. The system he used was that of John West, who published it in Edinburgh in 1784 under the title *A system of shorthand/with plain and easy directions for writing it.* A copy of this rare pamphlet was found in New College Library, though not among the Chalmers papers, and appeared to tally with his script. Further evidence appears on a copy in the National Library of Scotland, which bears a pencil note: 'This is the system used by the Rev Dr Thomas Chalmers.' [21]

John West was a student at St Andrews from 1769, a contemporary in the mathematics class of Sir James Ivory and of Sir John Leslie, who later edited West's *Mathematical Treatises* of 1838. From 1780 to 1784 he was one of the long series of mathematical assistants to the ailing Professor Vilant, a position later held for one session by Chalmers himself. West preceded James Brown, who is said to have aroused Chalmers' interest in Mathematics and who remained his much respected friend. West left for Jamaica after publishing his shorthand system, and became rector of St Thomas' in the East, Morant Bay. His system does not appear to have been widely used, and is given an incorrect date in James Henry Lewis' *Historical Account of Shorthand*, 1816, and a brief mention in J E Rockwell's *The teaching, practice, and literature of shorthand*, Washington 1884. West does not claim originality for it, but says in his introduction that it is 'an improvement of Angel's.' Chalmers adapted the system for his own particular usage and left behind two 'shorthand keys' which give his own variants but do not by themselves enable a reader to decipher the manuscripts.

The first evidence we have of Chalmers' use of shorthand relates to the purpose for which he used it most, i.e. writing sermons. This practice appears first on his appointment to Kilmany in 1803, and the sermons he preached at that time occupied only two sides of a small sheet of paper. 'Read' sermons were unpopular at that time, and Hanna describes Chalmers' difficulty in extempore preaching: 'So very eager was he at this period of his ministry to communicate the impressions which glowed so fervidly within his own heart, that even when he had a written sermon to deliver, he often, as if dissatisfied with all that he had said, would try at the close to put the matter in simpler words, or present it in other lights, or urge it in more direct and affectionate address. But when the restraints of a written composition were thrown away, when not at the close only, but from the very beginning of his address, this powerful impulse operated, he often found that, instead of getting over the ground marked down in his study to be traversed, the whole allotted time was consumed while yet he was labouring away with the first or second preliminary idea.'[22] He overcame this drawback partly by the vehemence of his oratory and partly through his use of shorthand. An article on oratory in *The British Quarterly Review* of 1857 described how he made use of it particularly for speeches:

> In the case of Dr Chalmers, it is worth remarking that the manuscripts from which he read were always, or nearly always, in short-hand. This permitted him, as it seemed, to take in a larger number of words per glance, as his eye crossed the paper, and so to have a larger proportion of his attention free for the aspect of his audience. Indeed, unless one was near him so as to observe the fact, it was difficult to know that he was reading. A favourite plan of his in a public meeting was to post himself where he could, as it were casually, rest his left hand, with his note-book in it, on the back of a chair or some such slight support, leaving his body, and especially his right arm, free for movement and gesticulation. Then, moving his head and shoulders in a peculiar acquired curve, one point of which brought him within eyeshot of the paper, he took his glances cunningly at regular intervals, delivering the result of each in a corresponding volley. [23]

It was in the early years at Kilmany that he formed the habit of writing two forms of sermons, 'short-handers and long-handers', the latter being a more careful preparation to be produced once a month.

Perhaps it is surprising that Chalmers did not use shorthand for his journals, which he kept up intermittently from 1810. It was chiefly reserved for spoken material, and its convenience for this medium is illustrated in an article published in the *Phonetic Journal* in 1895 by John M Warden, [24] who cites the address to the first General Assembly of the Free Church of Scotland as an example of the minimal expanse of notes required for a long speech. Most of Chalmers' lectures are written out in longhand, with shorthand additions on the opposite sheets which are left blank. His published works show various states of composition in different forms. The multiplicity of shorthand notes for speeches, toasts, addresses and prayers indicates that Chalmers was never happy to speak without a paper in his hand; even such a comparatively informal occasion as the presentation of Walton's Polyglot Bible by the students on his retirement from St Andrews required a small sheet of shorthand to guide him through his speech.

I have found no evidence that William Hanna mastered the shorthand, but three of the daughters—Margaret, Helen and

Fanny—were able to transcribe it. This may have been for the purpose of publication in Chalmers' lifetime or for the assistance of William Hanna. The keys found among the papers are in Helen's hand, and many of the sermons bear notes such as 'transcribed into long-hand, H J C'. These transcriptions are of great value to anyone wanting to master the shorthand. John M Warden, in the article already mentioned, said that Mrs William Wood (Margaret Chalmers) 'is still accustomed to read her distinguished father's shorthand papers.' Transcriptions from longhand were made at various times by Mrs Chalmers and all the daughters.

Though so much of Chalmers' work was published by the indefatigable Hanna, and so much has been discovered recently among the letters, journals and printed papers, there still remains a great deal to be studied in the shorthand material, as well as in the anecdotes and comments in his daughters' letters. The cataloguing of all these papers has been virtually completed.

Notes to Chapter XI

1 Chalmers Papers, New College Library, Edinburgh (*CP*), CHA 2.27.89.
2 e.g. S J Brown, *Thomas Chalmers and the Godly Commonwealth in Scotland* (Oxford, 1982); F Voges, *Das Denken von Thomas Chalmers in Kirchen—und Sozialgeschichtlichen Kontext* (Frankfurt, 1894); W P Huie, 'The Theology of Thomas Chalmers' (Edinburgh University PhD thesis, 1949); I F Maciver, 'The General Assembly of the Church, the State, and Society in Scotland: Some Aspects of their Relationships, 1815-1843' (Edinburgh University MLitt thesis, 1976); D F Rice, 'The Theology of Thomas Chalmers' (Drew University PhD thesis, 1966); J Roxborogh, 'Thomas Chalmers and the Mission of the Church with special reference to the Rise of the Missionary Movement in Scotland' (University of Aberdeen PhD thesis, 1979); S J Brown, 'The Disruption and Urban Poverty: Thomas Chalmers and the West Port Operation in Edinburgh, 1844-47', *Records of the Scottish Church History Society*, vol. XX pt. 1 (1978), pp.65-89; G I T Machin, 'The Disruption and British Politics, 1834-43', *Scottish Historical Review*, vol. XI (April 1972), pp.20-52; I F Maciver, 'The Evangelical Party and the Eldership in the General Assemblies, 1820-1843', *Records of the Scottish Church History Society*, vol. XX, pt. 1 (1978), pp.1-13; D Shaw, 'The Moderatorship Controversy in 1836 and 1837', *Records of the Scottish Church History Society*, vol. XVII (1972), pp.115-30. The most extensive bibliography of Chalmers' material presently available is contained in S J Brown's *Chalmers*, listed above, pp.417-29.
3 David Keir, *The House of Collins* (1952), *CP*, CHA 5.3, 4, 5.
4 ibid.
5 *CP*, Journal no. 9, CHA 6.1.14.

6 Scottish Record Office. SC 70/4/4.
7 Anne S Chalmers (Hanna) to Anne Parker (Cardwell), 20 Jan. 1848, *CP*, CHA 2.14.51.
8 *CP*, CHA 2.14.37.
9 John Mackenzie to Grace Chalmers, CHA 2.
10 John Campbell to William Hanna, 25 Nov.-19 Dec. 1849, *CP*, CHA 2.33.58, 60.
11 SRO RD 15/W/4/8.
12 Letters from Grace Pratt Chalmers to Anne Brown, *CP*, CHA 2.54.80ff.
13 Thomas Chalmers to Mrs Dunlop, Skirling, 8 June 1842, *The Correspondence of the late Thomas Chalmers, DD, LLD*, William Hanna (ed.) (1852), p.132.
14 *The road and the resting-place* by Grace Pratt Chalmers (1864).
15 'Notabilia of papa's conversations with me—Church-hill', *CP*, CHA 2.57.4.
16 Thomas Constable to Grace Pratt Chalmers, 5 Dec. 1850, *CP*, CHA 2.56.40.
17 Thomas Constable to Margaret Parker Chalmers, 9 Jan. 1852, *CP*, CHA 2.
18 SRO RD 15/W/4/A.
19 William Gemmill Chalmers Hanna to Adam Mitchell Hunter, 20 Nov. 1939, *CP*, CHA 2.
20 Marjorie Penney to John A Lamb, *CP*, CHA 2.
21 National Library of Scotland, Wn 875.
22 William Hanna, *Memoirs of Dr Chalmers*, vol. I (Edinburgh, 1850), p.339.
23 *British Quarterly Review*, April 1, 1857, p.453.
24 *Phonetic Journal*, vol. 54, 1895.

I wish to acknowledge the kind assistance of the following in the preparation of this article: Professor David Abercrombie; National Library of Scotland; Scottish Record Office.

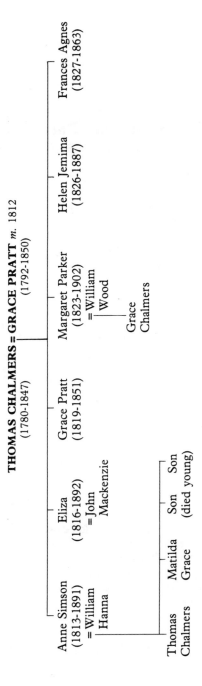

THOMAS CHALMERS ≡ GRACE PRATT *m.* 1812
(1780-1847) (1792-1850)

Anne Simson (1813-1891) = William Hanna

Thomas Chalmers — Matilda Grace — Son — Son (died young)

Eliza (1816-1892) = John Mackenzie

Grace Pratt (1819-1851)

Margaret Parker (1823-1902) = William Wood — Grace Chalmers

Helen Jemima (1826-1887)

Frances Agnes (1827-1863)

XII
The Chalmers Portraits
J Patricia Campbell

The features of Thomas Chalmers must be amongst the best known from 19th-century Scotland. Oil, pencil, watercolour, silhouette, calotype, engraving, marble and bronze were employed by a wide range of Scottish artists, the portraits ranging in scale from life-size heroic full-lengths to intimate cabinet pictures and vindictive cartoons.

By 1826 Chalmers' fame encouraged minor artists to importune him for sittings, seeing a commission from him as an opportunity to build their fame on his. B W Crombie [1] begged, through family contacts, to be allowed to publish Chalmers' portrait 'in a group of other worthies', promising to do it with 'the most marvellous expedition'. Patrick Park declared that he could produce a marble bust after only six sittings, and promised 'the most immediate attention'. [2] In 1838 F C Lewis, averring that his great object was to possess portraits of as many public characters as he possibly could, offered to take Chalmers' likeness 'at no expense' in daily sittings of two hours per day. [3] Unfortunately neither of the leading painters of the early 19th century, Raeburn and Lawrence, recorded Chalmers' features, and only one of Sir John Steell's [4] portrait busts was carved during Chalmers' lifetime.

Very little is known of Chalmers' own attitudes to art and artists, but rather conflicting impressions are gleaned from a consideration of what he read on painting, and of the type of pictures he himself commissioned. By 1821 Chalmers was familiar with the work of Sir Joshua Reynolds. [5] Reynolds' *Discourses on Art* advocates 'general effect' rather than 'exact expression of the peculiarities, or minute discrimination of the parts.' [6] This could be achieved by dressing sitters 'with the general air of the antique for the sake of dignity and preserving something of the modern for the sake of likeness.' [7] Perhaps the early bust by Samuel Joseph, [8] dated 1 November 1820, partially follows Reynolds' austere principles, but two commissions for which Chalmers himself engaged the portraitist reveal a much more domestic taste.

The first painted portrait we know of Thomas Chalmers is that by Andrew Geddes. [9] This commission was arranged through a series of letters [10] between John Smith, bookseller and publisher, and David

Wilkie, [11] already an established and famous painter in London, in connection with an intended frontispiece for a publication of Chalmers' sermons. Chalmers had originally intended that Wilkie should undertake the commission. He claimed Wilkie as 'an old and intimate friend' [12]; his wife Grace had known Wilkie during their schooldays at Cupar. Chalmers visited London for the first time in 1807. [13] His diaries reveal that his imagination was gripped by exhibitions of cork models and mechanical curiosities rather than by works of art [14]; he did, however, make two visits to the Royal Academy Exhibition. [15] He was deeply impressed by the particular admiration paid to Wilkie's painting 'The Blind Fiddler'. The painstaking minute handling in the manner of Dutch 17th-century interiors, combined with truthful characterisation, made Wilkie's pictures very attractive to a wide audience. Chalmers' admiration extended to the man himself, 'a man of genius and excellent sense, with all the simplicity which accompanies talent and firmness to resist the corruptions of flattery.' [16]

Friendship flourished between artist and author in 1808 when Wilkie went to great trouble searching for a London publisher for Chalmers' *Enquiry into the Extent and Stability of National Resources.* [17] The men met at the manse at Cults, when Wilkie came to see his parents, and there Wilkie's father and Chalmers found mutual interests both in the ministry and in mathematics. [18]

It was much later, during the summer of 1817, that the project of Chalmers' portrait began. Wilkie, who was travelling round the West of Scotland collecting material for subject painting, visited Glasgow. There he 'saw a great deal of Dr Chalmers', [19] and made a number of slight sketches of his friend. When he had returned to London he was contacted by John Smith, who asked for a copy of one of these drawings. [20] None was, however, considered to be sufficiently complete for the purpose, although Wilkie had originally considered one of them to be 'one of the Lions of [his] portfolio.' [21] Arrangements for sittings during Chalmers' rushed visits to London were mooted but abandoned; eventually Wilkie urged his friend, who at first 'refused to sit to any artist except Wilkie', [22] to employ Geddes. Wilkie had previously approached Sir Henry Raeburn, who had expressed 'a strong desire' to take the portrait; Sir Thomas Lawrence (who had heard Chalmers preach at Hatton Garden) had also stated that he would feel 'as much delight in painting the unassuming Presbyterian [sic] as in portraying the imposing figure and attire of His Holiness the Pope' [23]; unfortunately, neither artist was free at the time to accept the commission.

Geddes himself was pressing strongly for the commission [24] and wisely sent Chalmers an impression of a print after one of his most attractive and best-known portraits: a full-length little cabinet picture of Wilkie, [25] rather in Wilkie's own detailed, accessible manner.

O

Wilkie's recommendation was accepted, the matter was at last resolved, and the little picture of Chalmers as author resulted. He is shown seated informally at his table with its brightly-patterned turkey cover, his waistcoat partly unbuttoned for comfort, pen and paper immediately to hand. 'Rendered with scrupulous finish and crisp detail', [26] it is an appropriate interpretation for translation into an engraved frontispiece, although as an image of the man it is perhaps over-truthful. His accentuated eyes, quarrelsome expression and heavy body lack the inherent impressive power demanded by the exacting Sir Joshua Reynolds. The painting was sufficiently popular, however, to be reproduced in mezzotint by William Ward for general sale.

Later portraits emphasise Chalmers' impressive bulk, his high forehead and heavy-lidded eyes. A study of Chalmers' death mask at the Bicentenary Exhibition at New College, Edinburgh, confirmed the report on his features by the Phrenological Society:

> The size of his head is great, and hence the powerful impression which he has made in the public mind. His Benevolence, Veneration, Ideality, Wonder and Compassion are all large. Dr Chalmers is likewise distinguished for extensive chemical and mathematical knowledge. His size, weight and locality are very large. Acquisitiveness is well developed. [27]

Artists, unfortunately, were usually unable fully to express these qualities in their oil portraits of Chalmers. During the long sittings Chalmers' features settled into a completely passive and immobile mask suggesting an oppressive weightiness rather than an impression of patriarchal wisdom. Cartoonists of the 1840s, however, found his strongly-marked features a boon; his figure is easily recognised in many lithographs and engravings of the Disruption with an enormous head and expressionless face. [28]

A more lively, inspired interpretation of Chalmers as author and thinker is the very successful half-length seated portrait of 1843 by Thomas Duncan. [29] In this painting the noble size of Chalmers' head has been animated by an alert, turning pose, as if the attention of the sitter had been arrested by a developing idea. Duncan's ability to 'escape all trace of that ready-made tradesman-like look' [30] by searching character and lively arrangement is entirely missed by other painters such as William Bonnar [31]; these qualities made this portrait a favourite choice for engravers. Chalmers' autograph on an 1845 mezzotint by Edward Burton suggests that the sitter also approved of Duncan's image.

It was while speaking that Chalmers' particular powers were most felt, and artists preferred to show him in action, heavy features animated, hands gesturing. August Edouard, [32] a silhouette cutter who 'had an eye for the important feature' was certainly approved of by Chalmers, for he was employed 'at the usual fee' [33] in 1830 to take likenesses of all the members of the Chalmers family. In the same year Edouard captured several of Chalmers' characteristic preaching attitudes in silhouettes. It was, however, David Wilkie who produced the most memorable image of Chalmers' power to move his hearers, when he used drawings made of his friend during the famous sermon for the London Missionary Society at Rowland Hill's Surrey Chapel [34] as the basis for his painting of 'John Knox Preaching before the Lords of the Congregation'.[35] A slight pen drawing[36] taken during one of Chalmers' sermons shows Chalmers in a crowded church; figures press up the pulpit stairs behind the preacher, intent on the passionately eloquent words of Chalmers. For the dramatic subject picture of 'Knox', Wilkie simply reversed and amplified this design, retaining Chalmers' expressive pose and gestures for Knox himself.

A very different modern history painting also used Chalmers' figure as its linchpin: in D O Hill's huge commemorative picture of 'The Deed of Demission' [37] his central figure, occupying the moderatorial chair, gains its authority from its calm stillness and frontal pose among a ranked mass of excited protagonists. Begun in 1843 and not completed until 1865, this painting was one of the first in which photographs rather than portrait sketches were used as reference material for the painter.

The advent of photography profoundly affected artists' interpretations of Chalmers' heavy features. As Hill explained in connection with his picture of the Disruption, 'by the use of the Daguerrotype and Calotype . . . the sitter is detained only a very short time, the whole process being effected in a few minutes.'[38] The benefit of these short sittings, entailing no fatigue, is evident in the alert expressions of the late daguerrotypes of Chalmers. Even in the calotype of Chalmers preaching,[39] when a support for his arm was necessary during the exposure, the impression is vivid and lively. His settled, bulky figure is seen slightly turning as if about to speak, his mouth mobile, eyes sparkling. In another calotype he is even breaking into a smile, revealing a warm, humorous aspect of his character otherwise hinted at only in the 1838 oil by Watson Gordon. The most moving of these calotypes is the late full-length of Chalmers turning stiffly in his chair to look right, eyes glinting sharply despite physical infirmities.

This group of calotypes, made from 1843 onwards, was used by other painters as the basis for their work, which encouraged an even more minute inspection and recording of physical features than in Geddes' early oil. Rather than the presentation of an idealised hero, they led to an investigation of the private qualities of the family man. D O Hill based the design of his small oil, 'Dr Chalmers and his Grandson Thomas Hanna',[40] on an 1844 calotype taken in Merchiston Gardens, where Charles Chalmers had founded a school, and where Thomas Chalmers enjoyed walking. The 1849 engraving by John Le Conte[41] after this painting shows a very literal treatment of a family relationship in domestic circumstances rather than a public man engaged in national events. The portrait becomes a subject picture, filled with descriptive detail and allusions—in the butterflies, sundial and scythe—to the passage of time.

It is ironic that Kenneth McLeay[42] was obliged to depend for both of his posthumous, exquisitely-finished watercolours of Chalmers on calotypes, for the increasing popularity of photography lost him his market. The portrait in an imaginary sun-drenched interior[43] shows McLeay at the height of his powers, before he turned to oil painting and lost his fine sense of lighting and colour, becoming hard and minute in handling. Even although the half-length of 1847[44] retains a sepia tint in the head, McLeay transforms the photographic image by delicate modelling and strong lighting.

Most of the portraits mentioned so far consistently tend towards the analytical, illustrative type of presentation, concentrating on physical appearance rather than on character. There are, however, two splendid full-length life-size oils which portray Chalmers in a heroic manner. John Faed's[45] commemorative portrait of 1849 showing Chalmers as first Principal of New College must also have relied heavily on calotypes and prints, and bears the common fault of over-precision in the head. The general effect is, however, impressive, despite the overall linear, flat, hard handling of paint resulting from Faed's early training as a miniaturist. Chalmers is shown standing by a table in gown and bands, a small book in his right hand, spectacles, with which he emphasises a point, in his left. A large mezzotint (23 in × 15¾ in) was published in 1849 by John's brother James; this shows much greater detail than is now visible in the damaged oil, although after cleaning in 1980 much of the background of the oil, including the great red chair and book-laden table, became visible.[46] Faed followed the common 19th-century practice of mixing his pigments in bitumen to give a rich tone. The bitumen has subsequently moved and darkened, so that the entire detail in the robes is concealed. In spite of this disfigurement, Chalmers emerges from the damaged, gloomy background as an influential, dignified public figure. The picture formed part of a group of portraits commissioned for New College some time after Faed's marriage in 1849, when he was working in Edinburgh; the series was a coup for the painter.[47]

The second, very different interpretation of Chalmers as hero is by Sir John Watson Gordon,[48] PRSA, and comes nearest to Reynolds' ideal in portraiture. This striking full-length, showing Chalmers in his robes of Moderator of the General Assembly, was probably commissioned by the Moderator and members of the General Assembly: James Anderson considered that the most appropriate dedication of Lupton's 1837 engraving would be either to this group or to the Lord High Commissioner, Lord Belhaven. [49] Watson Gordon had become the leading practitioner of portraiture in Edinburgh after the death of Raeburn in 1823, and was the obvious choice for a portrait in the grand manner. Sittings were under way by 13 November 1835, when Miss A S Chalmers wrote to Miss Parker: "I went with Papa to Watson Gordon's where he is having a full-length portrait taken', [50] but no more is mentioned until James Chalmers saw it hanging in the Royal Academy Exhibition of 1837. He wrote unenthusiastically to Thomas: 'had a view of your portrait by Mr Watson Gordon; it may be a good painting but I do not think it is a very striking likeness—Lewis, Mr McClellan's friend, would have done you greater justice.' [51] Others, however, including John Anderson, found the likeness excellent. Watson Gordon was usually successful with strongly-characterised male figures 'distinguished by intellect or by Scotch shrewdness'. [52] This painting has all the fine qualities of his most baroque period: his colour is rich and varied, though far more restrained than Lawrence's flamboyant settings; the paint handling is unmuddied and assured; and the arrangement of figure and background unusually well proportioned. The main light of the picture is reserved for the head and hands, which are more firmly modelled than the rest of the freely-painted figure.

Recent cleaning for the Bicentenary Exhibition [53] revealed much more of the rich setting: through creamy pillars glimpses of blue sky can be seen against a heavy swag of red curtain falling behind a scarlet upholstered chair. Nothing much could be done to disguise the deep bitumen cracking around the head (originally a rich deep brown foil to the flesh tones), and the thinly-painted black clad figure of Chalmers is still difficult to read in parts. The dramatic low viewpoint and effective strong lighting, however, capture the essence of the orator and public figure in a manner which is as welcome as it is rare in portrayals of Chalmers.

Notes to Chapter XII

1 *CP*, CHA 4.63.39. Benjamin W Crombie drew and etched a series of portraits including Chalmers, and published them under the title 'Modern Athenians' between 1837 and 1847.

2 *CP*, CHA 4.268.1. Patrick Park (1811-55), specialist in portrait busts.

3 *CP*, CHA 4.271.110.

4 Sir John Steell (1804-91). A posthumous white bust, height 24 in, dated 1877, is in New College, Edinburgh University, from a first version of 1845. The large-scale bronze standing at the junction of Castle Street and

George Street was completed in 1878 and is the best-known image of Chalmers as a preacher.

5 *CP*, CHA 4.18.64. D Wilkie to T Chalmers. Wilkie called the Discourses 'a text book and by far the most philosophical writings upon the subject that have ever been produced.'

6 Sir Joshua Reynolds, *Discourses on Art* (1959), Discourse XI, lines 308-10.

7 ibid., Discourse VII, lines 740-41.

8 Samuel Joseph (1791-1850). Plaster bust, height 28 in, Senate Hall, New College, Edinburgh University.

9 Andrew Geddes (1783-1844). Portraitist and friend of Sir David Wilkie. 1806: studied at the RA in London. 1810: opened a studio in York Place, Edinburgh. 1821: exhibited 70 works in Waterloo Place. 1823: established in London and refused to fill Raeburn's place as Edinburgh's portraitist. 1827-31: travelled on the Continent.

10 *CP*, CHA 4.9.49., CHA 4.14.39., CHA 4.11.45.f236., NLS Acc 6236 f.5; NLS Acc 5236. *Dictionary of National Biography*, vol. 21, pp.101-2.

11 Sir David Wilkie, RA (1785-1841). Born in Cults, Fife. 1799-1804: studied at the Trustee Academy, Edinburgh. 1804-5: painted portraits in Fife. 1805-41: established in London. *Lit:* A Cunningham, *Life of Sir David Wilkie* (1843), King's Painter to George IV, William IV and Queen Victoria.

12 W Hanna, *Memoirs of the Life and Writings of Thomas Chalmers* (4 vols., 1851-52), vol. I, p.217.

13 ibid., vol. I, pp.103ff.

14 ibid., vol. I, p.109.

15 ibid., vol. I, pp.108, 110.

16 ibid., vol. I, p.115.

17 ibid., vol. I, pp.133-36; also Cunningham, op.cit., vol. I, pp.175-80.

18 Hanna, *Memoirs*, vol. I, p.217.

19 Cunningham, op.cit., vol. I, pp.464f.

20 NLS Acc 6236 f.5.

21 NLS Acc 6236. This was presumably not the slight 4 in × 2½ in pencil sketch by Wilkie in the National Gallery of Scotland, no. D4725, entitled 'Dr Chalmers'.

22 *CP*, CHA 4.9.49.

23 *CP*, CHA 4.14.39.

24 *CP*, CHA 4.9.49.

25 *CP*, CHA 2.11.45. f.236.

26 DNB, vol. 21, 1890, pp.101-2.

27 Records of the Phrenological Society, Gen. 608.

28 Four cartoons from the collection at the National Library of Scotland were included in the Bicentenary Exhibition. They included a typical lithograph by Nichol of 'The Reel of Bogie' which shows Chalmers, Cunningham and Candlish dancing with Charles Hope, Lord President of the Court of Session, as avenging angel.

29 Thomas Duncan (1807-45). *Chambers Biographical Dictionary of Eminent Scotsmen* (1868), p.507.

30 J L Caw, *Scottish Painting 1620-1908*, pp.110-12.

31 William Bonnar (1800-53).

32 August Edouard (1789-1861). Advertised in the local press in Edinburgh and Glasgow in 1830 and 1831.

33 Mrs E N Jackson, *Silhouette Notes and Dictionary* (1938), p.20. Scottish National Portrait Gallery, no. 836, height 8¼ in; no. 1211, silhouette on watercolour background, 10 in × 7 in; no. 2150, height 6 in (1830), signed; no. 2282, height 6 in (1831), signed.

34 J P Campbell, Unpublished thesis, 'Catalogue and assessment of drawings by Sir David Wilkie', vol. II, pp.97-99. Hanna, *Memoirs*, vol. I, pp.98-99.

35 Completed in 1832; now at Petworth House.

36 'Dr Chalmers Preaching' (1817), by Sir David Wilkie. Pen and brown ink; 6¼ in × 7¼ in. Private collection.

37 'The First General Assembly of the Free Church of Scotland. Signing the Act of Separation and Deed of Demission at Tanfield, Edinburgh, May 1843' by D O Hill (1802-70). Oil on canvas; 11 ft 4 in × 5 ft. Free Church of Scotland. *Lit.* D MacKinnon, *The Disruption Picture* (Edinburgh 1943). K Michaelson, *Catalogue of a Centenary Exhibition of the Work of David Octavius Hill and Robert Adamson* (Scotish Arts Council, Edinburgh 1970).

38 NC MS., Aut. Cab. 240.

39 One of the collection of daguerrotypes and calotypes of Chalmers in the SNPG.

40 SNPG no. 2365.

41 John le Conte (1816-87), 'Dr Chalmers and his grandson Thomas Hanna, 1849'. Engraving after an oil painting by D O Hill (note 40); 16⅛ in × 12 in.

42 Kenneth McLeay (younger) (1802-78). Miniature painter and one of the founder members of the RSA in 1826. *Lit.* DNB 1890, vol. 35, pp.205-6.

43 'Dr Chalmers seated in an imaginary setting'. Posthumous, c.1847. Watercolour and gouache, 9⅞ in × 8½ in. Private collection. A second variant known only through an allegedly life-size photograph, 19¼ in × 15⅜ in, is signed and dated 'K McLeay, RSA, 1847'. Provenance unknown.

44 SNPG no. 591. Watercolour 3½ in × 3 in, signed and dated 'K McLeay, RSA, 1847', and inscribed 'To Geo. Bell MD'.

45 John Faed (1819-1902), 'Dr Chalmers, First Principal of New College'. Oil on canvas; 7 ft 9 in × 4 ft 9½ in. New College, Edinburgh University. *Lit.* M. McKerrow, *The Faeds—A Biography* (1982).

46 R Shearer, painting restorer, reported in October 1979 that the painting had suffered damage resulting in a hole towards the bottom of the canvas, and that the varnish was very badly discoloured. A bloom of mildew obscured the picture. The mildew was removed, the rent repaired by a patch and a simple surface cleaning given in order not to disturb the thin bituminous paint layer.

47 John Faed kept roughly chronological but imperfectly dated notebooks which confirm, after the entry about his marriage in 1849, that he had painted portraits of Duff, Cunningham and Chalmers and had made a drawing of Candlish for New College. Private communication, M McKerrow.

48 Sir John Watson Gordon, PRSA (1778-1864), 'Dr Thomas Chalmers'. Oil on canvas; 7 ft 9 in × 4 ft 10 in. New College, Edinburgh University. *Lit.* CP, CHA 4.248.25., CHA 4.258.27., CHA 4.258.29., CHA 4.271.110., CHA 4.271.112. D and F Irwin, *Scottish Painters at Home and Abroad*

(1975). Watson Gordon also painted a posthumous portrait of Chalmers, SNPG.

49 *CP*, CHA 4.208.27.
50 *CP*, CHA 2.8.103-4.
51 *CP*, CHA 4.260.57-8.
52 DNB, vol. 22, pp.218-19.
53 R Shearer reported on 17 October 1979 that the painting was sound but marred by discoloured and shrunken varnish. J Dick, Conservator of paintings for the National Gallery of Scotland, advised against cleaning off the darkened varnish as bitumen pigment might be disturbed, and remedial work by 19th-century restorers would certainly be removed from the wide cracks, entailing unrealistically expensive and hazardous restoration work. The painting was surface cleaned by R Shearer.

Notes on Contributors

Margot Butt: Manuscripts Assistant, New College Library, Edinburgh, 1972-83. Sorter and cataloguer of the Chalmers papers there, and organiser of the Chalmers Bicentenary Exhibition, 1980.

J Patricia Campbell: Lecturer in Fine Art, University of Edinburgh, specialising in Northern European Art in the 17th-19th centuries. Publications include *The Torrie Collection Catalogue* (1983), and articles on Scottish painting. In preparation: a bicentenary monograph on Sir David Wilkie.

Owen Chadwick: Regius Professor of Modern History at Cambridge, 1968-83. His many publications include *The Victorian Church, part I* (3rd edn., 1971), *The Victorian Church, part II* (3rd edn., 1979), *The Secularisation of the European Mind in the Nineteenth Century* (1976) and *The Popes and European Revolution* (1981).

Olive Checkland: Honorary Research Fellow in Scottish History, University of Glasgow. Publications: *Philanthropy in Victorian Scotland* (1980), *Health Care as Social History: the Glasgow Case* (1982) (editor), and with S G Checkland, *Industry and Ethos, Scotland 1832-1914* (1984).

Alexander C Cheyne: Professor of Ecclesiastical History in the University of Edinburgh since 1964, and Principal of New College since 1984. Publications include *The Transforming of the Kirk: Victorian Scotland's Religious Revolution* (1983).

Mary T Furgol: Postgraduate student in the Department of History, University of Edinburgh.

Boyd Hilton: Fellow, Tutor, and Lecturer in History, Trinity College, Cambridge. Publications include articles on Peel, Gladstone and 19th-century evangelicalism, and *Corn Cash Commerce. The Economic Policies of the Tory Governments 1815-1830* (1977). Presently working on volume 1783-1846 for the projected *New Oxford History of England*.

John McCaffrey: Senior Lecturer in Scottish History, University of Glasgow. Contributor to various scholarly periodicals, including *Innes Review, Records of the Scottish Church History Society*, and *Scottish Historical Review*, and editor of *Glasgow 1858. Reprint of Shadow's Midnight Scenes and Social Photographs* (1976).

206 *The Practical and the Pious*

Iain F Maciver: Assistant Keeper in the Department of Manuscripts, National Library of Scotland, since 1968. Publications: articles in *Records of the Scottish Church History Society*, and 'Cockburn and the Church' in A S Bell (ed.), *Lord Cockburn: A Bicentenary Commemoration* (1979).

Ian A Muirhead: Lecturer in Ecclesiastical History, University of Glasgow, 1964-79. Minister of St James', Forfar, 1940-48, of Brandon, Motherwell, 1948-64, and of Monymusk with Blairdaff, 1979-82. Died 1983. Contributor to various learned journals, including *Innes Review, Records of the Scottish Church History Society* and *Scottish Journal of Theology*.

W John Roxborogh: Minister of the Presbyterian Church of New Zealand, formerly at Brooklyn and Kelburn, Wellington, and now teaching at Seminari Theoloji Malaysia, Kuala Lumpur. Thesis on 'Thomas Chalmers and the Mission of the Church' was awarded PhD degree by the University of Aberdeen, 1979.

Henry R Sefton: Lecturer in Church History, University of Aberdeen, since 1972 and Master of Christ's College since 1982. Publications include '"Neulights and Preachers Legall": some observations on the beginnings of Moderatism in the Church of Scotland' in N Macdougall (ed.), *Church, Politics and Society: Scotland 1408-1929* (1983) and articles in various learned journals.

Friedhelm Voges: Lutheran minister in Stade, West Germany. Publications include *Das Denken von Thomas Chalmers im kirchen—und sozialgeschichtlichen Kontext* (1984).

Index

207